The MAVERICK MAHARAJA

His Highness Maharaja Jayachamarajendra Wadiyar (1919-1974)

The MAVERICK MAHARAJA

The Life and Times of His Highness Maharaja Jayachamarajendra Wadiyar

With Best Regards,
Deepti

DEEPTI NAVARATNA

HarperCollins *Publishers* India

First published in India by HarperCollins *Publishers* 2022
4th Floor, Tower A, Building No. 10, Phase II, DLF Cyber City,
Gurugram, Haryana – 122002
www.harpercollins.co.in

2 4 6 8 10 9 7 5 3 1

P-ISBN: 978-93-5489-244-8
E-ISBN: 978-93-5489-252-3

Typeset in 11/15.5 Sabon LT Std at
Manipal Technologies Limited, Manipal

Printed and bound at
Thomson Press (India) Ltd

HarperCollinsIn

MIX
Paper
FSC FSC® C010615

This book is produced from independently certified FSC® paper
to ensure responsible forest management.

This book is dedicated to Shri Rajachandra Urs, the son-in-law of Maharaja Jayachamarajendra Wadiyar and his most ardent chronicler. Without his blessings, this book would not have come to fruition.

CONTENTS

ACKNOWLEDGEMENTS

It was on Makara Sankranthi day in 2019 that I expressed my wish to write a book on Maharaja Jayachamarajendra Wadiyar (JCW) to my parents. By then, they were aware of the fact that I was consumed by his music and was getting increasingly infatuated with studying the layered history of Mysore during his reign. They did not even bat an eyelid before they said that I must start right away! For them, this meant many nights and days of taking care of my infant daughter, Gowri, and relieving me of responsibilities, so I could write. This book is dedicated to their love, affection and unwavering support. My husband, Navneeth Kowdle, has affectionately witnessed the many joys and moans that go into sculpting good prose. I thank him for holding the fort down as I wrote well into the wee hours, revelling in research and writing.

This book would not have come into this world without Shri Rajachandra Urs. He fed my need for information and insight into the life of JCW, helped me reframe content and put them in perspective. It was he who initially seeded the idea of a good biography in English, which contextualized JCW's life to the extraordinary times it was lived in. Smt. Indrakashi Devi Wadiyar, daughter of JCW, has been affectionate and immensely supportive of this endeavour. I am grateful to Smt. Kamakshi Devi Wadiyar, daughter of JCW, for sharing some photographs from the family collection and for providing so many insights into his life.

It is a phenomenal responsibility to write about a multifaceted genius like the Maharaja. The inexplicable connection I felt to him and his music has made it possible to understand and locate his maverick virtuosity in so many creative areas. I have done my best to present his life; any deficiencies found in the book are my own, and do not reflect on his singularly extraordinary life.

MESSAGE BY HIS EXCELLENCY SHRI VENKAIAH NAIDU

सत्यमेव जयते

भारत के उपराष्ट्रपति

VICE-PRESIDENT OF INDIA

September 06, 2021

Dear Dr. Deepti Navaratna ji,

Namasthe!

I am happy to know about your upcoming book 'The Maverick Maharaja' on the illustrious life of Mysore Maharaja Sri Jayachamarajendra Wadiyar.

Sri Jayachamarajendra Wadiyar was a remarkable ruler and an able administrator who provided visionary leadership for the development of Mysore as one of the most progressive and self-reliant states in pre-Independence India.

A democrat at heart, the Maharaja was a true people's ruler who believed that people must be empowered to govern themselves. After independence, Mysore was the first major State to accept the recommendation of the Constituent Assembly and join the Indian Union. This speaks volumes about his strong nationalistic vision.

Sri Jayachamarajendra Wadiyar was a perfect blend of ancient traditional values of Indian civilization and the modernism of the western world. Recognizing the need for rapid industrialization, he actively encouraged the establishment of several institutions of national importance including Hindustan Aeronautics, Central Food Technological Research Institute and the National Tuberculosis Institute.

His unparalleled patronage to arts, literature and culture earned him the moniker 'Dakshina Bhoja'. I hope this English biography of the Maharaja Sri Jayachamarajendra Wadiyar will provide interesting insights into his multifaceted personality and showcase his many contributions for the cause of nation building before and after our country's independence.

I wish you all the very best in this noble endeavour.

Yours sincerely,

Naidu

(M. Venkaiah Naidu)

Dr. Deepti Navaratna

COMMEMORATIVE NOTE

By Bharat Ratna Dr C.N.R. Rao

Linus Pauling Research Professor & Honorary President
Jawaharlal Nehru Centre for Advanced Scientific Research,
Bangalore, India

The Maharaja of Mysuru, Jayachamarajendra Wadiyar, was a scholar who was well versed in Western music as well as Indian music. He was a composer par excellence, his kritis shine upon his rare musical brilliance and the cultural ethos of the Mysore kingdom. Besides Mysuru being the jewel in the crown of the British Empire, the Maharajas believed in making Mysuru progressive industrially, scientifically, and culturally. The contribution of JCW and the kings of the Wadiyar dynasty in this regard is significant.

Another great aspect of his personality was that he was generous and indeed a great benefactor to all those who deserved it. Even after his reign ended, and when he was made the Rajapramukh on our gaining freedom, he continued his scholarly ventures for the greater benefit of his people and Indian culture. Notably, the *Jayachamarajendra Granthamala* series, especially *Jayachamarajendra Vedaratnamala,* made available the entire *Rigveda Samhita* with the original Sanskrit verses followed by a word-to-word Kannada translation of the Vedic verses. His contributions to the preservation of Indian knowledge systems and Indian philosophical thought are immense. The very essence of Karnataka's culture was laid down in Mysore's exalted culture. I become nostalgic whenever I think of the Maharajas of Mysuru. I wish Dr Deepti Navaratna great success in her attempt through this biography to revisit and showcase this legacy for the generations to come.

FOREWORD

By Shri Tejasvi Surya

Member of Parliament, Bengaluru South, &
National President, Bharatiya Janata Yuva Morcha

Maharaja Jayachamarajendra Wadiyar was a marvel, whom the people of my generation heard a lot about, but never got to see. This generation, however, is fortunate to experience the legacy of the Maharaja through such biographic explorations. The sprawling locality of Jayanagar in my constituency of Bengaluru South, the educational, technological and innovation hubs of Bangalore today: the Hindustan Aeronautics Limited (HAL), the Raman Research Institute, National Tuberculosis Institute, the Indian Institute of Science, and even the forever bike JAWA are all blessed to receive the royal touch of the Maharaja. The story of Bengaluru's development and its status as the capital of the Mysore State can be understood by knowing the life and contributions of JCW.

This book, *The Maverick Maharaja*, while exploring the different facets of JCW, also goes on to provide a detailed account of life in Mysore and Bengaluru, the two great cities of Karnataka today. The book also encapsulates the journey of Mysore and JCW during an unpredictable era in the country, the post-World War chaos, events leading to the formation of the Indian dominion, the Union of India, the assertion of Republic status and the rudiments of post-Independent India. JCW was among the first to sign the Instrument of Accession with the Republic of India. In doing so, he set an example for all of the country's other princely states and made way for the creation of the Indian Union.

Today's Bengaluru has a lot to thank JCW for. As the Maharaja of Mysore, he took an egalitarian approach to governance, using his policies to guarantee every individual enjoyed a good standard of living in the kingdom. While many parts of the country were grappling with poverty, the Mysore kingdom stood as an example of how the Maharaja's sound policies in irrigation, food technology, agriculture, sericulture and forestry can steer the kingdom away from famine and food shortages. JCW, in particular, was heavily invested in wildlife conservation, ecological studies and the protection of green cover, his governmental policies for sustainability are still relevant several decades later.

The most remarkable aspect of JCW's tenure is that he coupled industrial development and modernization with the popularization of arts, music, and technology. With the composition of more than 100 Carnatic kritis and several essays on Indian philosophy, such as the Sanskrit text of *Avadhuta Gita* (Song of the Free Soul), he gave a fillip to Indian traditional knowledge systems. Having a deep interest in Western compositions and music, JCW quietly contributed to curating the musical legacies of the London-based Philharmonic Orchestra and introduced little-known Russian composer Nikolai Medtner to the world. If the city of Mysore stands majestically as a heritage icon of India, it is only because of the vision of JCW and his predecessors.

JCW sponsored the translation of several ancient and religious texts from Sanskrit to the Kannada language. One of his most remarkable achievements is the *Jayachamarajendra Granthamala*, running into more than 2.5 lakh pages, which, including the *Vedaratnamala*, remains the most rigourous, systematic, comprehensive, and monumental work in Kannada literature. His democratic ideals of creating access to Indian heritage and knowledge are exemplified by this colossal undertaking, for no other translation of the Rigveda Samhita exists in any other language of the world—a gift for Kannada and Kannadigas for generations to come.

The contemporary relevance of JCW can be seen in several policies of successive governments, which have replicated or remodelled the administrative policies during his reign. From being the first king to constitute a five-year planning commission to selecting villages from every region to develop civic amenities, industries and educational institutions, the roots of many current government schemes can be traced back to the days of JCW.

Many kings have come and gone. Some continue to draw imperial strength even today from their erstwhile position in India. But JCW is something special—he was a people's king. There is so much more that makes Maharaja Jayachamarajendra Wadiyar a true maverick. Hence, his legacy is powered by the gratitude and pride that people from his generation and our generation feel and nurture in our hearts. This magnificent piece of work provides a deep insight into the wonder that is JCW and the legacy he has left behind.

FOREWORD

By Maharajakumari Smt. Indrakshi Devi Wadiyar
Daughter of Maharaja Jayachamarajendra Wadiyar

I am very happy to write this foreword to the book *The Maverick Maharaja*—a biography of my dear and revered daddy, Late Maharaja of Mysore, Sri Jayachamarajendra Wadiyar, by Dr Deepti Navaratna.

The title of the book is as intriguing as the person my father was! Famous playwright and wordsmith William Shakespeare in his play *Twelfth Night* tells us not to fear greatness: 'Some are born great, some achieve greatness, and some have greatness thrust upon them.' My father, no doubt, was born great but he achieved greatness by his innate talent. But ironically, greatness was never thrust on him. In 1954, when he was just 35 years old, he sums up his own persona quite eloquently. Speaking on the occasion of Maharaja's College Day Celebrations as chief guest, he said:

> Several positions of honour and dignity, I have held in my life as a result of the circumstances of my birth, but there is one position, one destiny, I have carved out for myself and that is as a student, shall I say, as an advanced student of literature, history, philosophy, music and above all, our ancient culture

which illumines my path and which serves as a perpetual refreshment for my mind and soul.

In life he tried his best to conform to what Avadhuta Gita says:

'rāgadvesha-vinirmuktahsarvabhūya-hiteratah
drudha-bodsh ca dhīras ca sa gaccetparamampadam'

||*Avadhuta Gita: II. 24*||

Meaning:

The person who is free from attachment and hatred (aversion), who is intent upon doing good to all creatures, whose knowledge is stable and who is un-defied (courageous) attains to highest Truth

English poet and lexicographer Samuel Johnson once said: 'The true measure of a man is how he treats someone who can do him no good.' This aspect of my father's personality leaps out of the very large reservoir of his talents and capacities. The values he lived with, his kindness, altruism, empathy for others, although sublime and often overlooked as passive traits, have powered his personal successes. The fact that he was very much in touch with his own humanity as with that of others' is a great personal success. We often succumb to the notion that greatness belies an isolationist tower of vanity; in his life we see that greatness is achieved and lived by connecting to the human and divine within and around—all at once. His many acts of benevolence suggest that he lived with this spirituality—connected within and to all aspects of cosmic divine—its energies and beings. His religiosity, rooted in the Advaitha Vedanta, enabled him in this process, as a king, statesman, scholar, musician, person, and 'student of culture', as he himself professed. It is far harder to bring out the man amidst the myriad list of his sparkling achievements. I am indeed very happy that this biography has focused on this aspect and makes an effort to showcase it.

Alas! He lived at a time when India was going through the cauldron of World War II, Freedom at Midnight and all the pangs and tribulations of a nascent and evolving constitutional civilization. How he bowed to the present with such a complex and laced past is very well narrated through the story of *The Happy Prince and Other Tales* written by Oscar Wilde. Drawing parallels between the storyline and the life of my father, the many travesties and triumphs of his life after his reign ended have been ingeniously inter-woven.

Just two years ago, I hardly knew the author of this delightful biography! When my husband chose her to sing an invocation and speak about my father during the Centenary Celebrations we hosted at the Mysore Palace and Bangalore Palace, it was a revelation. She astounded the selected audience not only with her mellifluous singing but also by her authoritative speech on the Maharaja and his extraordinary talent in Western music and its profound and innovative influence in his compositions of Carnatic music. She is not a mere classical singer but a musicologist and neuroscientist and an achiever sadhaki! Now with this book, she has proved she is equally adept at being a wordsmith. All this at a young age! I wish this work will spur her to greater glory and success!

INTRODUCTION

By Maharajakumari Kamakshi Devi Wadiyar

It is my great pleasure to write an introduction to this wonderful book about my venerable father Sri Jayachamarajendra Wadiyar, erstwhile Maharaja of Mysore. Smt. Deepti gives us rare insight into the life and times of my father, and not just a chronicle of his life. The biography delves deeper into his psyche, makes an effort to understand him as the person he was—a father, a scholar, a king, and administrator of a kingdom. We were in awe of how he managed all of his duties and found time for his greatest passion, music, and his philosophical writings. In his life and legacy, we find many inspiring messages for the future generations to come. Through Deepti's rich tapestry of words, this aspect is well-showcased. His life was not merely extraordinary by circumstances of his lineage, but by the sheer grace and will with which he braved the extraordinary times in which his life was lived. His extraordinary appetite for knowledge, for the arts, for music, for wildlife, for photography, and creative pursuits was beautifully set in the light of his philosophical bent. Another extraordinary trait of his was his ability to embrace new realities and turn adversity of any nature into an opportunity. Often his creative side is spoken of more often than his successes as a king. Without a doubt, the documented history of Mysore speaks volumes of the staggering amount of work, diplomacy, administration, and innovative thinking that went into his reign. His reign was most definitely set in the politically turbulent times of India's birth and the decision to join the Indian Republic. I am very happy to note that several chapters of this book devote much time to this aspect of his legacy. The chapters on his music are refreshingly eloquent on the importance of his compositions in the larger culture-scape of South India and India. Kindness and empathy are two great values enshrined in him, and the chapter 'The Happy Prince' most heart-warmingly captures his life after his tenure as Governor of Mysore and Madras ended. One finds that he practiced his Rajadharma long after he relinquished the throne—his many acts of benefaction and his service to music, Kannada, and his countrymen continued throughout his life. To relinquish one kind of power and to find a life of significance—that according to me, in essence is the crown jewel in his story.

I thank Deepti for devoting so much of her time, for such in-depth research and for bringing together this beautiful book. Thank you, Deepti, I appreciate what you have done from the bottom of my heart!

1

A CROWN OF BARBS AND A SONG WITHIN

There he strides in majestic gloom
A wholesaler of ideas in bloom
Crown of barbs and a song within
A steady sail in all that din!

Maharaja. The word evokes powerful imageries. Erstwhile power. A silhouette of past glory. A medieval vestige. A glimmer blunted by the monochrome of contemporaneity.

A Maharaja in today's world is thought of as a relic. A vestigial figure drowned by colonial sovereignty, vanquished and defeated; imagined to have led a languid life lurking around colourful corridors in vain. The history of history itself is testament to the fact that it is the handmaiden of the agendas that engender its documentation. The lives of Indian princes have indeed escaped respectful attention in the accounts of Indian history during colonial times. After all, one may ask, what can be remarkable about these 'vassals' of the great British Empire? Why should the ruminations of history be bothered about these men who were 'free' under colonial siege? Despite such stereotyping, if one delves deeper into the chronicles of princely kingdoms, many scholars, thinkers, composers, philosophers and statesmen emerge from behind the veil of dismissal. Many Indian princes lived a life of value, valour and vigour, influencing events and destinies not just for their kingdoms but for the world even, their personas and personalities shining brighter than their crowns.

Is the kingliness only about the crown? Can the king emerge from the shadows of his crown? Perhaps only the one who knows how to be a king within. One whose inner light outshines the dismal darkness of duty. Unfazed by conditions, and unconditionally hell-bent on being himself first. One such maverick maharaja is the hero of this book; the legacy of the last Maharaja of Mysore has outlasted his throne, precisely for this reason.

Maharaja Jayachamarajendra Wadiyar's life (18 July 1919–23 September 1974) highlights the significance of an inner kingly enterprise that asserted will over destiny. The gifts of his precocious insight and vision continue on as sovereign souvenirs to Mysore and India at large. Post World War II, William Douglas Pawley, an aircraft manufacturing entrepreneur, and Walchand Hirachand, an Indian businessman, happened to rendezvous with the just-coronated 21-year-old Mysore Maharaja Jayachamaraja Wadiyar (JCW). It was a mid-air collision of great minds and interests, which, after a smooth 'landing' gesture by JCW, cleared the runway for India's first aircraft manufacturing company: the Hindustan Aircraft Limited. This was a watershed moment for Indian defence aerospace industry and research—the company has now grown into India's largest defence and aerospace company: the Hindustan Aeronautics Limited in Bengaluru. Imagine India's jaw-dropping success with the Mars Orbiter Mission (MOM), also called Mangalyaan, would not have been possible if the Maharaja had not seen the promise of the premise.

It was all on paper. Papyrus. The witness of many a transformation. The instrument of accession. Outdated currencies of the princely states. The substance of 'minting dreams'; the papyrus of pomp. Only that this maverick Maharaja dreamt of minting reams of pedantic papyrus; he curated the only translation of the terse 10,552 mantras of the *Rigveda Samhita* to Kannada, so his people could access that treasure. A distinct inner freedom within him sanctioned seemingly anachronistic behaviour. Despite being the man with a heavy privy purse and an empty wallet post-Independence, he liquidated his assets to support the Philharmonia Concert Society in London! Far, far away from Mysore, an eighty-four-year-old German composer, Richard Strauss, wrote his farewell to the world through his *Four Last Songs*, after having expressed the desire to have them sung by the reigning Wagnerian soprano, Kirsten Flagstad. He died with his wish unfulfilled. His wish, however, travelled half the globe to Mysore and JCW commissioned the only recording of this music for a whopping $5,000 in 1949! This act of benefaction came ironically at a time when his own sovereignty was being decommissioned to the idea of a Republic of India.

His benefaction and love for music knew no boundaries. When the world was polling out monarchies, unfazed, JCW was designing the world's first ever music psychology-based opinion poll with *Gramophone* magazine and a British record label, the Electric and Musical Industries Ltd. (EMI). The findings of the poll not only decided the roadmap for the Western Classical music production giant, but also changed the course of what would eventually be recorded and adored in its history. But for his foresight, many breathtaking masterpieces of Western classical music embodying the philharmonic spirit would never been available for posterity. Between 1946 and 1948, when most Rajahs were twiddling their thumbs about how to wrestle power, our Maharaja was instead plumbing the depths of quiescent Ragas to anchor his soul. When national chaos pervaded, a still music arose in his heart. How can one be 'instrumental' in music, when you are an instrument of accession? Yet, when national chaos erupted, when the maps dissolved, the nagging demands of civic duties stung, when the pageantry mellowed, this maverick's inner melody reigned. In such trying times, he furiously composed a set of Carnatic classical compositions, melding harmonic ideas into Carnatic vocabulary. It was as if the poetry of Richard Strauss's 'Im Abendrot' of the *Four Last Songs* were prophetic of his tussle with his times; only two larks soared musingly into the haze, him and his inner lark.

> Around us, the valleys bow,
> the air already darkens.
> Only two larks soar
> musingly into the haze.

Even more perplexing, in the maze of his personality are the values he embodied, often paradoxical at first sight, but singing in unity upon reflection. Can one revere ancient knowledge while being fully aware of its limitations? Can a mind steeped in symbols of Agamas and Advaitha find beauty in symbols, metaphors, and the music of a post-modernist West? Can one be a strong advocate for *Arthashastra* and yet study European diplomacy for solutions? Can one be contemporary and classical at the same time? Can someone find the divine in a Carnatic kriti and a symphony? Wildlife conservation, philately, photography, music, statesmanship, philosophy—all converged in his consciousness like perfectly fitting pieces of a giant jigsaw puzzle. It is as if his consciousness transcended the time-space-culture continuum, life spoke to him in beautiful metaphors, understood by few. It is not very often that the man emerges from the shadows of his crown. That is precisely why his story has to be told.

2
THE PHILOSOPHER ON THE THRONE

'We live in deeds, not years; in thoughts, not breaths;
In feelings, not figures on a dial.
We should count time by heart-throbs
He most lives who thinks most, feels the noblest and
acts the best.'

– Philip James Bailey, English poet (1816–1902)

The *Bhagavad Gita*, arguably the most acclaimed Hindu scripture, is expounded by Krishna to Arjuna on the battlefield. The *Gita*'s setting is no accident; in fact it brings together two words that are otherwise not thought of in the same breath: philosophy and action. Most of Western philosophy has focussed on 'problematizing', and therefore, a philosopher questioned, critically analysed, discussed and rationalized larger and smaller conundrums of life and society. The 'thinking man' as a speculating agent in the world is born out of this orientation in the history of the Western philosophy. Not surprisingly then, a continued power tussle between monarchy and men of enlightenment is documented in history, something that has sparked the many French revolutions, anti-monarchy movements in Europe and England leading to the expulsion of thinkers, artists and men seeking liberty, science, democracy and freedom of expression.

Monarchy was seen as the structure embodying religious dogmas, enforcing the 'divine right of kings'[1] to rule the less-ordained, and perpetuating the doctrines of religious institutions such as the Roman Catholic church. In this milieu, the idea of a philosopher-king is viewed with the same discomfort as an anthropomorphic figure. A philosophizing Maharaja, prone to reason and spirituality, was assumed to have great internal and external strife with the mantle.

Philosopher Voltaire visualized an absolute monarch[2] as one who is dictated by reason and a sense of inner justice—which in many ways, is a philosopher-king. Yet, the mainstream perception of a king was that of a beast that ran on brute testosterone rather than oxytocin! One that thought less and spoke more with the sword than the pen. Right from the chronicles of Ashoka, the Mauryan king who had a change of heart after the Battle of Kalinga and sent Buddhist missions across the world, to JCW, a contemplative bent is seen as the last qualifier for a Maharaja. Arguably, the soil of India has by far seen more philosopher-scholar-kings than any other part of the world. One does not find in accounts of Great Britain or Europe, as many scholar-musician-philosopher kings who themselves drank from the creative fountain of the inner muse. India for long, has been the land of learning, and hence the learned man was held above the warrior king, the statesmen and the gentry. This also explains why India's history is not marked by long-drawn power struggles between the men of hard power and the men of knowledge, like in the West. A long and documented history of wise kings consulting wise rajgurus exists in India, including the very famous duo of Rajguru Chanakya and Chandragupta Maurya, who consolidated one of the largest Hindu kingdoms in the Indian subcontinent between 321–298 BCE. The *Rig Veda* teaches: 'Let there be for the benefit of the rulers and the ruled three assemblies. 1. Religious 2. Legislative 3. Educational. Let each discuss and decide subjects that concern it, and adorn all men with knowledge, culture, righteousness, independence, and wealth, and thereby make them happy.' Thus, the goal of governance was to promote a society which journeys from physical security to material abundance to spiritual upliftment. From Chikka Devaraja Wadiyar, the founder of the Wadiyar dynasty, to JCW, almost all of the kings of the Wadiyar dynasty were philosophers, composers, musicians. A creative side, 'a light side of the force' in *Star Wars* lingo, shone through their souls. The contribution of their philosophical and spiritual leadership to the creation of an exalted Mysorean culture is immense. Dr M.V. Krishna Rao (1901–1971), political scientist and historian, describes the philosophy of the Mysore's culture thus: 'Freedom, toleration, immunity from arbitrary arrest and reasonable hope of redress, the willing acceptance of the law and the growing universal desire to check excessive privilege—these were a few of Mysore's classical characteristics.' In fact, the exertion of power as monarch is in direct opposition to the culturing of a certain inner freedom of spirit in his subjects—for this makes them immune to the claustrophobic notions of authority. Yet, this was made possible in Mysore, to a great extent because of the equanimous minds that occupied the Mysore Gaddi.

The monist philosophies of the Advaitha Vedanta, the oldest and most premier school of Vedanta, anchored the mind of JCW. He was a Srividya Upasaka, an ardent student of the practice of Srividya, which imparts knowledge of the self through an alchemy of tantra, mantra and yantra. In his life, one finds a shining example of how religious practice can engineer a mind that's capable of transcending the binaries of reason and faith, as understood by the West. The core ideas of Western enlightenment were built around the centrality of thought and reason; it believed in the absolutism of the evidence of the senses, of observation and inference, as primary sources of gaining knowledge. 'I think therefore I am', the famous quote of Descartes is quite illustrative of this obsession with rational thought as a means to unravel human experience. In his essay, 'Avadhuta—Reason and Reverence,' JCW observes that:

> In the Western world today, logic has led to the infructuous method of logical analysis or philosophical analysis—to give it a more respectable name. A more barren study than logical analysis as it is expounded today in the West is hard to

> conceive. No doubt this is the result of pushing empiricism and realism much too far; so far that it has ended in mere verbal analysis and paradoxical statements.

Core Hindu texts and tenets like the *Gita*, the hermeneutic literatures of Darshana do not exalt thought and reason to highest order of human acuity. The reasoning thought is no king. The concepts of the Avadhuta, the Jivanmukta, the Stitapragna, the Kshetragna have all strongly pointed to the imagery of an equanimous man—in whom reason and reverence, thought and action have their honoured seats in the court of the self. JCW observes, 'Mysticism all the world over confesses to this ultimate ineffability of this great reality in linguistic and conceptual terms. "Naisatarkenamatirapaneya," says an Upanishad. This higher insight cannot be gained by mere logic.'[3] In fact, Advaitha Vedantic principles offer a more realistic and democratic view of the mind—where reason, rationality, sensory perception, and discrimination barter with previous memories, prejudice, false notions, belief systems, collective memories and autobiographical attitudes. This noisy cacophony of the inner self, needs a conductor, who can, through the prudent use of all of his 'players', produce the heady concoction called human experience. Inner truth and self knowledge, thus, is simply the knowledge of this hierarchy, knowing who-is-who in your mental court, enabling the right counsel within to pervade your antahkarana based on the context and problem on hand. In such a mental ensemble, there is only one king, the one who knows the limits of each of his 'courtiers' and conducts himself like one. In such a model, the philosopher is king and enabling action is at the heart of philosophy.

Advaitha Vedanta also set the tone for his understanding of Rajadharma. The inner life of men is but a battle of binaries—between engagement and detachment, thought and action, time and space, religion and science, perception and truth, and so on. This battle is more loaded with stakes for a king. How does one navigate such complexity? Hindu ideologies of dharma come in handy while tackling such conflicts. Dharma can be understood as the equivalent of the concept of the 'internet of things' (IOT). In the IOT model, the unique identifiers (UIDs) provide a framework for the interrelatedness of components, from computing and mechanical devices, and other digital objects—an ontology of who, when and what. With such intelligence vested in the 'identifiers', decision-making is somewhat automated with minimal or no human or computer interventions. Similarly, dharmic role prescriptions are meant to specify 'identifiers' to work within the decision-making process, especially when conflicting situations arise. In the *Bhagavad Gita*, Krishna reminds Arjuna must choose his Kshatradharma over others, and fight for his rights, rather than be weakened by his Bhratrudharma, and bemoan the reality of fighting with his kinsmen. JCW's grounding in Advaitha Vedanta enabled him to navigate the most complicated of times, soon after his coronation. How a leader perceives reality has implications far beyond his personal space. A monarch's mind, a battleground of dharma, a mind that processes impressions, vested interests, and temptations of the now needs philosophical grounding more than the renounced sadhu in the Himalayas. After all, the mind that maketh the law is a tide that takes many small boats ashore. When it was wise to fight against the Axis, he rallied with Britain and allies to bolster victory. If India had fallen into Japanese occupation, for instance, the next few centuries of India's history would not have been the same. JCW's decisive leadership during World War II spearheaded British India's fight against the Axis.[4] Had he been steeped in short-sighted patriotism, in the face of war, he could never have made the hard choice of rallying Mysore's resources for India's greater good.

JCW's writings on philosophy clearly indicate how his study of both Indian and Western philosophies informed a strong perspective on Indian philosophical matters. His study of Pigou, Bertrand Russel, Spinoza and Kant were offset by his study of *Vedas, Upanishads*, Vedanta and Adi Shankara. The body of JCW's writings reflect his penchant for life's binaries: *Avadhuta—Reason and Reverence, Atman and Brahman, Religion and Man, Dattatreya: The Way and the Goal, The Gita and Indian Culture*. In 1956, C. Rajagopalachari, former Governor General of India and writer–activist statesman, in the preface to the book *Atman and Brahman* describes the writing prowess of JCW as lucid yet powerful:

> His Highness Sri Jaya Chamaraja Wadiyar, Maharaja of Mysore, is a philosopher among our princes. In addition, His Highness also came under the influence of the great saint, His Holiness Sri Chandrasekhara Bharati Swamigal, the late Sankaracharya of Sringeri and also of the reputed savant and thinker, the late Sri V. Subrahmanya Aiyer.
>
> Schooled in the philosophy of Advaitha, his highness develops the thesis that the realization of the identity of the individual Atman and the universal Brahman represents the acme of our ancient civilization. In a small compass, His Highness has provided a lucid account of the treatment of Atman and Brahman from the Advaitic point of view, in a manner which reveals his scholarship and conviction.

In the same book, JCW rants against the stereotyping of Eastern spirituality and Western materiality:

> It has become far too common to describe the two predominant viewpoints of the world as Western and Eastern. It has become the vogue these days, in keeping with the mania for labelling everything, to label the Western view as materialistic and the Eastern as spiritual. This is to rest on a false foundation. Perhaps, we may admit that there is much of truth in it, that by and large, the West has been more concerned with outside things pertaining to the world of matter more than with the inner things of the spirit. Equally well can the charge be sustained against the East that it became obsessed so much with the inner side of life that it forgot the existence of an external material world. Therefore, such generalizations do no one any good—least of all to the protagonists of such views.

His view on the problem of individual versus society is relevant as ever:

> The mind of the student must be impressed to understand that self-love and interests can never be secured by injury to the legitimate aspirations of the community, and love for culture and country are ultimately bound up by love and enthusiasm for humanity. No man can be called educated who has not a willingness and desire as well as trained ability to do his part in the world's work. Learn the dignity of work, labour with your hands, and with your brains and duty.

It is very clear from his magnum opus, *Dattatreya: The Way and the Goal,* and his other writings that JCW idolized the concept of an Avadhuta. Another seemingly paradoxical inclination, one might say. An Avadhuta is defined as one who has 'let go'. Coined from the roots Ava and Dhu, it means to 'shake off'. On the surface, the imminent contrast between a king and Avadhuta is clear. The Avadhuta is known for what he has let go and the king for what mortal things he has amassed. The paradox melts when one understands what the Avadhuta lets go of—excess and compulsivity. The personality of the Avadhuta, as described in the *Avadhuta Gita*, is a riddling mix of reason and reverence, tyaga and bhoga, of immersion and detachment with the world. In his lecture, 'Avadhuta: Reason and Reverence' at the Indian Institute for World Culture, JCW describes the equanimous state of an Avadhuta thus: 'He is described as the pure, sinless, aesthetically balanced bhogi, enjoyer of life. (Sudha niranjanasamarasabhogi). This indicates that the Avadhuta is adept in the art of life.' His fascination with the concept of an Avadhuta was perhaps because it was a philosophy closest to his reality. The *Avadhuta Gita* gave him the recipe to enjoy his royal material bhogas while consuming the redeeming spirituality of the arts, music and literature. Most importantly, it contextualized his incessant bhoga of knowledge, which he did in great amounts throughout his life. Dr M.V. Krishna Rao remarks: 'The Maharaja is of the order who would chase rainbows, than content himself with the purely material things of the world, which he has in abundant measure.' His balanced perception of life is also reflected in his vision to modernize Mysore with abundant material resources, while emphasizing on regenerating its spirit through the arts, study of vernacular languages, religion and Indic knowledge.

That one's philosophy can firmly entrench the mind and enable it to make the most difficult choices in trying times is what makes his story important in today's world. In his world, the pursuit of knowledge was not an aggrandized romance but an agency that can digest the unthinkable. Philosophy gave him the womb to incubate his inner world and the terra firma to operate out into the world; it gave the facility to traverse between thought and action seamlessly—much like the emblem of his dynasty, the Gandabherunda. Gandabherunda signifies an equanimous presence in the material and the transcendental, the now and the beyond and the iha (mortal) and para (transcendental). Speaking on the occasion of the Golden Jubilee celebrations of the Chamaraja Ursu Boarding Institute inauguration in Mysore on 22 December 1943, he says, 'If you want me to say the essential, I would at once say that I attach the greatest importance to character, the source of all of our inner aspirations and the origin of all our outward conduct. Freedom without discipline and liberty without self-control will leads to disorder.' Time and again, his values were tested during the political turbulences that birthed India, during personal loss and vagaries of power. Most paradoxically, it was his philosophical bent that gave a certain acuity to his administrative actions in these circumstances; he did what felt right for himself and what was right for Mysore as well. It also gave him the much needed detachment from the throne and to fully express himself creatively, as he did with his music, writings and scholarly offerings. How often could we imagine a king writing music at a time when his state melded into a nation? Almost beautifully irreverent to his realities, engaged in what matters to the man behind the royal robe—to root for the right note, when the orchestra has crumbled. In a lecture at the Institute for Ethics, in New York City, 20 April 1959, he alludes to the source of his strength: 'What ordinarily makes a man quail and tremble leaves the Sakta brave and unbent, for he has developed in him a calm strength and fearlessness which is his characteristic quality.' Speaking of his journey with Adhyatma, he says: 'The sudden demise of my father and uncle had struck a severe blow on my mind. My mind leaned more and more towards Adhyatma. I was face to face before the cycle of birth and death. I had to resolve the tangle [...].'

When asked how difficult it was to make the decision to give away his kingdom to the Indian Union, he replied: 'I was inclined towards *Vedanta* almost right from my childhood. It was not at all difficult to change to the new situation. We are all parts of *Paramatma*—the Great Soul, *Viswatma*—the Universal Soul. This is ruling over us. Democracy is a practical application of this universal principle.' By saying democracy is an application of the principle of Vishwatma, it is as if he stands on the shoulders of the Men of Enlightenment and the Advaitha at once to come to this simple acceptance. Of what use is philosophy if it does not help men ride their realities?

> *You have referred in your address to what your generosity has termed my 'sacrifice'. I do not look upon it as such. If destiny had decreed that over the past few centuries, the progress and the prosperity of the people of this beloved State, should be in the hands of the Wadeyars of Mysore, then that same destiny now ordains that the time is ripe for the people, now grown to full political stature in a free democratic Republic, to rule themselves...the rule of the Maharajas has indeed fulfilled its purpose, the purpose of making the people fit to rule themselves.*
>
> **—On his 37th birthday, in his reply to an address presented to him by the Chief Minister on 29 July 1956.**

3
THE WADIYAR LEGACY

The Stench of Imperial Perceptions

A great stench emanates from the collective body of colonial literature and documentation of princely lives. The large archives of official communications and memoirs by British residents, civil servants, officers and military men who served in India, rarely paint a respectful picture of the princely men.

In historian Barbara Ramusack's pioneering study on the Indian princes and their states, she states: 'Many were consummate politicians, who exercised considerable degrees of autonomy until the disintegration of the princely states after Independence.' Many generations of Indians after Independence were culturally conditioned to believe in these colonially coloured stories on the quality of leaders India has produced. An insight into JCW's life is crucial in understanding and reframing this narrative too.

The colonial perception of princes is as old as the East India Company's need to meddle with local politics for their gain. Lord Wellesley's dispatch in 1804, even drew moral and ethical justification for East India company's meddling. He substantiates that 'subsidiary alliances may enable us to preserve the tranquillity of India by exercising a general control over those states calculated to prevent the operation of that restless spirit of ambition and violence, which is characteristic of every Asiatic government'. Strangely, despite the princely kingdoms being a noisy barrack of quarrelling neighbours, the 'restless spirit of ambition and violence' that Wellesley framed on these bickering men, was actually characteristic of the machinations that powered the avarice of the East India Company's policy in the 1700s. He further justifies his imperialist stance: 'This object can alone be accomplished by the operation of a general control over the principal states of India, established in the hands of a superior power and exercised with equity and moderation through the medium of alliances.' He definitely made an excellent case for arrogant imperialism and racial construction of Indian politics; a moral justification was sought to exert a 'general control over the principal states of India, established in the hands of a superior power' that could finally restore tranquillity in the Indian subcontinent. Undoubtedly, his strategy worked and permanently set the perception of the princes as being 'petty', 'bickering', 'subsidiary' men with no real clout or power.

Such bias has affected acceptance of 'royal enterprise' in much of South India. The music of the royal composers, their original scholarship or even statesmanship for that matter, is viewed by many Indians even today as being suspect. Every book, or music or scholarly output by royal princes is shrouded in suspicion. The snigger remains that maybe a more 'unroyal courtier' wrote it for him. There is a general discomfort in accepting that scholarship and royalty can actually sit on the same shoulders and permeate the same mind. The life of JCW challenges such prejudice sold by colonial histriographies and internalized by many in the Indian populace.

Many who read colonial history are left with this nagging question as to why the British did not do away with the Nawabs, the Hindu hereditary rulers or the Nizams? If these men were so petty and disposable with no real value addition to either the people they ruled or the British vested interest, then why bother with the subsidiary alliances? The treaties? The large pensions that were given to protect certain rulers? If the military might of the British was so large, they could have very well done away with the administrative nightmare of having to watch, supervise and rule indirectly. The truth is but sublime. Contrary to the idea of a British monolithic rule, what actually ruled India was an elaborate chain of command, from the Crown to the Viceroy to the Resident or an agent in the princely states. The big-five 21-gun salute princely states of India, namely, the Kingdoms of Mysore, Baroda, Gwalior, Hyderabad and Jammu and Kashmir were called 'autonomous self-governing dependencies'. The phrase is indicative of the paradoxical chain of command, and more importantly, it is indicative of the two major vested interests of the British Raj: the Maharaja seeking autonomy and the right to collect taxes, and the British government's interest to maximize revenue from the colonies while keeping administrative burdens to a minimum. This answers the question of why the British presence was not too keen on annexing every part of India nor enthusiastic about providing 'tranquillity and order', as Lord Wellesley waxed. With the major ports of India, the fertile, agrarian lands and lucratively taxable regions grouped up as presidencies, it was far more pragmatic to rule indirectly and not burden the exchequer with internal administration, civic and legal affairs. It was the colonial version of hiring an agency to bring in men, rather than hire a large workforce yourself. This large continuum of princely states included 'autonomous self-governing dependencies' like Mysore and Hyderabad, the treaty-states (the states that were created by the British to offset the power of local tribals or neighbours), states that received handsome pensions from the British government of India just to be 'on paper' and so on. They developed an intricate system of annex-some, administer-some, acquire-but-install-hereditary-figures approach to their conquest of India. Historian Barbara Ramusack, in her book, *The Indian Princes and their States* explains, 'First and foremost, the princes remained as inexpensive means of providing for administration of large tracts of unproductive or geographically inaccessible lands.'[1] She also accounts for their contributions to imperial military establishments, which without the princely contribution were quite meagre. More importantly, in the Indian milieu, with no access to and knowledge of local societal norms, communal politics and housekeeping, it just made sense to use that structure of power than topple it.

Mysore was also an autonomous self-governing dependent state, which meant that Mysore did have considerable say in certain matters concerning the state. A layered chain of command and administrative apparatus ensured that an autonomous and self governing Mysore functioned as a 'dependency' to the crown's sovereignty. The presence of a 'Resident' who participated in active governance along with the administrative structure of the Maharaja, with the Diwan being its head, somewhat created this 'dy-archy' of sorts. The Diwan governed, the Maharaja ruled and the Resident made sure this apparatus did not forget their dependency on the British Crown. After the third Anglo–Mysore War in 1799 and the fall of Tippu Sultan, the kingdom of Mysore was restored to Mummadi Krishnaraja Wadiyar, albeit with the appointment of the Mysore Resident. A Government House was built in Mysore as the node for such a dual-administrative set-up in the kingdom. Rumour has it that the posting of Resident Sir Barry Close was initially a reaction to Mummadi appointing a Diwan to head administration. The first Resident is said to have been appointed in 1799, guarding against the interests of the colonial vassal. There are some instances where the Maharaja had a great say in the appointment of the Resident too, Chamaraja Wadiyar X is said to have appointed his guardian, Sir James Gordon, as the first Resident post-rendition.

A map of British India, showing political divisions of British-administered provinces and princely kingdoms

To broker the cause of imperialism and to curate such an extensive hierarchy of power, there was an elaborate system of recognising and honouring these kingdoms and kings with gun salutes, gestures of pageantry, awards, honours and titles—which held this imperial rule in place, even as Britain itself plunged into economic and political chaos after the World War I. Princely Mysore was a 21-gun salute state, which meant that it was a part of the big-five princely states recognized as political structures in direct political relations with the Crown. Other princely kingdoms were either classified as 9-gun salute states or 12-gun salute states, based on the level of credence the British Crown gave its presence in India. It was also a means to create a hierarchy of allies, whose status of preference by the British government, precedence and priority were clear. It was a matter of great prestige to be a 21-gun salute state head, which the Maharaja of Mysore was entitled to. Various princely states enjoyed the prestige of odd and even numbers of gun salutes ranging from three to twenty-one. The heads of the big-five princely states received a 21-gun salute as well—the Nizam of Hyderabad, the Maharaja of Mysore, the Maharaja of Jammu and Kashmir state, the Maharaja Gaekwad of Baroda and the Maharaja Scindia of Gwalior. Such recognitions are awards of chivalry, having origins in the medieval sentiments of knighthood during the crusades. Contemporary Britain expanded the scope of such recognitions to include the princes and prominent figures in the British Raj. A new order of knighthood was created, and on 25 June 1861, the following proclamation was issued by the Queen:

> The Queen, being desirous of affording to the Princes, Chiefs and People of the Indian Empire, a public and signal testimony of Her regard, by the Institution of an Order of knighthood, whereby Her resolution to take upon Herself the Government of the Territories in India may be commemorated, and by which Her Majesty may be enabled to reward conspicuous merit and loyalty, has been graciously pleased, by Letters

> Patent under the Great Seal of the United Kingdom of Great Britain and Ireland, to institute, erect, constitute, and create, an Order of Knighthood, to be known by, and have forever hereafter, the name, style, and designation, of 'The Most Exalted Order of the Star of India'.

In 1945, as a mark of regard for his leadership efforts during World War II, JCW was awarded the Knight Grand Commander of the Most Exalted Order of the Star of India, abbreviated as GCSI. JCW also received the enviable Knight Grand Cross of the Most Honourable Order of the Bath which is abbreviated as GCB, next to his name in official records. The official notes pertaining to the investiture of his Order of the Bath, are an interesting read. The long and tenuous chain of correspondences between the Mysore Resident, the Diwan's Office, the Office of His Excellency the Viceroy of India, the Office of the High Commissioner for the United Kingdom in India, and their intermediaries paint a fascinating picture of the layers of diplomacy that existed between Mysore and Britain. The Mysore Resident in 1947, G.E.B. Abell, after noting that the Maharaja has missed several 'investiture' ceremonies in the past, inquires with Arcot Ramaswamy, the Diwan, if it is a matter of prestige or shyness. He receives a response back affirming that JCW is rather shy of receiving such awards. The Resident reports in his letter that he too believes that JCW's absence could be owing to his 'shyness', which he notes is very becoming of him. Over the course of a year and a half, the many offices in Mysore, Delhi and UK scramble to arrange for him to either attend the 'cold weather' Viceregal investiture or a ceremony when 'His Highness JCW' travels to New Delhi. Even a private ceremony in Mysore is suggested, when his Excellency the Viceroy travels to Mysore. In a 'top-secret' note by the personal secretary to the Viceroy, a small excerpt from Arcot Ramaswamy Mudaliar's interview is available, where he reports that the Maharaja is pained by Lord Archibald Percival Wavell's statement that Indian civil servants will not be considered for the British empire's decorations. Lord Wavell was a decorated British Imperialist and soldier, the penultimate Viceroy of India before Lord Mountbatten.[2] Between 1943 and 1947, Wavell's many plans—including the 'Wavell's plan' and the 'Breakdown plan'—tried in vain to keep Indian factions united in working towards an Indian Independence. Yet, he is a little-known figure in history. This report of anguish by Arcot Ramaswamy, the rather perceptive Resident, reads as Arcot himself seeking an award prior to the Maharaja's receipt of GCB. From January 1946 to June 1947, over 50 pages of notes and letters tell the tale of the possible 'shyness' of JCW and the eagerness of the British officials to fan the tentacles of power vested with Indian princes such as JCW.

OFFICE OF THE PRIVATE SECRETARY TO HIS EXCELLENCY THE VICEROY

NOTIFICATION

New Delhi, the 1st January 1946

ORDER OF THE BATH

No. 2-H.—His Imperial Majesty The KING, EMPEROR OF INDIA, has been graciously pleased to give orders for the following appointment to the Most Honourable Order of the Bath:—

To be a Knight Grand Cross
Civil Division

HIS HIGHNESS MAHARAJA SIR SRI JAYA CHAMARAJA WADIYAR BAHADUR, G.C.S.I., Maharaja of Mysore.

G. E. B. ABELL, Private Secy.

GIPD—(S) 92 PStoV—1).1.46—6

Official notification conferring the Knight Grand Cross and appointment to the Most Honourable Order of the Bath to JCW

The Order of the Bath vestiture. 'Rays of silver issuing from a centre and charged with three Imperial Crowns, one and two, within a circle whereon is inscribed the motto of the Order in gold : TRIA JUNCTA IN UNO ("three joined in one")'

Design of the Order of the Bath vestiture. The Order of the Bath is the fourth-most senior of the British Orders of Chivalry, after The Most Noble Order of the Garter, The Most Ancient and Most Noble Order of the Thistle, and The Most Illustrious Order of St Patrick

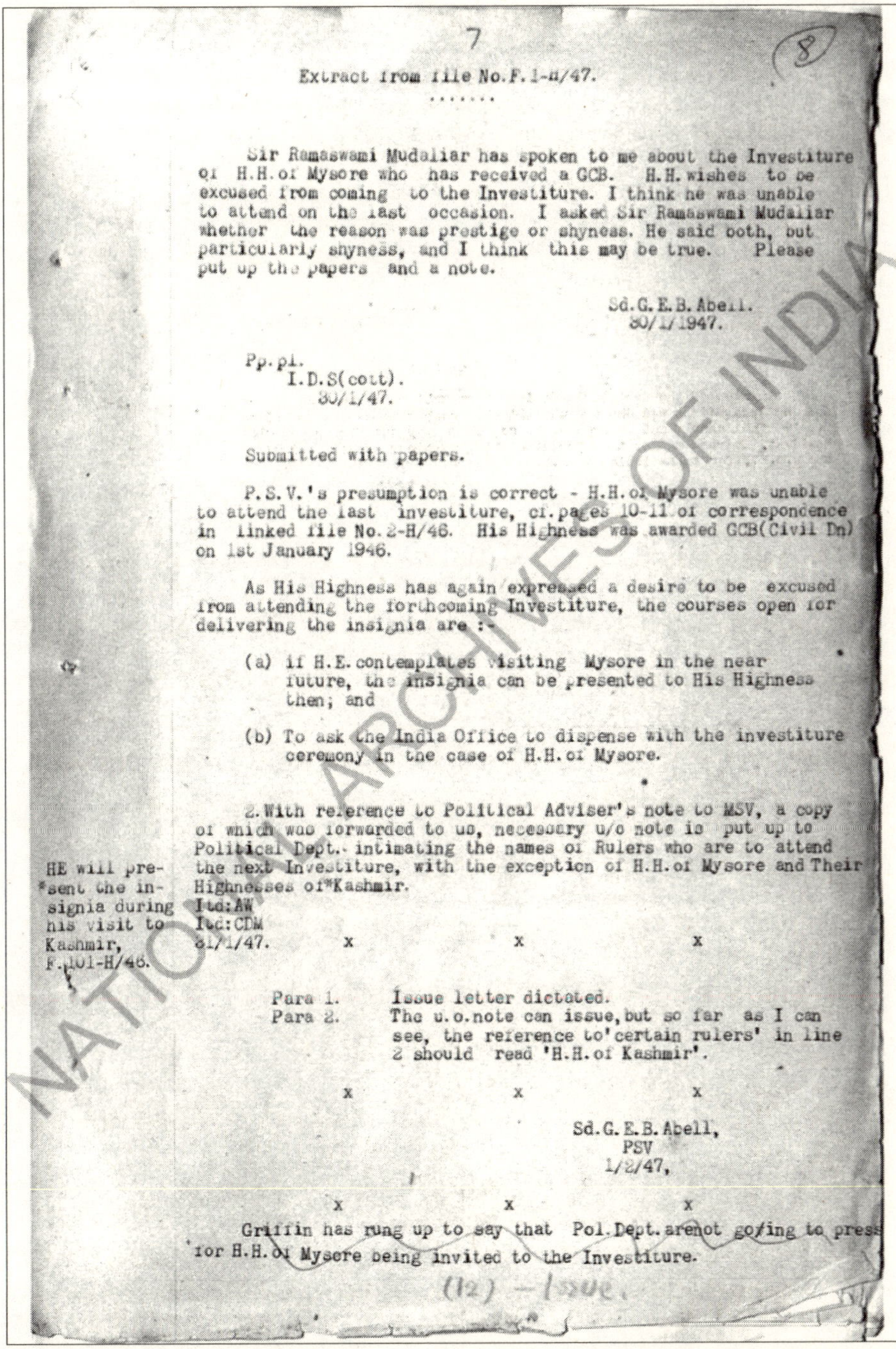

7

(8)

Extract from file No.F.1-H/47.

....

Sir Ramaswami Mudaliar has spoken to me about the Investiture of H.H.of Mysore who has received a GCB. H.H.wishes to be excused from coming to the Investiture. I think he was unable to attend on the last occasion. I asked Sir Ramaswami Mudaliar whether the reason was prestige or shyness. He said both, but particularly shyness, and I think this may be true. Please put up the papers and a note.

Sd.G.E.B.Abell.
30/1/1947.

Pp.pl.
I.D.S(cott).
30/1/47.

Submitted with papers.

P.S.V.'s presumption is correct - H.H.of Mysore was unable to attend the last investiture, cf.pages 10-11 of correspondence in linked file No.2-H/46. His Highness was awarded GCB(Civil Dn) on 1st January 1946.

As His Highness has again expressed a desire to be excused from attending the forthcoming Investiture, the courses open for delivering the insignia are :-

(a) if H.E.contemplates visiting Mysore in the near future, the insignia can be presented to His Highness then; and

(b) To ask the India Office to dispense with the investiture ceremony in the case of H.H.of Mysore.

2.With reference to Political Adviser's note to MSV, a copy of which was forwarded to us, necessary u/o note is put up to Political Dept. intimating the names of Rulers who are to attend the next Investiture, with the exception of H.H.of Mysore and Their Highnesses of Kashmir.

HE will present the insignia during his visit to Kashmir, F.101-H/46.

Itd:AW
Itd:CDM
31/1/47.

x x x

Para 1. Issue letter dictated.
Para 2. The u.o.note can issue,but so far as I can see, the reference to'certain rulers' in line 2 should read 'H.H.of Kashmir'.

x x x

Sd.G.E.B.Abell,
PSV
1/2/47.

x x x

Griffin has rung up to say that Pol.Dept.arenot going to press for H.H.of Mysore being invited to the Investiture.

(12) - Issue.

Communications from the Viceroy's office to the Mysore Resident about JCW's hesitation to receive the honour

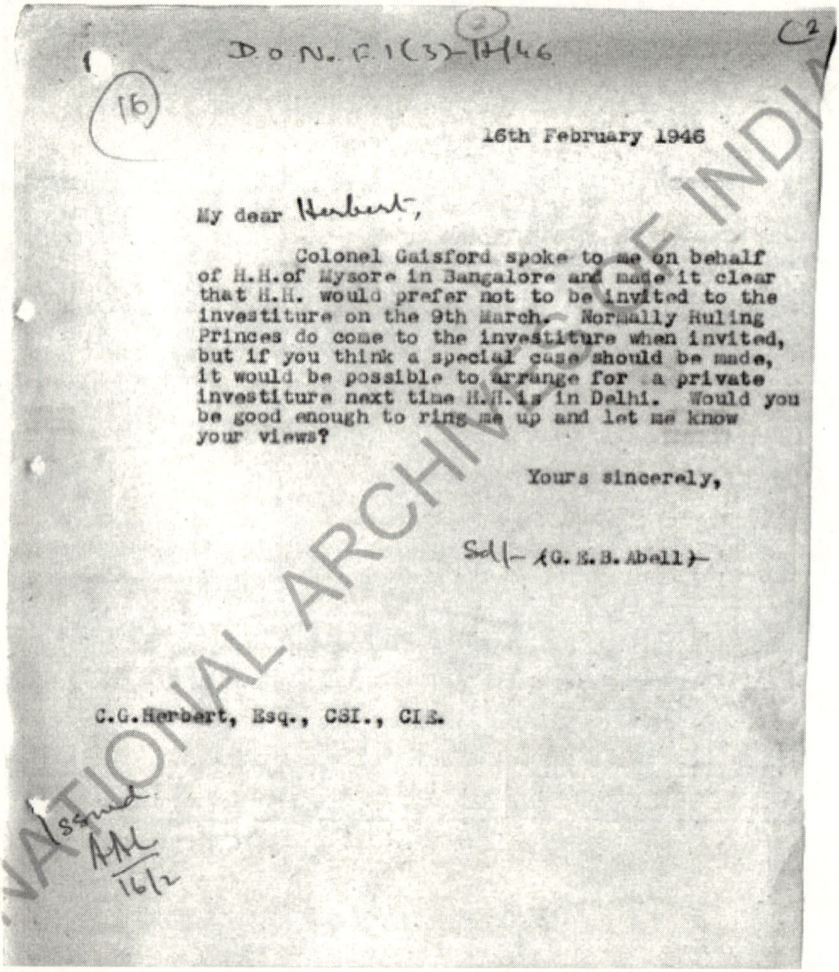

D.O.No. F.1(3)-H/46

(16)

16th February 1946

My dear Herbert,

Colonel Gaisford spoke to me on behalf of H.H.of Mysore in Bangalore and made it clear that H.H. would prefer not to be invited to the investiture on the 9th March. Normally Ruling Princes do come to the investiture when invited, but if you think a special case should be made, it would be possible to arrange for a private investiture next time H.H.is in Delhi. Would you be good enough to ring me up and let me know your views?

Yours sincerely,

Sd/- (G. E. B. Abell)

C.G.Herbert, Esq., CSI., CIE.

Issued AAL 16/2

Excerpt from official communications; a special private investiture ceremony was proposed to 'ensure' that he received the honour

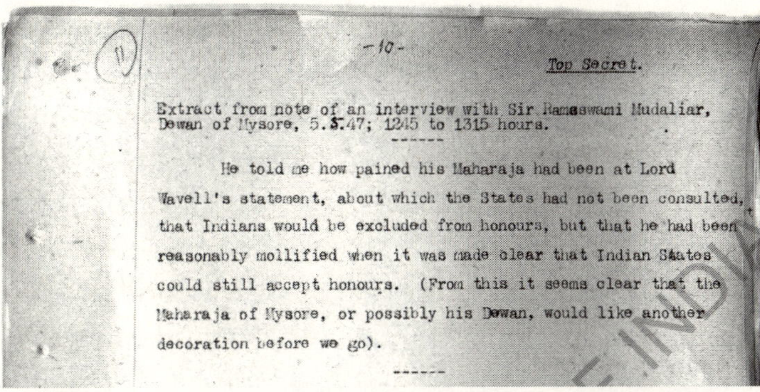

-10-

Top Secret.

Extract from note of an interview with Sir Ramaswami Mudaliar, Dewan of Mysore, 5.5.47; 1245 to 1315 hours.

He told me how pained his Maharaja had been at Lord Wavell's statement, about which the States had not been consulted, that Indians would be excluded from honours, but that he had been reasonably mollified when it was made clear that Indian States could still accept honours. (From this it seems clear that the Maharaja of Mysore, or possibly his Dewan, would like another decoration before we go).

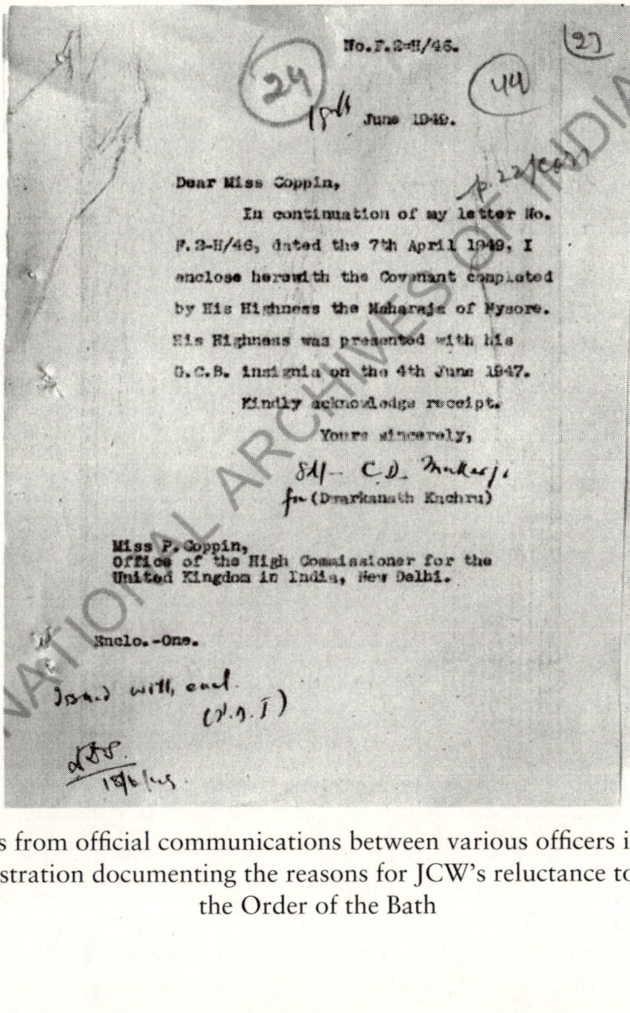

No.F.2-H/46.

18th June 1949.

Dear Miss Coppin,

In continuation of my letter No. F.2-H/46, dated the 7th April 1949, I enclose herewith the Covenant completed by His Highness the Maharaja of Mysore. His Highness was presented with his G.C.B. insignia on the 4th June 1947.

Kindly acknowledge receipt.

Yours sincerely,

Sd/- C.D. Mukerji

for (Dwarkanath Kachru)

Miss P. Coppin,
Office of the High Commissioner for the United Kingdom in India, New Delhi.

Enclo.-One.

Excerpts from official communications between various officers in British administration documenting the reasons for JCW's reluctance to accept the Order of the Bath

Another interesting story is that of the 'Order of Gandabherunda' initiated by Chamaraja Wadiyar X, the grandfather of JCW, along the lines of British civilian awards. He intended to institute this award for meritorious service to the Mysore gaddi by civil servants, philanthropists, teachers, scholars and artists. According to R.N. Singh of Ramsons Pratishthana, Mysore, the Mysore Resident initially was not approving of such an order, as it 'invests' in the local power of the Maharaja, away from the British Crown.[3] He notes:

> The British had made it clear that the Order, or for that matter, any other princely order or title could not be placed in a superior position on the chest to any award given by and on behalf of the King Emperor. The courtiers of Mysore, when the Order of the Gandabherunda was designed, instead made it a chain to be worn around the neck with the pendant close to the throat. So the Gandabherunda Order fits snugly at the base of the throat, making it quite clear what was superior! Thus the Mysore royals cocked a snook at the King-Emperor's diktats.[4]

The 'Palace Annual Gradation Lists' in the State Archives lists the awardees and between 1892 and 26 January 1950, about 300 people were awarded the Order of the Gandabherunda. The last such award was given by JCW on his birthday in 1949. The historical significance of these awards and vestitures highlight the social and local significance the Maharaja enjoyed in Mysore.

The Gandabherunda

Karnata janapada sampadadhistana bhuta
Nikhila kalanidhi kulakramagatha rajakshitipaala
Makara Sharabhsalva ghandaberunda ityaadaneka birudankita
Shri divyaratna simhasanarudha Shri Jayachamarajendra Bhoomipala
Paraak, paraak, Bahuparaak

In the paraak (benedictory praise) of JCW, he is described as the hereditary king, the treasure of knowledge, who adorns the star-studded throne of Mysore. An interesting reference is made to the Gandabherunda, the royal emblem of Wadiyars. The Gandabherunda is hailed to have an order higher than that of the Makara, the mascot of the Hoysala dynasty[5] and Sharabha[6], a symbol of the Chola period. This assertion of the Gandabherunda's higher power in the Wadiyar royal emblem over symbols of erstwhile dynasties, was perhaps deliberate.

In several streams of Hindu, Buddhist and Jain ideologies, the Gandabherunda signifies watchful equanimity—a mindfulness in the present and past, blurring binaries of time and space, the mortal and immortal. This unusual two-headed bird motif on the base of a stupa in Takshashila intrigued John Marshall, a colonial archaeologist and an English Director General of the Indian Archaeological Survey (1902–31). One head of the bird looked ahead and the other head faced the opposite direction, symbolic of the contrasting meanings it embodies.[7]

The Gandabherunda, the Royal Emblem of Mysore State

In several temples across Karnataka (especially Belur), the Gandabherunda is depicted as being at the top of an animistic 'chain of power'. On the sculpture at the Chennakeshava temple of Belur (1113 CE), the metaphors of power and the chain of destruction are clear. A big python preys on a deer, which in turn is tamed by an elephant. A lion attacks the elephant, which is usurped by the Sharabha, an-eight-legged part-lion and part-bird beast, which is finally killed by the Gandabherunda. The Wadiyar dynasty's choice of the royal emblem is somewhat symbolic of their resilient presence in the history of South India—one of the longest ruling dynasties of India, from 1399 to 1761 and from 1799 to 1950. JCW was the 25th king in a long line of kings who held power in many configurations. The Gandabherunda–Wadiyar symbolism has prevailed in Mysore—starting as warlords under the Vijayanagara dynasty to independent warrior kings, from kings who negotiated power with the rise of the Dalvoys Hyder Ali and Tipu to the kings who ruled Mysore under the indirect rule of the British empire.

The Gandabherunda as a symbol of power has existed in crests and seals from the Chalukyas to the Hoysalas, and from the Kadambas to the Vijayanagara empire. Historian Professor P.V. Nanjaraje Urs notes that the Gandabherunda was first used as a sign on coins of the Vijayanagara empire. The founder of the Wadiyar dynasty, Adi Yaduraya (Vijaya Raja Wodeyar, 1371–1423), a warrior and trusted vassal under six emperors of the Sangama dynasty, formalized a victory flag with the word 'Sathymevodhbhavaramyaham' and the Gandabherunda. The bird was flanked by an elephant-headed lion on either side and a lion with the demon Mahishasura in its mouth in the centre—alluding to the mythological tale of Mahishasura, the buffalo demon being slain by Durga, as chronicled in the Devi Mahatmya in the Markandeya Purana. With this triangulation of myth, legend and folklore, the Gandabherunda connect explains the presence of strong tantric and Shakta traditions in Mysore.

Illustration of the mystical Gandabherunda in H.H. Mummadi Krishnaraja Wadiyar's magnum opus, Sritattvanidhi

The Markandeya Purana and Shiva Purana tell the tale of a drunk-on-anger Lord Narasimha, who after having slain Hiranyakashapu raged on unable to rest. In the interest of the nether worlds, his aroused energies had to be captured, because energy can neither be created nor destroyed! So our 'cool dude' Shiva, comes down in the energetic bird-animal-human hybrid form called Sharabha, only to meet the energy-incarnate of Narasimha—the Gandabherunda. As the two major powers battled, somewhat reminiscent of the Vaishnavite and Shaivite power struggles for legitimacy, Shakti is said to have snatched this opportunity to create Pratyangira Devi, a fierce Devi incarnate, whose divine presence in Mysore is affirmed every year during the Dasara festival and Navaratri.

The Gandabherunda served another purpose, as a symbol of divine power, to fuse in people's consciousness two major loyalties to king and God, to faith and state. Much like James VI of Scotland (1567–1625), who promulgated the doctrine of the Divine Right of Kings, which asserts the power of the monarch from the shoulders of the Godhead—a legitimacy drawn not just from his military power or any mortal authority. Such symbolic assertions still live on as the British Anthem that prays that 'God Save the Queen' and informs the habit of all American Presidents ending their historic speeches with 'God bless America'. In 1750, Marthanda Varma gave up his kingdom of Travancore to Lord Padmanabha, and asserted that he and his descendants would rule on behalf of Lord Padmanabha. Since then, his title and those of his descendants would start with 'Padmanabha Dasa'. Such contemporary symbolism still exists in the imagery of the Bharata Mata, standing in Devi form, contoured by the map of India. The Gandabherunda symbolism over centuries stands as an emblem of a certain kind of Shakti, which transcends form, frame, physical strength and evolutionary advantages. It became the symbol of a dynasty, which sought to assert power in the very difficult political scenario of Mughal invasions, regional dalvoy and feudal lordship upsurges, declining presence of Hindu kingdoms and anarchies created by layers of fractured empires in the South.

Such anthropomorphic representations of power, such as the Sharabha and Gandabherunda have existed in many Oriental cultures. Such ideologies in visual form serve as powerful devices for consolidating power, which cannot be garnered by diplomacy, arms and administrative acumen. Alan Dundes, an anthropologist from the University of California, in his book, *Sacred Narrative Readings in the Theory of Myth*, explains a myth as 'a story that serves to define the fundamental worldview of a culture by explaining aspects of the natural world and delineating the psychological, social practices and ideals of a society'.[8] The evoking of such a Shakti was required to stay put and consolidate power for the dynasty and the Gandabherunda stood just for that. After joining the Indian Republic, the Gandabherunda reigned as the Mysore state emblem and continues as the Karnataka state emblem. The Gandabherunda insignia today is found on all buildings, heritage sites and communications of royal loyalties in Mysore.

The Wadiyar Legacy

Chiramapi vardhataam yadukula santana shri
May the tribe of Yadu continue to thrive eternally

The Wadiyars are said to have descended from King Yadu, whose successors, Yaduvamshis, were noted in the Rig Veda as one of the five Indian tribes called 'Panchajana'. Several historians contest this view, but claim that they were local lords who sought this legend to create legitimacy, much like many dynasties in India have in the past. Hence Shri Krishna is a significant deity for the dynasty, as he was a Yaduvamshi, also called Yadava[9] in many mythological references.

In an ode to JCW, Mysore Vasudevacharya seeks the grace of Krishna to protect the Yadukula Varidhi, whose personality is as luminous as the moon:

Nirupama chakradheeshwara karuna poornam sudhimanistutyam
Jaya Chamaraja bhoopam rakshasu satatam krpanidhihi krishnaha
Shri madyadukula varidhi rakchandram sushila gunasandram
Jaya Chamarajavaryam kripaya suciram shriyaha patihi payat

Monarch with no equal, an embodiment of compassion, celebrated by the wise.

Oh Krishna! You, who are the treasure of grace, protect and guide Jaya

Chamaraja, the mighty king Oh, torchbearer of the Yadukula clan, iridescent as the moon, scrupulous and virtuous.

May the revered Jayachamaraja be blessed with prosperity for a long time to come!

'Odeya' in Kannada means 'lord' or 'owner'. In spoken Kannada, when one calls another 'nanna Odeya' or 'my lord,' it implies, in addition to ownership of the subject, a reciprocity of care from the lord. In political parlance, an Odeya was one who would not just rule and collect taxes from his subjects but also give back in welfare. In chronicles of Indian history, the word is either spelt as 'Wodeyar' or 'Odeyar', but the official English spelling on records is 'Wadiyar'.

Adi Yaduraya, also known as Vijaya Raja Wodeyar, ruled over the Mysore area from 1399–1423 as a chieftain and trusted ally of the Sangama dynasty kings. The Wadiyars were from the Arasu-Wodeyar community of Karnataka, who during the Vijayanagara empire ruled the Nanjangud taluk near Mysore called Hadinaru. Another legend exists on the origins of how the Wadiyars came to power. Chamaraja, the king of Hadinaru, passed away suddenly, leaving his kingdom unattended. He also had a beautiful daughter whom many local noblemen wanted to marry. Many local chieftains also hoped to win her hand and the kingdom all at once. One such suitor, Mara Nayaka, harassed the widow Devajammanni, taking advantage of the anarchy in the land. The queen-mother sought the help of Yaduraya and his brother Krishnaraya, who sent a message to Mara Nayaka that Devajammanni's daughter had agreed to wed him. In the wedding procession, the brothers stealthily killed him, much to the relief of the royal family and the subjects of the kingdom. In return, Devajammanni gave her daughter's hand in marriage to Yaduraya and he was crowned the ruler of Hadinaru in 1399. There is an alternative plot to this legend, common in folklore of Mysore. Yaduraya and Krishnaraya are said to have travelled from Dwaraka to Melukote as pilgrims. Goddess Chamundeshwari is said to have appeared in Yaduraya's dreams, directing him to go save Hadinaru. This version of the origins of Yaduraya is rendered suspect by many historians, after ethnographic studies on the royal gentry of the Urs/Ursu and Wodeyar clans who populated Hadinaru at the time. Noted historian Prof. P.V. Nanjaraje Urs argues that Yaduraya and Krishnaraya were not from Dwaraka, as is the belief among some, but had come from Vijayanagar or some other region around the then Mysore province.[10] Having heard of their valour, the queen-mother invited them to the palace to slay Mara Nayaka, he says.

The neo-Mysore kingdom under the Vijayanagara empire was compact with the Chamundi hills and surrounding plains as its epicentre. After the fall of the Vijayanagara empire in 1565, the kings of the Wadiyar dynasty came to be independent rulers until 1799. Raja Wadiyar proclaimed himself as a sovereign ruler of Mysore and ruled from 1578 to 1617. The capital of the kingdom was shifted to Srirangapatna, a strategically located island created by the Kaveri close to Mysore, making attacks difficult. The size of Mysore was perhaps at its largest during the reign of Kanthirava Narasaraja, who ruled from 1638 to 1659. Mysore kingdom now had reached into the deep South, gaining strength as the Maratha Confederacy in the South was weakening. It is Chikka Devaraja, who ruled from 1673 to 1704, who is remembered for his statesmanship, administrative acumen and military valour, as he for the first time, organized his kingdom into 18 Chavadis, and introduced a reliable system of taxation.[11]

During the time of Krishnaraja Wadiyar II (1761–66), the kingdom experienced many uprisings of Dalvoys and ministers. Hyder Ali rose to prominence in his tenure and functioned as the 'Sarvadhikari' of Mysore, a titular alternative to the Maharaja. Nanjaraja Wadiyar, Chamaraja Wadiyar VIII and Chamaraja Wadiyar IX kept the dynasty's presence in Mysore through the death of Hyder Ali and the Anglo–Mysore Wars. After the death of Chamaraja Wadiyar IX in 1796, Tipu ruled Mysore for three years, establishing the Mysore Sultanate, till his death in 1799.

The installation of the five-year-old Krishnaraja Wadiyar III, as a subsidiary king of the East India Company and the Maharaja of Mysore in 1799 started the indirect rule of Mysore. In 1831, however, the East India Company under the pretext of maladministration usurped Mysore during the reign of Krishnaraja Wadiyar III (1799–1868). For the next five decades, Mysore was ruled directly by many British Commissioners, including Lieutenant–General Mark Cubbon, who served from 1834 to 1861. The First War of Indian Independence of 1857 led to the Government of India Act of 1858 and the British Crown taking over the administration of the Indian subcontinent. It was officially the start of the British Raj in India. With the dissolution of the East India Company, and after an extended diplomacy lobby by Chamaraja Wadiyar X, the Privy Council of the United Kingdom restored the princely status of Mysore by the Rendition Act of 1881, putting Chamaraja Wadiyar X on the throne in 1881. When a compacted kingdom of Mysore was returned to Chamaraja Wadiyar X with a Rendition Agreement, an additional title of Bahadur was added to the successors of the dynasty thereon. Following his death, Vani Vilasa Sannidhana, the queen of Chamaraja Wadiyar X, was Regent from 1894–1902, followed by Nalvadi Krishnaraja Wadiyar,

A unique painting of the kings of Wadiyar dynasty located in the Jaganmohana Palace, Mysore

whose reign as a contemporary monarch is celebrated as the pinnacle of Mysorean glory (1894–1940).[12]

In many streams of Indian history and the accounts of South India, the period of tussle between the East India Company and Hyder Ali and his son Tipu Sultan captures a great deal of imagination (1734–96). The exaggerated documentation of the valour of Tipu Sultan, the 'Tiger of Mysore' in East India Company Records is contrasted with the somewhat poorly understood kings of the Wadiyar dynasty, who battled their diminishing dominance over Mysore. Tipu's economic success, valour and military prowess did throw quite a spanner in the growth of the East India Company in the South. In Mysore, during his reign, the average per-capita income was five times higher than subsistence level[13] and Mysore emerged as a dominant economic power with productive agriculture and textile manufacturing bases. After the death of Tipu in the Fourth Anglo–Mysore War, parts of this rich Mysore were divided between the English, the Marathas and the Nizam of Hyderabad. A very compacted Mysore was rendered back to Chamaraja Wadiyar X with a Rendition Agreement—that made it difficult for Mysore to emerge from restraints posed on taxation policies, natural resource sharing and industrial development. From the wealth Mysore experienced during Tippu's rule to the Mysore famine of 1876, the back stories tell the grim tale of how British policies reduced a thriving economic powerhouse into a famine-stricken economy. They are perhaps the most well-kept secrets of that time, buried in reams of colonial administrative gunk. How Mysore extricated itself from such a burgeoning economic state to the Ramarajya of Nalvadi is a heartening struggle of vision; a victory of Mysorean will amidst British bureaucratic indifference. Vikram Sampath, in his book, *Splendours of Royal Mysore: The Untold Story of the Wodeyars*,[14] writes that the state's debt stood at a whopping Rs 80 lakh after the Mysore famine. To move from this state to a most well-administered Mysore, would not have been possible without the leadership of Chamarajendra Wadiyar X, Queen

Mother Kempananjammani Vani Vilasa Sannidhana, Krishnaraja Wadiyar IV, and finally, Jayachamarajendra Wadiyar. The tensions between the Maharaja's office and the Diwan notwithstanding, the four Diwans of Mysore actuated this conjoint transformation of Mysore. Sampath attributes the administrative marvels of Mysore to the famous 'quartet' of Rangacharlu (1881–83), K. Seshadri Iyer (1883–1900), M. Vishveshwaraiah (1912–18) and Mirza Ismail (1926–41).

Significance of the JCW Reign

JCW ascended the throne on 8 September 1940. His reign, though short, is significant for many reasons. He held Mysore together through the most difficult decade, 1940–50. First, the war-ravaged British paramountcy was failing in India, British provinces after World War I suffered from excessive taxation and lack of welfare measures. India saw a spate of devastating famines, from 1765 to 1947, including the Great Famine of Mysore in 1876, which claimed over ten million lives. During World War II, food shortage and drought in Mysore were pushing the needle towards another famine, like in Bengal, had it not been brilliantly managed by him and his Diwan N. Madhav Rao. British apathy and legitimate demands for Swaraj had intensified; several anarchist movements masquerading as 'peoples parties' in India and Mysore alike were fanned by vested interests. The Quit India Movement gave local Congress a national standing, increasing their public agitations in Mysore against the British occupancy. In this rather complicated hierarchy, JCW had the daunting task of navigating the maze of his own nationalist and democratic sentiments, the propriety of his crown as a subsidiary of British rule, asserting his kingly powers and tempering voices which ran amok. To some, the Indian National loyalists, he perhaps appeared as the local face of an imperial monster. The Issur rebellion and tragedy under his rule, illustrates his tight-rope balancing act with great accuracy.[15]

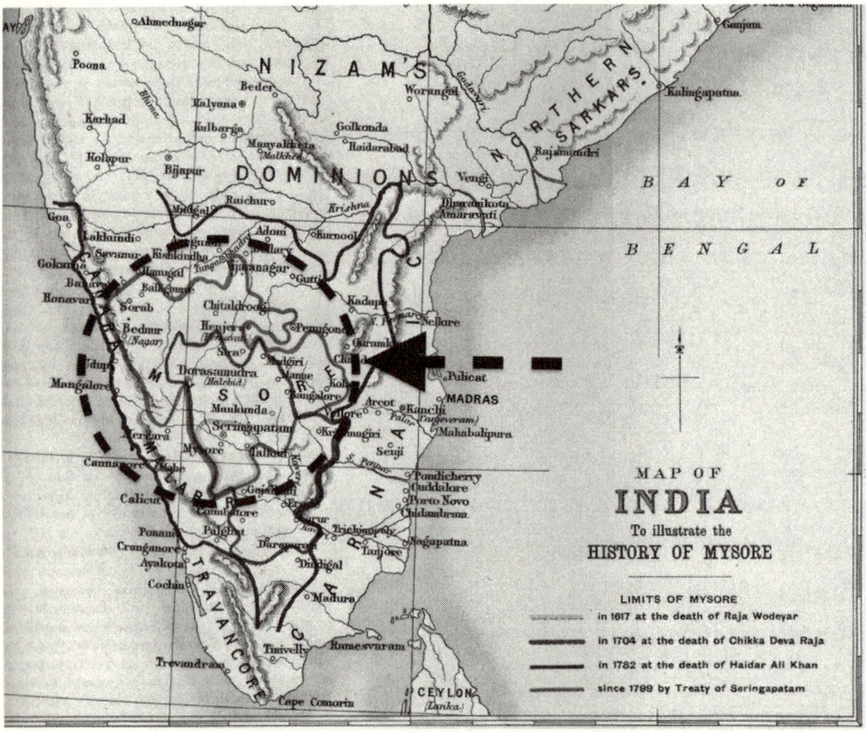

Map of South India showing the various limits of Mysore State from 1617 (death of Raja Wadiyar) to 1799 (Treaty of Srirangapatna). The boundaries of Mysore Kingdom in 1799 are shown inside inset circle

With the holding of Constituent Assembly elections in India, there was tremendous pressure to lead Mysore into a stable post-independent set-up, in a way that did not undo the many decades of industrial, social, cultural and political integrity it had built. His curious term as a free monarch in the Indian Dominion (1947–50) tested his statesmanship and diplomacy in balancing national powers with those who could misuse the legislative structure in Mysore for short-sighted gains. When he accepted the recommendation of his Legislative Assembly to join the Indian Union, he rested the long tenure of the Wadiyars on the Gaddi of Mysore. He was to be the last Maharaja. Technically, he was also the only sovereign after Krishnaraja Wadiyar II to rule Mysore between August 1947 and 26 January 1950. His son Srikantadatta Wadiyar and his successor Yaduveer Chamaraja Wadiyar continue to hold only ceremonial titles, after de-recognition of the titles of Maharaja and the cancellation of privy purse by the 26th amendment of the Indian constitution in 1971.

The man at the helm of all this showed remarkable valour—with a song in his heart, the surrender of a saint and the stoic will of a king. When Mysore exited his world, another avatar arose. What makes his story unique is that unlike many other last Maharajas, his journey towards a more immortal significance had just begun. As Swami Vivekananda describes, it was a 'a power that is not power, a shade in dazzling light!'

Behold, it comes in might,
The power that is not power,
The light that is in darkness,
The shade in dazzling light.
It is death between two lives,
And lull between two storms,
The void whence rose creation,
And that where it returns.

4

THE BHOGI OF KNOWLEDGE

The Maharaja had a major vice. He gambled avidly with the faculties of his mind, in pursuit of knowledge. A true follower of the Vedic mantra, '*Aano bhadrah kravato yantu vishwataha*' (Let noble thoughts come to us from the world), he sought knowledge from all sources. His pursuit of knowledge was marked by the classical and the exotic. His words on the occasion of Mysore Maharaja's College Day Celebrations on 8 January 1954, beautifully sum up how his personality was enshrined in the identity of a knowledge-seeker:

> Several positions of honour and dignity, I have held in my life as a result of the circumstances of my birth, but there is one position… one destiny, I have carved out for myself, and that is as a student, shall I say, as an advanced student of literature, history, philosophy, music, and above all, our ancient culture, which illumined my path, and which serves as a perpetual refreshment for my mind and soul.

The only son to Yuvaraja His Highness Sri Kanthirava Narasimharaja Wadiyar and Yuvarani Kempu Cheluvaja Ammanni, he was also the heir to his father's scholarship and multifarious interests—from world history to cultural entrepreneurship to jazz.

> Those who had a very great influence over me in my younger days were my mother, Kempu Cheluvaja Ammanni. The other was my maternal grandmother. My mother was largely responsible in shaping my personality. She kindled my interest in spiritualism—Adhyatma. It has the first place in my life.

He credits his mother and maternal grandmother with being the architects of his inner life, fortifying it, preparing him for life's bounties and barbs.

> My mother was a staunch believer of our old tradition. She had a great faith in the Shastras. My mother and grandmother moulded my inner life and made me mentally strong enough to face the harsh realities of life. They showered their affection on me and had sympathy, understanding and forbearance. Their affection was like a solid phalanx in my battle of life. These two revered ladies were like my guardian angels. Their words often reverberate in my mind.

JCW lived, witnessed and experienced what is heralded as the Golden era in Mysore. Nalvadi Krishnaraja Wadiyar's kingdom was hailed as 'Ramarajya' by even Mahatma Gandhi. JCW describes the role played by his uncle: 'He was my great guru, friend, philosopher and guide. He was my beacon light along the corridors of life. He was a royal sage, a man of few words—words, which always were very effective. The influence wielded by my father was different. He had an open mind and was large-hearted.'

JCW's kindness and empathy were qualities celebrated by many in his family, peers and subjects alike. His daughter, Maharajakumari Meenakshi Devi, reminisces: 'The word "no" was never there for anything with him. He was kind-hearted and generous to a fault. As a father, he was one of the best persons in my world. He used to be very fond of all his children. He used to spend time with all of us in spite of his busy schedule.' The very first adjective that Maharajakumari Kamakshi Devi used to describe her father was 'kind'. 'He was an extraordinarily busy man, yet he always had a sense of priority. He always gave us time, attention, and was in touch with our big and small likes, dislikes, fears and dreams,' Kamakshi Devi recollects. This river of compassion must have helped him navigate some very difficult personal times. The sudden death of his father Yuvaraja Narasimharaja Wadiyar on 11 March 1940 at the anchorage in Bombay, followed by the death of his uncle Krishnaraja Wadiyar IV, a few months later on 3 August 1940 shook his world in more ways than one. His marriage to Maharani Satya Prema Kumari, was failing soon after his wedding on 15 May 1938. His coronation on 8 September 1940 and taking on the reigns of Mysore was in such dire personal circumstances. Yet, he prevailed because of his inner faith and compassion—which allowed him to cope well with grief while dispensing his duties with passion. In the years to come, he turned his life around, on the personal front as well, arranged for the marriage of his sisters, married Maharani Tripura Sundari Ammanni Avaru on 6 May 1942, was blessed with six children and a home bustling with young, eager minds!

JCW credits this most exalted education in empathy and emotional intelligence to his mother:

> Another great quality of my mother was kindness. She had an open mind and was large-hearted, and she always tried to understand others' points of view. She would say, if you do not like another's thoughts and actions, don't lose your patience. Try to be calm. Count numbers from one to ten. You regain equanimity. You can then clearly see the other's viewpoint. I have followed her precept on many occasions and every time I have succeeded.

His mother gave him another gift to tide over the mortal and the mundane. 'My mother was an accomplished piano player. She would forget the whole world when she sat before it.' So did he. His first musical passion was the piano, and perhaps remained his

JCW meets piano virtuoso Rachimanoff while on a Europe trip.
Also seen is his sister Rani Vijaya Devi to his left

A rare picture of JCW with his
piano teacher Sister Ignatius,
mother and sisters

most ardent instrument of expression. Sister Ignatius from the Good Shepherd Convent in Mysore taught the young prince the majesty of the piano. His sister Rani Vijaya Devi remembers that his talent was precocious. His huge record collection made up for his inability to hear concerts live, and he kept abreast of all the latest developments, musical tastes, and styles in Europe. His expansive knowledge of Western classical music and piano was enough to baffle Walter Legge, a British classical music producer, who said, 'The visit to Mysore was a fantastic experience. The Maharajah was a young man, not yet thirty. In one of his palaces, he had a record library containing every imaginable recording of serious music, a large range of loudspeakers, and several concert grand pianos...' JCW became a Licentiate of the Guildhall School of Music, London, and was granted an honorary Fellowship of the Trinity College London in 1945—stupendous achievements for a man in his mid-twenties then. Shortly before his coronation, he is said to have visited Sergei Rachimanoff, a legendary pianist in Switzerland, seeking his mentorship in studying piano and composition. Compose he did, but much later, not for the piano but for himself, and as an offering to the Mother Goddess. His music most definitely anchored his soul and fortified his inner experience, in ways that intellectual fascinations could not. It also gave him the vocabulary to ignite his mind to the call of the Srividya, in the form of his musical kritis in Carnatic music. Even though his compositional tenure was short, he composed nearly a hundred compositions between 1945 and 1950, only to move onto his other creative pursuits of writing, curating the future of the Philharmonia Concert and lecturing overseas as a cultural ambassador of India.

JCW also grew up in a Mysore that was living its intellectually and spiritually most exalted state. In fact, the prefix 'Jaya' was added to his name, after his birth on 18 July 1919, to commemorate the victorious high experienced after World War I was won. Mysore, along with the many large and capable princely kingdoms, had played a significant role in bolstering the strength of British armies in war. To commemorate this victory of the Allied Forces, the word

'Jaya' was added to the name of the heir apparent of Mysore. It was somewhat prophetic, because Jayachamarajendra Wadiyar's life indeed was marked by the many battles he was to emerge victorious from. A victory over his circumstances. Treaties with his tribulations. Triumphs over his trials. It is clear from the chronicles of Mysore that the intellectual quotient everywhere around him ran high. The Mysorean sensibilities balanced the cosmopolitan with the traditional and a Western model of life with an Eastern spirit. Dr M.V. Krishna Rao notes:

> It was a period when the glamour and fascination of Western culture had laid under their spell all young, ardent and generous minds and when the best spirits of the land were eager to mould their life after the models of the West. Though they were steeped in the culture and education of Europe, they never lost the balance and sanity of mind, nor shut their eyes to the superior spiritual validity of Hindu civilisation.

The Maharaja's initial world was perhaps filled with British scholars, writers, and aesthetes such as H.A.L. Fisher, Henry Green and Harold Acton, but this was offset by his exposure to the indigenous scholarship that shone in his uncle's court.

His early education was at the Royal School, a school sculpted inside the palace with the children of elite gentry of Mysore. Dr M.V. Krishna Rao notes that while in school he 'exhibited high powers of application and distinguished himself by his robustness and modesty of deportment'. An Indian Civil Service officer, C.J. Turner, was appointed his tutor to train him in aspects that would prepare him for office later. Like most princes in his era, he was trained in horse riding, swimming, hunting and tennis. His classmate in Royal School, Chaduranga, a Kannada writer, remembers his interactions with the Maharaja:

It was my fortune to have been associated with him when both of us were young. I was one among the five or six lucky youngsters who were chosen to study with him in the Royal School. All fingers of the human hand are not equal. Similarly not all men are equal in the wealth of their personality. Human beings differ with one another in their innate qualities. Some are the specially chosen. They are endowed with special qualities. But such persons are rare and I found such a rare person in Sri Jayachamaraja Wadiyar, the ex-ruler of Mysore.

Chaduranga remembers that the Maharaja would often quote Robert Southey, an English poet of the Romantic school:

My days among the Dead are past;
Around me I behold,
Where'er these casual eyes are cast,
The mighty minds of old;
My never-failing friends are they,
With whom I converse day by day.

Perhaps, like the poet, the Maharaja's world was full of books, histories, historical figures, musicians and composers of yore who inspired him and stimulated his insatiable curiosity. In his mind, perhaps, he had many a conversation with this intellectual 'cohort'!

After completing studies at Yuvaraja's College (then called Intermediate College), it is reported that his uncle suggested that JCW attend Maharaja's College, to prepare for a kingsmanship that was sharpened by his interactions with all factions of the society.

I am ever grateful to my beloved uncle for his foresight. This experience helped me to equip myself to play the great role I had to play as the ruler of a great State, and later, as a common and loyal subject of our great nation. I acquired great friends and gained wisdom, thanks to my teachers like Prof. Rollo, Prof. Wadia, Dr M.H. Krishna, Dr Gopal, Prof. Satyagirinathan and Prof. D'souza.

Growing up in Mysore, JCW was aware of the reality that it was a Mysore that had already heard the faint strains of Indian Independence on the anvil. Several socialist movements with a strong base in student-run organization had begun. Dr M.V. Krishna Rao notes this awareness in him: 'With the admission to the Intermediate class, he gave definite instructions that no difference was to be made in the treatment given to him and to the other students.' Most of his peers remember him for his voracious consumption of knowledge in a variety of subjects. Professor Krishnaswamy, a noted Kannada columnist, essayist, novelist, critic, and teacher of economics at Mysore University strikes it right:

> Some are born great, as Shakespeare says, some acquire greatness through hard work, and greatness is thrust on some others. Jayachamaraja Wadiyar, the last Maharaja of the erstwhile native State of Mysore, was great not just because of his birth. Greatness was not thrust on him. He was great not only because he belonged to a great and ancient dynasty. Much of his true greatness was acquired by him through hard work.

At Maharaja's College, he showed a keen interest in the study of international affairs, history, politics and economics. International and national political problems fascinated him, an aptitude that was to come in handy in dispensing many public administration issues later in life. He was sent abroad to Japan and China in 1937, and Europe in 1939, just before the commencement of World War II, to understand world affairs and further expand his exposure to contemporary affairs. His uncle, Maharaja Nalwadi Krishnaraja Wadiyar ensured that his shoes would be filled by someone who knew his state well enough to rule it. JCW often accompanied his uncle during his tours within the state, to gain a personal knowledge of the conditions prevailing in the state. Dr M.V. Krishna Rao notes:

> His study of international affairs was a special feature of his work in the University. He was unanimously elected Honorary President of the History Association of the Maharaja's College, and as its President, he delivered the Inaugural Address of the Association in July 1937, which at a comparatively early age with almost uncanny insight, he discerned and foretold serious complications in the Sino-Japanese relations, which would ultimately prepare the ground for a major and global catastrophe.

He remembers the Maharaja highlighting a particular passage in H.A.L Fisher's *A History of Europe* marked deep in pencil:

> Men wiser and more learned than I have discerned in history a plot, a rhythm, a predetermined pattern. These harmonies are concealed from me. I can see only one emergency following upon another as wave follows upon wave, only one great fact with respect to which, since it is unique, there can be no generalisations, only one safe rule for the historian; that he should recognize in the development of human destiny the play of the contingent and the unforeseen.

It is as if back then, he had an inkling of how the Maharaja's life was soon to be dropped amidst a world chaos of wars, the Quit India Movement and power uprisings. Nobody could have predicted that the contingent and the unforeseen events of 1940s would change the course of everything he had been till then.

JCW graduated from Maharaja's College, Mysore, in 1938, earning five awards and gold medals. In a memoir of JCW, J.M. Imam, who was named 'Mushir ul-Mulk' ('Advisor of the Kingdom') in 1945 by JCW, notes the glee and pride on Krishnaraja Wadiyar's face as he watched his nephew garner gold medals: 'I was present at the convocation as a member of the Senate and I could see His Highness the Chancellor Sree Krishnaraja Wadiyar beaming with pride when he presented the medals to his nephew.'

Even though his formal education ended, he remained an avid consumer of knowledge till the very end. It is clear from his writings and creative offerings that he loved to unbox and integrate knowledge from various sources. His deep knowledge of Western intellectual traditions, gave him a vantage point to examine Indic intellectual traditions. His compositional offerings in Carnatic music underscore a deep and fundamental knowledge in the Ragas enmeshed with Western classical music syntax. Music and philosophy were most definitely his larger love interests. He also loved to deep dive into exotic subjects—knowledge sabbaticals of sort, where he would explore an unknown territory—going on a research tour to Scandinavian countries to study how border issues could be negotiated or a tour to Africa to study the seminal connections between India and Africa. His pursuit of knowledge not only irrigated his psyche but his administrative approaches as well. His study of the economic and ecological aspects of large irrigational projects formed the basis for the signature irrigation projects taken up in Mysore during his reign—such as the Bhadra reservoir, Thunga Anekattu, and Kabini reservoirs.

His self-directed journey with knowledge informed a distinct approach to revitalizing Mysore's education system as a Maharaja later. His vision for education was crystal clear: an education that is scientific, technical and professional, fully embodied in a mind that is knowledgeable of the country, its literature, history and philosophy: 'We look to education to restore to man his peace, the condition in which all his faculties would be in harmony with one another and in deep rhythm with the nature of things.' His goal was to create an educational ecosystem that would transcend the binary of contemporaneity and the ancient:

> The close association in ancient India between learning and religion gave education a spiritual rather than a secular significance. The ancient emphasis upon distinction of human worth, the free spirit in search for truth, goodness and beauty, the breath of human understanding—all these were embraced in the classical tradition and they are the very things necessary for the humanization of our scientific and industrial age. Where is the wisdom we have lost in knowledge? Where is the knowledge we have lost in information? Our national education should be something distinctive of India, something that shows that India has come to a collective consciousness of itself.

Contrary to some popular perceptions that princely kings in the nineteenth century were indeed 'Macaulay's children', the Maharaja's views appear grounded in the intellectual traditions of India. Thomas Babington Macaulay is hailed as the 'pioneer of India's modern education', for his extraordinary educational vision of an assembly line that spewed literate Indian officers fully divorced from their roots—well-groomed hand puppets of cultural imperialism that Macaulay so successfully slapped on the Indian subcontinent. Educational policies in India are still haggling over a 'golden mix' of the traditional and the modern, the vernacular and English, of institutionalized education versus the traditional gurukula model. In an interview with ace biographer and journalist Dr H.S. Krishnamurthy published in the *Star of Mysore* dated 3 October 2006, JCW remarks, 'It is regrettable that we are quarrelling among ourselves in the name of language. When a decision is taken on the official language, we should all make concerted efforts to develop it. One can never afford to neglect the regional language. English is the window to the world.'

Education, predictably, was a major administrative thrust area during his tenure. In a rather short time, the starting of nearly one thousand primary schools, hundreds of middle schools, and several higher education and polytechnic institutes strengthened Mysore's primary education. The Maharaja as the Chancellor of Mysore University revitalized its vision, time and again, by starting the Department of Music, Department of Ancient History and Archaeology, and mooting the idea of a chair in Indology. He continued to support institutes of higher education, such as the Indian Institute of Science, Bengaluru, and niche organizations such as the Mythic Society and the Indian Institute of World Culture. His tireless pursuit of knowledge was decorated by many doctorates: a Doctor of Literature from the University of Queensland, Australia, and Annamalai University, Tamil Nadu; a Doctor of Law from Banaras Hindu University; and a Doctor of Laws, honoris causa from the University of Mysore, 1962.

It would be no hyperbole to say that the one knowledge he sought with greater passion and desire than the rest was the knowledge of the self. His mother and grandmother had seeded a contemplative bent in him, which later blossomed into a desire for a rich inner life. 'No man is free, who is not master of himself,' said Epictetus, a Greek philosopher. Swami Vivekananda affirms: 'All knowledge that the world has ever received comes from the mind; the infinite library of the universe is in our own mind.' JCW's study of Vedanta, Adhyatma, Puranas and the mainstay of his Srividya practice were all aimed at pursuing this knowledge of the self. This pursuit was his crowning glory. After all, of what use is one's ability to write a piece of music, if the song does not sing within? Of what use is studying history, if one does not believe in its transformative power? How can one believe in an awakened society, if that awakened light is first not felt within?

Photographs of JCW with Family Members. Also Photographs of His Student Days, Coronation and Foreign Tours as Yuvaraja

A painting of JCW as a child from family archives

JCW with mother, Yuvarani Kempu Cheluvaja Ammanni, and sisters Maharajakumaris Vijaya Lakshmi Ammanni, Sujaya Kantha Ammanni and Jaya Chamunda Ammanni

Maharani Tripura Sundari Ammanni with Princess Gayatri Devi, Princess Meenakshi Devi, Prince Srikantadatta Narasimharaja Wadiyar, Princess Kamakshi Devi and Princess Indrakshi Devi

Official photograph of JCW with his sisters at Mysore Palace

JCW, just after his graduation from Maharaja's College, Mysore

JCW with foreign guests while on a hunting expedition during his college days

A painting of JCW with his sisters during his teenage years

JCW with his mother, sisters and extended family

JCW with his father, Yuvaraja Narasimharaja Wadiyar, mother and the Mysore delegation on a trip to Europe in 1940

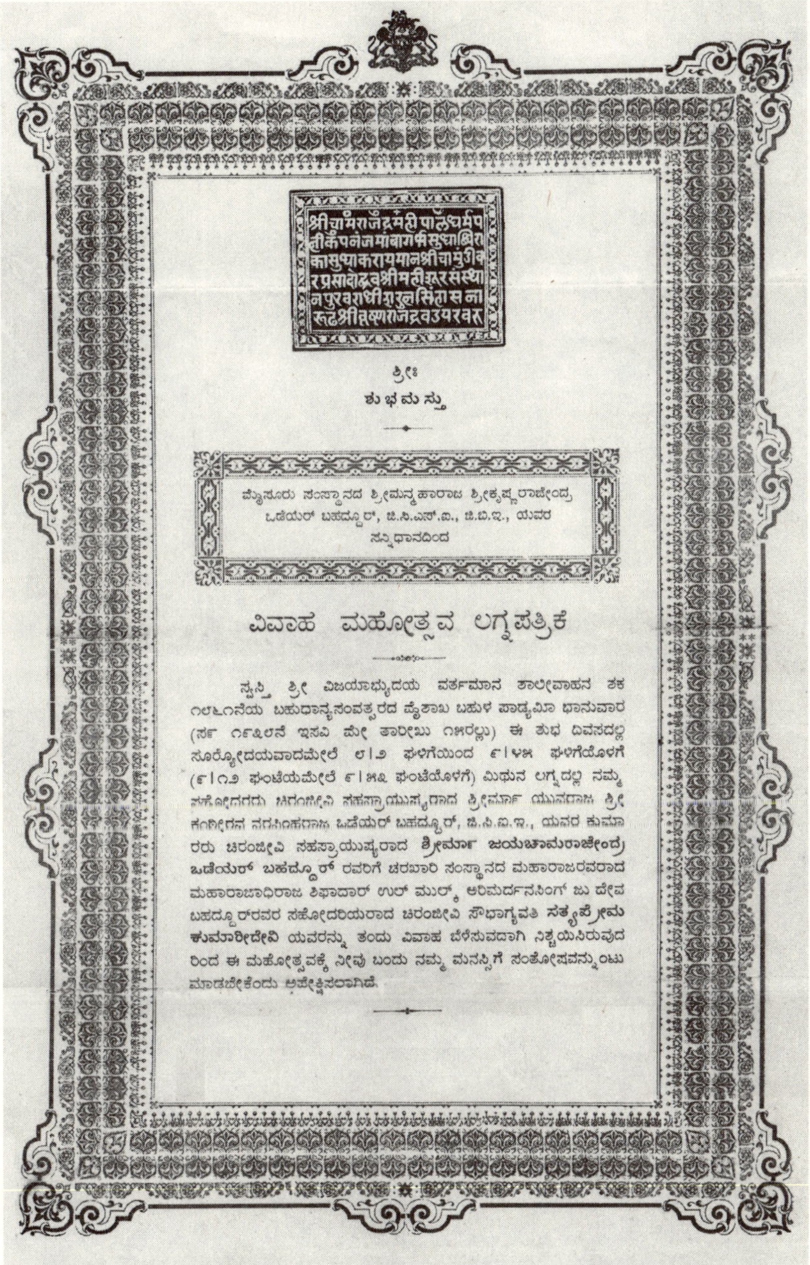

श्रीचामराजेन्द्रमहीपालचरमप
त्नीकेंपनंजमाबामणिसुधाब्धिरा
कासुधाकरायमानश्रीचामुंडीव
रप्रसादोद्भवश्रीमहीशूरसंस्था
नपुरवराधीश्वरकुलसिंहासना
रूढश्रीकृष्णराजेन्द्रवडेयरवर

ಶ್ರೀಃ

ಶುಭಮಸ್ತು

ಮೈಸೂರು ಸಂಸ್ಥಾನದ ಶ್ರೀಮನ್ಮಹಾರಾಜ ಶ್ರೀಕೃಷ್ಣರಾಜೇಂದ್ರ
ಒಡೆಯರ್ ಬಹದ್ದೂರ್, ಜಿ.ಸಿ.ಎಸ್.ಐ., ಜಿ.ಬಿ.ಇ., ಯವರ
ಸನ್ನಿಧಾನದಿಂದ

ವಿವಾಹ ಮಹೋತ್ಸವ ಲಗ್ನಪತ್ರಿಕೆ

ಸ್ವಸ್ತಿ ಶ್ರೀ ವಿಜಯಾಭ್ಯುದಯ ವರ್ತಮಾನ ಶಾಲೀವಾಹನ ಶಕ ೧೮೬೧ನೆಯ ಬಹುಧಾನ್ಯಸಂವತ್ಸರದ ವೈಶಾಖ ಬಹುಳ ಪಾಡ್ಯಮಿ ಭಾನುವಾರ (ಸನ್ ೧೯೩೮ನೆ ಇಸವಿ ಮೇ ತಾರೀಖು ೧೫ರಲ್ಲು) ಈ ಶುಭ ದಿವಸದಲ್ಲ ಸೂರ್ಯೋದಯವಾದಮೇಲೆ ೮।೨ ಘಳಿಗೆಯಿಂದ ೯।೪೫ ಘಳಿಗೆಯೊಳಗೆ (೯।೧೨ ಘಂಟೆಯಮೇಲೆ ೯।೫೩ ಘಂಟೆಯೊಳಗೆ) ಮಿಥುನ ಲಗ್ನದಲ್ಲಿ ನಮ್ಮ ಸಹೋದರರು ಚಿರಂಜೀವಿ ಸಹಸ್ರಾಯುಷ್ಯರಾದ ಶ್ರೀಮನ್ಯುವರಾಜ ಶ್ರೀ ಕಂಠೀರವ ನರಸಿಂಹರಾಜ ಒಡೆಯರ್ ಬಹದ್ದೂರ್, ಜಿ.ಸಿ.ಐ.ಇ., ಯವರ ಕುಮಾರರು ಚಿರಂಜೀವಿ ಸಹಸ್ರಾಯುಷ್ಯರಾದ **ಶ್ರೀಮನ್ ಜಯಚಾಮರಾಜೇಂದ್ರ ಒಡೆಯರ್ ಬಹದ್ದೂರ್** ರವರಿಗೆ ಚರಖಾರಿ ಸಂಸ್ಥಾನದ ಮಹಾರಾಜರವರಾದ ಮಹಾರಾಜಾಧಿರಾಜ ಶಿಫಾದಾರ್ ಉಲ್ ಮುಲ್ಕ್ ಅರಿಮರ್ದನಸಿಂಗ್ ಜು ದೇವ ಬಹದ್ದೂರ್‌ರವರ ಸಹೋದರಿಯರಾದ ಚಿರಂಜೀವಿ ಸೌಭಾಗ್ಯವತಿ **ಸತ್ಯಪ್ರೇಮ ಕುಮಾರೀದೇವಿ** ಯವರನ್ನು ತಂದು ವಿವಾಹ ಬೆಳೆಸುವದಾಗಿ ನಿಶ್ಚಯಿಸಿರುವುದರಿಂದ ಈ ಮಹೋತ್ಸವಕ್ಕೆ ನೀವು ಬಂದು ನಮ್ಮ ಮನಸ್ಸಿಗೆ ಸಂತೋಷವನ್ನುಂಟು ಮಾಡಬೇಕೆಂದು ಅಪೇಕ್ಷಿಸಲಾಗಿದೆ.

Official wedding invitation for JCW's wedding with Maharani Satya Prema Kumari of Jigni. It has the Royal Mudra (see the rectangular black inset with Devanagari script below the Gandabherunda emblem). Traditionally, the invite is called a 'Lagnapatrike' in Kannada

The coronation of JCW on 8 September 1941 following the demise of his father and Krishnaraja Wadiyar IV

Photos from the coronation of JCW and his ascent to the Mysore throne in September 1941

More photos of the coronation of JCW on 8 September 1941

Krishnaraja Wadiyar IV, Yuvaraja Narasimharaja Wadiyar and JCW arrive at his convocation at Mysore University campus

Pictures of a young JCW on a tour of Japan and Far East nations to study diplomacy and emergent political situations prior to World War II

Young JCW while on a foreign tour

JCW addressing a gathering of guests prior to the famous Khedda operations in Mysore

5
BRANDISHING A MYSORE BRAND

Almost all of history has remembered kings for their valour. Conquest. Rule. Power. Ambition. From Raja Raja Cholan to Chhatrapati Shivaji, the accounts of a king almost always revolve around how much land he amassed and how long he was able to keep it. This has been the prototypical measure of his leadership. Rarely has a king's success been measured by the culture he created in his land. Such a vision is often not recognized as true leadership either. In the colonial accounts of Maharajas, who were vassals of the British government, such leadership is mocked, as if cultural leadership was the only thing they could do anyway. Therefore the quintessential image of a Maharaja as a patron of all sensory pleasures was permanently lodged in the discourses of Indian history. The Maharaja, who instead of fighting for his land (warrior's duty; kshatradharma) and his way to an exalted death (a warrior's death; veeramarana), flirted with music, letters or chess. Popular Bollywood depictions of the Maharaja enslaved by his own idiosyncrasies are way too common, such as in the movie *Shatranj Ke Khilari*, where the chess-crazy Maharaja spends all his genius on winning the game on black-and-white checker boards rather than in his own checkered life. The popular celluloid images sold repeatedly are that of a vain king, always indulging in a lazy 'mujrah' or dance performance of a damsel, after having sold his soil and self-respect to the white man. Serfoji II, who after the annexation of Tanjore by the British, focused his energies on creating a multicultural, plural and energetic culture bursting at its seams with artistic and scholastic achievements, is also seen as a weak figure who could not do much else anyways. Such an attitude in viewing the lives of the Wadiyars of Mysore is not uncommon. A stark contrast to the image of a Jhansi Ki Rani, who tried to fight the British and died on the battlefield. Or a Chattrapati Shivaji, who threw quite a few daggers at the heart of British supremacy before the Maratha Confederacy fell to the cunning viles of the East India Company. The Maharajas under colonial rule, however, are dominantly seen as the antithesis of a nationalist hero, the perpetuators of the indirect rule of the British, often depicted as 'stooges' of the British empire, with no real personality or vision left in them to lead. Therefore philosophy also was seen as an attribute that suited such a silhouette.

Even his role as a patron of culture, religion and scholarship, his 'Rajadharma', is pandered with. The popular notion is that the administration and policy-making was handled between the powerful Diwan and the Resident of the British Empire. The job of showing the glorified path to divinity and self-liberation was left to the spiritual masters, the gurus, the sadhus and the religious men. The social reformers were on the important job of guiding civic and social narratives for justice, equality and societal transformations. With the merry men making music, the ladies engaged in dancing, the scholars chipping away at the sculpture of Indic knowledge, what was the Maharaja to do, really? Such dominant stereotypes have succeeded in only bringing stories of the erratic and the indulgent behaviour of the Maharajas to the fore. There have been such Maharajas in this land indeed. Myths intersect facts in circulated stories about such vanity affairs, a Maharaja who organized wedding parties for his cat or one who used a Rolls Royce to collect trash in his kingdom! Colonial narratives depict their personal tastes in poor light, as if their affinity to scents and Western colognes, was to ward off the internal stench that pervaded their souls.

Even in the chronicles of JCW such subtle programming can be seen. He is often praised for relinquishing the throne. Kuvempu, regarded one of the greatest Kannada poets of the twentieth century, is said to have eulogized him by saying, 'Many monarchs in history have become kings by ascending thrones, while he became the greatest king by descending one'. Grossly overlooked are his successes as a king, his cultural leadership and administrative successes in a reign that was perhaps most turbulent for Mysore and India at large. In a world where monarchies across Europe and the rest of the world were being overthrown and exiled for good, Mysore, under the leadership of his uncle Nalvadi Krishnaraja Wadiyar had achieved a certain sophisticated civil society—way ahead of not just other princely states in India but other provinces of the world as well. Nalvadi's ingenious administrative acumen and notions of social justice won him the title 'Rajarshi', the saint ruler. This title is far more remembered in the annals of history than any other titles given to him by the British government, because it was given by the people. A befitting inheritor of Nalvadi's legacy, JCW gave new meaning to the phrase, 'the people's Maharaja'.

The marvels of Mysore were enshrined in its administrative and societal enterprises. No wonder Lord John Sankey, humanist and Lord High Chancellor of Great Britain, remarked that 'Mysore was one of the best administered states in the world' at the First Round Table Conference at the Royal Gallery House of Lords, London, in 1930. By the twentieth century, Mysore was a brand with global recognition. There was the world famous Mysore Soap Factory. In a popular song, Dr Rajkumar, the icon of the Kannada film industry, quips, '*Navaduva nudiye Kannada nudi, naaviruva taanave gandhada gudi* (What we speak is Kannada and where we live is the temple of sandalwood)'. By the twentieth century, the Mysore kingdom exported its sandalwood to all corners of the globe, and was one of the largest producers globally. During World War I, Nalvadi Krishnaraja Wadiyar established the Government Soap Factory in Bengaluru to use the large pile of unexported sandalwood in 1916. Two factories to distill oil from sandalwood were started as feeder industries. Thus entered the Mysore Sandal Soap with sandalwood oil into the world of exotic soaps and perfumes.

Legend has it that Mysore Pak, the dessert, was an accidental success. Kakasura Madappa, the chief chef of Nalvadi Krishnaraja Wadiyar, on an occasion had to make a dessert rather quickly. Mixing gram flour and ghee to a sugar paka (concoction), the experimental 'Mysore paka' was presented with the royal thali, and it was an instant hit. Today, this Mysore pak is sold to gourmets all over the world, and is a standard staple in most sweetmeat stores.

When Nalvadi Krishnaraja Wadiyar attended Queen Victoria's jubilee celebrations, he was drawn to the machine-made silk fabric worn by British royalty. Of course, he had to have it at home, and ordered thirty-two power-looms from Switzerland to manufacture machine-made silk sarees in India. The first silk factory in India was established in Mysore in the year 1912. Today, the Mysore Silk Factory, incorporated as Karnataka Silk Industries Corporation, produces over 35,000 metres of pure silk fabric, the pride of many saree collectors across the globe. Since 2005, armed with Geographical Indication (GI) tag, the brand continues to put Mysore and silk on the global map.

Cultural historians and Mysoreans will agree that Mysore's most distinguished brand was one that could not be sold, but emulated and lived. The intellectual traditions of culture in Mysore were indeed a philharmonia of cultures of the East, West and pan-India. Mysore had its own 'bani' or a distinct aesthetic style of South Indian classical music. Mysore became synonymous with the instrument Veena, with famous Vainikas such as Veene Sheshanna, Veene Subbanna and Veene Venkatagiriyappa. A distinct style of traditional dance existed in Mysore, with dancer lineages of Jatti Thayamma (1857–1947) and K. Venkatalakshamma (1906–2002) at the forefront of this tradition. Mysore painting had evolved from the grammars and visual vocabularies of the Vijayanagara empire to a distinct art form. There was Raja Ravi Varma, who melded European academic art with Indian sensibilities. Mysore's literary world was abuzz with Kannada scholarship receiving both royal and societal patronage. The Oriental Research Institute (ORI) was started by Chamaraja Wadiyar X as a premiere institute for preservation and study of manuscripts and scripts of India. It is said to house over 75,000 literary and scientific studies in extant scripts of South India, Grantha, Nagari, Nandinagari, Tigalari, and Brahmi, among others. It is true that South India's knowledge systems were better preserved till the twentieth century because of the presence of the Wadiyars, the Marathas, and the Travencore dynasties. Could this have happened without a Serfoji creating the Saraswathi Mahal Library? Or without Chamaraja Wadiyar's vision to start the Oriental Research Institute (ORI) in Mysore? An even more remarkable aspect of the leadership of the Wadiyar kings is that the Mysorean cultural brand was brandished in a milieu of great intercultural prejudice in India. An India that was navigating a transgression of values held in the past because of a difficult polity backing several peddlers of imperialist impressions.

A Philharmonia of Cultures

An incident recorded by Margaret Cousins and James Cousins, in their book, *We Two Together,* notes the keen interest JCW showed in Western classical music as a young lad:

> While the rehearsal was proceeding, a handsome boy, little taller than the piano, came in. Gretta took him to be the son of some of the officers of the Palace, and smiled at him. He listened with rapt attention, and at the end of a piece said, 'Please play that again.' At the end, he said, 'Thank you' and went out. Gretta asked the aide who the charming little lad

was. 'That is Prince Jaya, son of His Highness the Yuvaraja, and expected to be the future Maharaja.'

Margaret Elizabeth Cousins, also known as Gretta Cousins (7 October 1878–11 March 1954) was an Irish–Indian theosophist and pianist, who moved to India in 1915. She is credited with having tuned the national anthem written by Rabindranath Tagore, which was then referred to as the 'Morning Song of India'. In their memoirs, they speak highly of the Western classical taste that prevailed in Mysore: 'The interest taken in good Western music by the Maharaja of Mysore led to a celebration of the bi-centenary of Beethoven in Bangalore, the commercial capital of Mysore State.'[1] A celebration of Beethoven in Mysore is reflective of a thriving adopted culture but also that of a certain digestive fire to assimilate colonial culture and realities that pervaded. Mysore's affair with Western art music ran deep in its social fabric. It produced trailblazers who straddled both worlds and identities with great ease and beauty. Mysore's Philomena Thumboochetty was the first Western violin prodigy to gain a Fellowship from the Trinity College London and the first Indian to be admitted to the Paris Conservatoire in 1926, when she was barely sixteen. In 1934, Philomena and her mother were presented at the court of King George V and Queen Mary. Homegrown talent had begun to make ripples in a world far, far away from home. Before she gave her first performance with the Mysore palace orchestra, she said, 'I am anxious to give my first recital in Mysore before His Highness the Maharaja, as a loyal subject of his ...' When such careers were taking off, the Yuvaraja was nursing his own dreams of a being a concert pianist, of a life immersed in music. When the concert with Philomena Thumboochetty and palace band was presented at the Jagan Mohana Palace, JCW was a teenager witnessing the impossible: a girl from a small kingdom in South India had returned to Mysore with the world at her feet, as she raised her bow. Some eclectic fare followed, Kreisler-Vivaldi Concerto, the spirited Saint-

Saëns Havanaise, and the romantic Bruch Violin Concerto to shorter, appealing pieces like Brahms' Hungarian Dance and Schubert's Moment Musicale arranged by Kreisler. This was the philharmonic spirit of Mysore, in which the musical sensibilities of JCW were groomed.

Mysore's intellectual and philharmonic culture could be best understood by the devices that celebrated this interculturality. Mysorean culture beautifully and paradoxically stood for a deep investment in its traditions and a keen desire to experience the contemporary. Mysore's attitude to interculturality was unique. It was not an identity-dissolving phenomenon, where East meeting the West was problematic, but an opportunity to live out a new aesthetic. When JCW was asked if it would it be possible to synthesize the musical systems of the north, the south, the east and the west, he replies cautiously, with no jingoism of either being less or more. Instead he shows an honest acceptance of the difficulties in embracing interculturalism. 'It is difficult. One can only make an attempt. Each system has its own inimitable features.' The literary and musical works of JCW are enshrined in such attempts and intercultural values, a remarkably unique cultural appetite for the new and the ancient—a chasm only a maverick can tread with ease.

The word 'philharmonic' comes from intellectual societies in England, who organized themselves based on certain artistic or knowledge-seeking orientations. In 1813, some of the nobility and socially influential thinkers of that time took charge of the art music scene by announcing an agenda for the Royal Philharmonic Society of London as being 'less conservative' than existing music concert organizations. One can trace the culture of philharmonia in the Mysore Court from an earlier time. The Mysore Court from the time of Krishnaraja Wadiyar III sported an English band, which played military music at several governmental ceremonies. Richard Caton Woodville, an English artist, who was invited to paint an equestrian lifesize portrait of H.H. Chamaraja Wadiyar X, notes:

> Daily, at noon, an A.D.C. would call to inquire if I desired a band to play during dinner, and the performance of the musicians was distinctly as good as could be desired. The Maharaja himself was a musician above the average, and his compositions, both European and native, as good as those of many a professional musician of high standing.

The encounters of this Western aesthetic with Carnatic sensibilities were not smooth at first. As early as 1813, M. Scott the Military Secretary to the Commander-in-Chief of Fort St. George noted: 'Our musick not being in much repute among the Natives of India'. He urged that military bands in the native regiments of East India Company be initiated, so that European culture and music would be better appreciated. One can find the salaries and emoluments given to the band in Kille Kutcheri records as early as the time of Mummadi Krishnaraja Wadiyar.[2]

In sync with the intellectual movement of the Philharmonia Societies in London, a philharmonic orchestra was started in 1921 by Nalvadi Krishnaraja Wadiyar. Unlike the English bands already existing in other princely kingdoms, the orchestra was envisioned with an exalted purpose of commissioning intercultural experiments and new music. Much like the Royal Philharmonic Orchestras of Europe, it boasted of bandmasters imported from the very best of the globe, commissioned new music for its signature repertoires and most importantly, it kick-started a renaissance of instrumental music, which looked at the Western classics and world music for inspiration at once. Lavish sums were spent on importing the very best of instruments, both classical and unconventional. The horn violin, the electronic theremin and calliaphone were reported to be part of such experimental encounters in Mysore.

The arrival of the military band in Mysore undoubtedly was a fresh encounter in the musical ecosystem in India. In addition to bringing in a new aesthetic, the 'band' brought in music from faraway lands, played oh-so-near. The military music of that time was rich with musical innovation, somewhat irreverent to boundaries on the map, power and prestige. A celtic melody on a dilruba somehow made sense musically. Suddenly, history was transcended in a way like never before. When a Tyagaraja's kriti eulogizing the valour of Lord Rama was decorated with orchestrations of a string and brass sections, and the tympani resounding the victory of Rama—suddenly time, space and cultures ceased to matter. In addition, the music of bands, and the 'philharmonic' orchestras in the Royal Courts in Mysore were doing another job altogether. They were pedalling a new taste, a new thinking, a high-brow musical taste that pushed the traditional on trial, experimented with the past, and strangely, through all this, attempted to express a certain unity in human experience.

JCW himself lead the way by inventing Ragas based on Western tonal vocabulary and by writing Carnatic compositions for Western instruments. Ragas invented by the JCW are not merely 'sisters' of allied Carnatic Ragas, they embody a grammar of Western, blues and jazz music brought into the world of Raga construction. These compositions speak eloquently about the sustained intercultural transactions that have impacted both these traditions of music. More importantly, they reflect well on the brave new ethos in the Mysore Court. One finds instances of people who moved across continents, assimilated in an alien culture, while adding their own distinct hue to the larger cultural canvas of Mysore. European composers and conductors who were brought to Mysore participated in a more organic influencing of each other's cultures. There was Veene Venkatagiriyappa, a celebrated veena player, who actively arranged music for the Carnatic orchestra, after having learnt Western classical music. Veene Sheshanna, superstar veena player of his times, also learnt the piano and Western harp. Several new genres of compositions were co-evolved in Mysore. The Hindustani performance format of 'Gat' inspired the 'Nagma' genre in Carnatic music. Many 'Carnatic airs' were composed during this time, which melded Carnatic, Hindustani, Western classical and jazz ideas. Many experiments failed, some lived on as Ragas, some became 'classical' kritis, some lives were forgotten, some celebrated. The memories of such a tapestry of lives, experiences and music lives on today, through the music of JCW.

Through JCW's benefaction, the philharmonia spirit was revitalized in England too. Post World War II, perhaps aware of the enlightened culture of Mysore and in his quest to revive the philharmonic culture, Walter Legge, a classical music record producer and the founder of the Philharmonia Society, approached JCW to resuscitate the ideals of the philharmonic spirit. He reports:

> In the weeks I stayed there, the Maharajah agreed to paying for the recordings of the Medtner piano concertos, an album of his songs, and some of his chamber music; he also agreed to give me a subvention of 10,000 pounds a year for three years, to enable me to put the Philharmonia Orchestra and the Philharmonia Concert Society on a firm basis ...[3]

This resulted in a historic series of concerts and recordings called the 'Mysore Concerts'[4] with the Philharmonia Concert Society. JCW commissioned recordings and performances with top-notch composers, eclectic fare, and hand-selected innovative musical pieces, so that the world could listen to the future—really. Later, he was the first president of the Philharmonia Concert Society, London, in 1948. The Maharaja's funding of the Philharmonia Society indicates deeper intellectual and spiritual connections between Mysore and England—of his love for music beyond colonial hierarchies.

6

CHITPRABHANANDA—ON THE THRONE OF MELODY

> *'Srividya Chitprabhananda Rajayogindra sannutam.'*
> (The Rajayogi basks in the effervescent bliss of the mind, evoked by the Srividya.)

In the very first kriti in *Atana*, *Shri Mahaganapatim,* the Maharaja clues us in on his motivations for composition. Chitprabhananda is understood as the sublime Ananda, the neurological and embodied ecstasy experienced when in 'union'. This truth is spoken about often in Hindu philosophy; Rajayoga is both the goal and the method of attaining this union within. According to Rajayoga philosophy, when a 'union' of the faculties of the mind sustains, when chittavritti (loosely translated as 'a thought-centric, non-centered experience') is transcended, satchitananda is what remains. The Hatha Yoga Pradipika also explains this rather abstract 'union', which we have come to understand as Samadhi, Unmani, Amartva, Laya, Advaitha, Niralamba, Jivanmukti, Sahaja, and Turiya:

> Just as how salt dissolved in water becomes one with it, so the union of Atma and Manas (mind) is denominated samadhi, When the breath becomes exhausted, and mind becomes

> Praliyate (still, reabsorbed), they fuse into union called samadhi. This equality, this oneness of the two, the living self and the absolute self, when all Sankalpa (desire, cravings) end is called samadhi.
>
> —*Hatha Yoga Pradipika*, 4.3–4.7

In Rajayoga methods, sound and music are used as vehicles to carry consciousness closer to jivanmukti. The Maharaja's compositional project was very clearly envisioned in this direction. This sentiment is reflected in almost all of his kritis *'Pahiman Satatam'*, *'Pahimam Shri Rajarajeshwari'* (Protect me always, Rajarajeshwari). A great number of the kritis are introverted, contemplative compositions bathed in dense Sanskrit—the expressive outpourings of a soul seeking a higher consciousness, not necessarily composed for Carnatic performance. Thus, one finds that lyric is the final crucible in his music, not a mere placeholder of melody but an ignited place from which melody, metaphor and meaning emanate. For it is in his lyrics that he encodes the gamut of our civilizational knowledge and his unique experience of it. In response to his sister Rani Vijaya Devi's question as why he took to music composition, he simply said, 'They are my humble offerings to the Devi.'

The practice of the Srividya tantrism involves incantations, visual and chant-based meditations in a phased manner, and one can find the clues of his Srividya journey in his compositions. The compositions are best described as an alchemy of sound, thought, word, action and symbolism: music was an offering, a vehicle of finding chitprabhananda, a medium to exalt the mind into higher states of consciousness. The Maharaja was initiated into Srividya Upasana by Siddalinga Swami, a saint and an ace sculptor, whose works adorn the many temples built by the Maharaja. Chitprabhananda was the name he chose for himself, in this new realized universe he was to pervade. It also fixed the major deity of all his compositions—the Devi, the one who reigns the Sriyantra, the Lalitha Tripura Sundari. Many kritis begin with the source of it all—'*Shri Vidyam Lalitham*' in *Nadabrahma* Raga or the '*Shri Vidye Pahi*' in *Lalitha Panchama*. After the Devi, Shiva becomes the deity of 13 of his kritis, followed by his son, Ganapati, who is invoked in about 11 kritis, followed by 4 kritis on Vishnu. The prosody in the kritis is heavy. They are not mere eulogies of Gods either. They carry stories of Hindu Puranic lore, they speak of kshetra-purana, sthala-purana, the interconnected symbolic relationships between objects, places, people and places. In *Kamaksheem Varalakshmeem* in Raga *Vasantha*, he refers to '*Kanchipuravasineem Kamithartha Pradayineem*', the Goddess who lives and reigns over Kanchi and is known to gift to her most deserving devotees their wishes. The kriti *Hatakeshwaram Bhajeham* in Raga *Hatahambari* refers to this remote temple, the Hatakeshwara temple, near Srisailam in Andhra Pradesh, where Adi Shankaracharya is supposed to have lived and composed many of his masterworks. In the anupallavi, he makes reference to an esoteric text called the *Haalasya Maahatmyam* as '*Hatakambaradharam Paratparam Haalasyanagaraadheeshwaram*', while in the charanam, he alludes to the puranic knowledge of Shiva as the master of Pataala—'*Pataalavasinam Sarveshwaram*'. In *Shreemad Bhagvat Purana,* Shiva is the master of gold mines in the Vitala, below Atala, and is thus known as 'Hatkeshwara'.

ततोऽधस्ताद्वितले हरो भगवान्हाटकेश्वरः स्वपार्षदभूतगणावृतः

tato dhastād vitale haro bhagavān hātakeśvarah sva-pārsada-
bhūta-ganāvrtah

It is this aspect of his musicality which reminds Carnatic musicologists of Muttuswami Dikshitar, who had the same attitude towards composition: the usage of compounded words in Sanskrit, carefully chiselled word groupings, references to the Hindu pantheon, iconographies of Gods, references to Vedas, Puranas and Yoga, the similarity in the kriti form such as using madhyamakala sahitya in most compositions, the terse and packed spacing between his words—these are aspects common to both. It is very clear that

Dikshitar's model of composition inspired JCW's choice in the form of the kriti, however, he stands on his own when you take into account the musical vistas he explored, and the relatively short number of kritis he composed.

Dr S. Krishnamurthy, the editor of the book *Srividya Gana Varidhi,* which for the first time published authenticated notations for JCW's kritis says:

> Wadiyar's prosody is not light. They are not garlands of eulogies either. They are cryptic, with references from tantra and mantrashastras. Even the pronunciation of his lyrical passages is difficult. In short, his compositions are not easy to reach; mastery and Siddi can come only by incessant and deep study.

The themes, journey, shlokas, the tantric metaphors of Srividya are liberally sprinkled in almost all his compositions: '*Om hrimkarekasaranuvagarthasvarupini*' in *Ambujakshi Pahimam*. '*Sarvanandamaya trikonantargata chakravasini*' in the kriti *Kameshwarim.* One also finds some personal prayers embedded in his kritis, he prays to the Jagatjanani as the '*Satputrapoutra kalatra dayini*', the one who bestows the gift of lineage, satputra (virtous son), poutra (grandchildren and kin) and kalatra (wife). One can find that he has laid out many cryptic crossword puzzles in his kritis, one can even find interesting personal titbits in his lyrics. He has brought in the names of all of his children: Gayatri Devi, Vishalakshi Devi, Meenakshi Devi, Indrakshi Devi and Srikantadatta in his kritis also!

The number of recovered compositions composed by JCW is only ninety-seven today, three compositions in *Bindumalini, Geethapriya* and *Sarasangi* were added to the list of surviving compositions at his Centenary Celebrations in Bengaluru, on 20 July 2019. The search is on for some 108 compositions he is supposed to have composed. What is masterful about this rather small body of compositions is that a whopping two-thirds of them are in rare, extant and new

Cover of the book Srividya Gana Varidhi, which contains published notations of available JCW compositions in Kannada script

Ragas, while the rest are in established Ragas of Carnatic music. The innovation quotient runs high in a rather small number of his offerings. A great number of Ragas were resuscitated from being mere scales in musicology texts. Ragas like *Lalitha Panchama, Bhupalapanchama, Shuddha Lalitha, Shuddha Todi, Bhairava* were given the form and life as a kriti. In this sense, many of the scales he brought to life as Ragas are his. Some forty-odd kritis are eka-Raga kritis, which means the only kriti available in these Ragas today are his. Example: *Bhogavasantham*, a very ancient Raga referred to in old musicological texts, comes to life through his beautiful composition of *Amba Shrirajarajeshwari*. Scholars differ on the number and name of Ragas invented by him, suggesting that an in-depth study of the new Ragas in his works is much warranted. Clearly,

Jayasamvardhini, Hamsanatini, Shivakambhoji, Nadabrahma, Hindoladeshika are strong contenders for this spot. In quintessential Ragas of Carnatic music, such as *Nata, Gambhira Nata, Hindola, Atana, Madhyamavati, Yadukula Kambhoji* and others, the Maharaja scores with majesty, holding his own. His *Sri Mahaganapatim* in *Atana, Chintayami Jagadamba* in *Hindola*, *Shri Jalandhara* in *Gambhira Nata* are extremely popular in Carnatic concerts.

The kritis are somewhat reflections of his own sensibilities, as a man of piety, religious devotion and an equally thinking spirit capable of incisive discrimination and logical reasoning. The overtly devotional lyric is balanced by innovative musical craftsmanship which is his own. The musical choices he makes as a composer are as vocal as his speeches or writings. One can find many parallels between his writings and his music. First, the problem he chooses is not simple. He is drawn to esoteric Ragas and the aspect of novelty. Not any Raga on the block, but one that has no surviving kriti—such as *Nagadhvani*. His composition in *Nagadhvani* is touted to be the only one, composed with its Raga lakshya and lakshana intact. It is clear that he was not interested in a great volume of output which did not make any strides musically. Each composition had to have something to say, something that it tries to accomplish in the world of music. The 'musical problems' he chose were deep musicological ones. Uncommon Ragas, extant Ragas, *Swarantara* Ragas, Ragas created by unusual rules of Raga construction, Ragas created through harmonic theory and so on. A shining example is his *Hindoladeshika*—a Raga created using Hindustani concept of 'ang' and 'jod' but applied to Venkatamakhi's tetrachordal construction of Ragas. The crooked ascending phrase 'SaMaRiGaMa' in the first tetrachord space enforces a typical Hindustani Desi kind of glide from Ma to Ri. The second half of the scale is another circular movement—'PaDaNiSaPa', ensuring directionality in phrases possible in the Raga. For example, a PDN-SNDP is not allowed. Also, it enforces another glide from Sa to Pa. The second half of this Raga is the typical 'ang' of *Ahiri* Raga in Hindustani music. While the elements of 'angs' or musical gestures is explored, he simply does not create a Raga like all other 'ang' Ragas. He applies this idea to the tetrachordal construction concept of Venkatamakhi, thus making the scale an interesting tetrachordal jod Raga, a new hybrid in itself. His manodharma is one that loves the synthesis of ideas, be it connecting the dichotomies of Atman or Brahman or Hindola and Durbar! One can find several 'thought experiments' in his compositions. The Ragas that we perform today have landed in contemporary performance through a long process of multistream evolution. Several of his Ragas attempt to bring back these concepts into performance. After having composed in *Lalitha*, he has explored ancient versions of the Raga, *Lalitha Panchama* and *Shuddha Lalitha* as well, which are older isotopes of the contemporary *Lalitha*. He experiments with the *Panchama-varjya Todi* called *Shuddha Todi*. In his choice of Ragas, one can find 'Ragaputras' and 'Raginis', from the time when Ragas were attributed humanoid characters of masculinity and feminity based on their swara-phrase and gestural quotients. Ragas in India were classified according to not just musicology but according to non-musical parameters such as time, seasons, gender, astrological symbolism. His revival of the kriya Ragas—*Gamakakriya, Gundakriya,* or the set of dhvani Ragas *Nagadhvani*, *Garudadhvani*—are noteworthy.

The one thing that screams out in every page of his compositions is that the compositions were the products of a pianist's mind at play. Hence, unlike a vocalist, he loved non-linear Ragas with large, intervallic gaps and jumps. A great number of his Ragas chosen have an empty first or second half either in ascending or descending aspects of the scale *(Nadabrahma, Hamsanatini)*. Perhaps such contraptions allowed for non-linear phrases, more directionality to Raga phrases, enabling certain harmonic treatment if orchestrated. One can find that several of his compositions are built on Western compositional ideas such as cadences, thematic movements, thematic development, voicing and such. The *Hindoladeshika Kriti* is one such example. A good 80 per cent of the kriti runs on three key motifs of (RiSaRiNiSa)

(SaPaDaNiSa) and (MaRiGaMa). The kriti lines always end with perfect or imperfect cadences, clearly written for orchestral ends. Another example is that of *Shivakambodhi*—a Western mixolydian-based scale, capable of generating a Kambodhi by an interesting Grahabheda. Such Western-ideas-meet-Carnatic-ends are tested out in his compositions—most of the times masquerading as normal-looking compositions bathed in heavy Sanskrit. This aspect again is a testament to his genius. It is far harder to innovate in an existing form, showing multiple possibilities than to rebel and find a new narrative. A lot like Beethoven, who is adored for having exalted the symphonic form to its most expressive state and for bringing in stylistic innovations that bridge the Classical and Romantic periods. Writing a concerto in *Shivakambhoji* or a jazz run is not as difficult as it is to bring that vocabulary to a Carnatic idiom and to birth a *'Kamakshi Pahiman'*—a perfectly Carnatic sounding melody playing hide-and-seek with its listeners' ears about its Western and Carnatic identities. Such musical hunting attracted him clearly, and he was a damn good shot at music, just as he was with his gun! In his musical thought laboratory, each kriti was a hypothesis, which he tested amply before a composition was born. Much like in his writings, he connects several rivers of knowledge to create a higher perception or to clarify an abstract problem. His penchant for unravelling the esoteric is reflected in both his writings and music. Be it a clarifying commentary on Dattatreya's *Avadhuta Gita,* an esoteric text understood by few, or composing in an esoteric Raga such as *Namanarayani*, he was drawn to the exotic.

His other musical decisions as a composer are quite firm. He stuck to one single form, the kriti, no javalis, varnams or thillanas. None of his compositions are in *Chaapu taalas* or unequal beat metre taalas, but in long ardous *Sulaadi taalas* like *Chaturashra matya, Mishra jhampe*. Perhaps no other composer in Carnatic music has so many kritis in *Suladi taalas* to his credit. His compositions are rather difficult to sing because of how the accents of prosodical phrases syncopate with rhythm weaving interesting rhythmic relationships between the prosodical structure and laya. The lengthy taalas for most of his kritis challenge the working memory of even the most experienced musician with their difficult word-to-beat placements, some prosodical phrases begin ahead of the taala cycle, while some lag, some parts of the kritis are offset from the starting beat to match the accents of the poetry with the accents of the taala. For a vocalist, the terse spacing of the poetry, will test the breath work and vocal stamina. More importantly, his kritis demand that the singer understand the words, the majesty of the prosody; one cannot treat them as mere consonants to anchor the melody.

The compositional form and melodic structure is experimented with too in many of his kritis. One finds cyclic expansive melodies like *Srirajarajeshwareem* in *Lalitha*. There is a typical Tyagaraja-style kriti in *'Shri Jalandhara'* of *Nata*, where he has developed multiple *sangatis* musically on a single line of sahitya (not to miss a tongue-twister chitteswara passage!). There are the Dikshitar-inspired prosody-centric compositions with almost no melodic or sangati variations. An almost lyric-dominant prabhandha style of composition is explored in *Sugnana Dayini* in Raga *Shuddhasalavi*. There are Hindustani instrumental *gat*-like compositions such as *'Vandeham Sada'* in *Hamsanatini*. The *Dhrupad*-like *'SriRajarajeshwareem'* or *'Chintayami Jagadamba'* can very well be contrasted by the other kritis such as *Shri Chamundeshwari* in *Madhyamavati*—which have more linear Carnatic melodic structures. Such Dhrupad-like kritis can be sung with a Hindustani khayal-like routine, unraveling layers of lyrics cycle after cycle with greater melodic complexity. While *Rupaka taala* is assigned for *Srirajarajeshwareem*, the accent pattern of the kriti fits very well to a cycle of Ektaal in Hindustani music. The Hindustani meend-like fluidity imagined and almost embedded in the composition is another interesting feature. The kriti is well-crafted to allow for interpretive exposition by an experienced singer, there is room for meditative reemphasis, long rests, long glides and nyasa. The kriti flows like a river in quiet contemplation, the sangatis are sparse, it is a meditation in Lalitha, for Lalitha—undoubtedly.

Tuning His Destiny

'It was the best of times, it was the worst of times,' said Charles Dickens about the French Revolution, describing the roller-coaster, socio-political changes of the nineteenth century. When Mysore agreed to be part of the Indian Union, it was a transfer of power from the British government to the vision of an Indian unity that flickered perilously in the dark hours of that night. As the cliché goes, the spell ended at midnight. As the Mysore state melded into a union, the words: royalty, empire, statehood, majesty, legacy, and power would all now hold new sway. The man at the helm of this tumultuous change, perhaps found a certain immunity to reality through his musical muse. The notions and meaning of everything that once defined him would soon change. One can almost be sure that the last Maharaja could not have been in an ideal 'state', pun intended, for some serious musical retreats. Wrong. When the contours of modern India were being mapped, JCW's mind sought to outline an ode to the Devi. As the tricolour flip-flopped in chaos, a prayer soared as *'Shri Vidya Pahi Mudam Dehi'* (Protect me, Oh! Srividya, grant me bliss). The fingers that signed the instrument of accession to the Indian union exuberantly keyed in a jubilant '*Bruhannayaki Jagatrakshaki,*' describing the larger-than-life valour of the Devi. It is as if he was invoking her presence to face the king-size changes in his life.

The timing of his 97-odd recovered musical compositions, the pace at which they were composed, the cultural ethos they embody, all reek of history. Music is auditory history. Sheathed within her radiant overtures of sound are unvoiced slices of the past. The silhouettes irradiate in rich technicolour the predicaments of a glory. If one analyses the life and passions of the Maharaja, his creative genius bloomed amidst gloom. Another interesting titbit about the pace at which these compositions were composed is that from 17 August 1945 to 19 December 1947, he furiously composed nearly a hundred kritis! He never perhaps went back to composition, strangely not bothering to preserve his own kritis by publishing them. Only the lyrics of his compositions were available in a booklet, sans notations or notes until, his most ardent chronicler, his son-in-law R. Rajachandra Urs published the original notations available with Dr S. Krishnamurthy, grandson of JCW's guru Mysore Vasudevacharya.

The Maharaja's music preserves a Mysorean ethos in song. It tells of a cultural alchemy in a world where the East met the West not as quick encounters, but as a daily negotiation. The Mysore Police band, which evolved from the Royal Carnatic Orchestra of JCW's court, plays some very rare compositions of his today, as part of state and national ceremonies in Karnataka. In a niche piece of history, in a D.O. letter, the Maharaja requests his composition teacher Mysore Vasudevacharya to review his compositions for the palace band:[1]

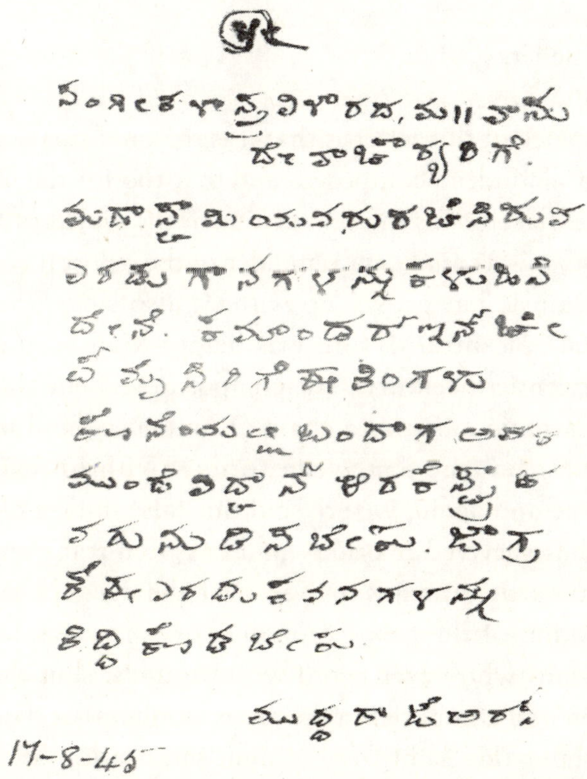
17-8-45

An official note from Muddaraje Urs, addressed to JCW's music guru, Mysore Vasudevacharya, regarding new compositions by the Maharaja

Dated 17-8-1945
Sangeetha shastra visharada shri Ma. Vasudevacharyarige.
(Salutations to Shri Mysore Vasudevacharya.)

Mahaswamigalu rachisiruva yeradu ganagalannu kaluhisiddene.
(Enclosed are two compositions by HH Maharaja Jayachamaraja Wadiyar)
Commander in chief e tingalu koneyalli mysoreige bandaaga avara munde vidwan orchestra ravarau nudisabeku.
(The orchestra is supposed to play these compositions in front of the commander-in-chief event later this month.)
Jagrathe e yeradu kavanagalannu tiddi kodabeku.
(Kindly carefully preserve and review the following compositions)
—Muddaraje Urs

The significance of this letter is that it is the only surviving proof that the Maharaja indeed composed, and that too for the band.

What is the place of his musical genius in the world of Carnatic music? For one, it is a significant reminder of the cultural encounters that Carnatic music has grown up with. It also sings a eulogy of what a musical epicentre Mysore was before Madras emerged as a hub in the twentieth century. The compositions belie the current branding of Carnatic music as a chain of untouched and unbroken musical genius from the Samaveda to now with no extraneous influences. Time and again, we are sold this false notion of a 'pure' music which has survived hybridity and has been transmitted with 'six sigma standards' of transmission over the ages. In an almost dumb imagination of the past, composers of yore are imagined as 'chaste' musicians who never heard world sounds, shut themselves off from reality and composed in the pious 'confines' of their minds. This also explains the 'saint-ization' and 'sanitization' of Carnatic memories, not including the fertile cultural influences Carnatic music has had—from Persian, Western and Oriental music. This despite the very clear modelling of Carnatic music along Western Art Music—what with the Carnatic 'Trinity' of Tyagaraja, Dikshitar and Shyama Shastri similar to the Trinity of Beethoven, Bach and Mozart, a Carnatic nineteenth-century obsession with written score and the development of the Carnatic kriti format along the lines of Western art compositional canons.

The Maharaja's work is significant as a body of compositions which expressed the sensibilities of a generation after the Trinity of Carnatic music. Despite the long line of Carnatic composers from Annamacharya to Arunagirinathar to Tyagaraja to Lalgudi Jayaraman, the tradition is producing fewer composers today. This has to do with exaggerated notions of genius in Carnatic thinking. For one, the overly zealous patrons of this culture exaggerate the intelligentsia required to sing let alone compose a kriti. Carnatic jingoism says all geniuses were so at birth, fully undermining the role of the individual will, effort and evolution of genius. Many people still believe that learning Western music will 'dilute' Carnatic classicism or if one listens to other styles of music, the influences of the 'other' will almost always interfere with the purity of the tradition. In addition, the imagery is overdone with claims that musical creativity 'just flowed' and came in 'flashes' of divine—hence the art of conscious composition is never really taught in the tradition. Many creative minds have thus perhaps relegated themselves to simply performing the music already composed. Also, there are not enough role models available of composers who made beautiful music while straddling other roles and lives.

The Maharaja's composition project is also a significant world music-meets-Carnatic initiative. In any conservatory today, a student of composition will 'study' different models of compositions available in a certain genre or from different genres to create his own distinct style of composition. That is exactly what JCW did. Dr S. Krishnamurthy in his book, *Sangeetha Samaya,* says that the Maharaja was actually advised to take this project up by his teacher Mysore Vasudevacharya, who noticed his intuitive gift for melody and tuning. In what is comparable to the processes of an academic dissertation project, with Mysore Vasudevacharya as his mentor, he is said to have launched into the vaggeyakara world, churning out 94 pieces in less than two years—at roughly 1 kriti every 15 days! Dr Krishnamurthy elaborates the method:

> The lyrics were first written by the Maharaja and tuned after. Later the *sargam* transcriptions would be prepared and sent to his mentor for review. Lengthy discussions on prosodical features, melodic line, form, metre used to follow. Later, these were given to musicians of the court to be sung as part of daily *pooja* rituals in the palace or disseminated to the Carnatic orchestra.

Shri Titte Iyyengar, court musician, remembers singing many of JCW's compositions as part of the daily poojas at the palace. Dr S. Krishnamurthy wonders how the Maharaja always seemed to find time to learn and compose amidst a packed daily schedule of administrative and political meetings!

The unusual life in which these compositions were composed is also refreshing. The Maharaja's world was full of the creative and the mundane, from administrative duties to royal obligations. Not a particularly idyllic saintly setting. Does not exactly sound like a life that may have music in it, does it? But it did. He may be no Saint Tyagaraja, but his music is not that of a wandering minstrel either. Another stereotype that the Maharaja's life breaks is the belief that one should do only one thing because it's the only thing that ensures mastery. Musicians all over the world are sold this narrow idea that they must focus all their energies on the one egg that is to hatch sound, otherwise they can never succeed. At the most, a musician may have a day job, something to offset the only kind of creativity he can experience in music. But to rule a kingdom, be passionate about Vedanta, to like jazz and Western classical music, is thought to almost preclude one from the single-minded claustrophobia needed to hash a kriti apparently!

The Maharaja's maverick life and renaissance-like genius presents many other inspiring messages. The world loves boxes and specialists. Intensity and excellence are measured by the one-life-one-passion axiom. Intensity is also measured by quantity rather than quality. There is a belief that excellence is the handmaiden of a certain type of pedigree, a certain kind of training, a certain kind of complete immersion to only passion. The Maharaja's life and his creative outpourings in a variety of seemingly disconnected domains of knowledge only point to a polymath mindset, which perhaps finds the same joy in composing a kriti as in writing a book on India and Africa (which he did!).

Can one be a purist and seek innovation?

How can one adore tradition while thinking beyond it?

Is questioning convention incompatible with honouring tradition?

Can one find the same quality of joy and anandatmanubhuti in researching and writing about Africa[2] and the deeply abstract philosophies of the Advaitha Vedanta?

Yes, in the lives of such mavericks, such questions find beautiful answers. That's where his life is his message. His art truly reflects an inner beauty, because as Aristotle said, 'The aim of art is to represent not the outward appearance of things, but their inward significance.'

Music sessions at the Mysore court during the Vardhanti and coronation of JCW

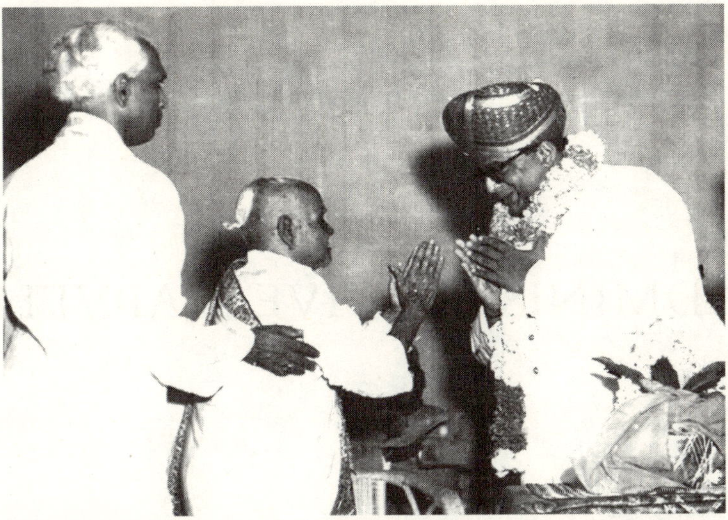

JCW with his teacher, Carnatic composer Mysore Vasudevacharya

JCW with noted Carnatic vocalist Ariyakudi Ramanuja Iyyengar in Madras

7
ADMINISTRATIVE MARVELS

Mirza Ismail, one of Mysore's most celebrated and longest serving Diwans wrote to the newly coronated JCW, 'The war presents unusual and unrivalled opportunities for starting key industries in the country and it is unforgivable to not make use of the situation.' He was hoping to counsel the young Maharaja about the promise of starting an automobile factory that would assemble Chrysler cars in Mysore. JCW, who had given the go ahead for the starting of the Hindustan Aircraft Factory earlier, had declined this. Charles Todhunter, private secretary to JCW wrote back to Mirza, 'His Highness is not prepared to agree to take such a prominent part as is proposed in a scheme which seems to him, to have little prospect of ultimate success.'[1] To which Mirza Ismail wrote back to give a prophetic warning about how his infant reign could be marred by the wrath of the people:

> I do not think His Highness realises the fact that he is ranging himself against the whole State in coming to such a decision. I hope I shall not be misunderstood if I utter a word of warning. The people of Mysore will not easily forget or forgive those responsible for deliberately missing such a splendid opportunity

of establishing an industry of such far-reaching importance in the State.

The answer to this was silence and a firm no.

In November 1940, Walchand Hirachand, an industrialist with multiple industrial bases from shipping to manufacturing gave Mirza Ismail a proposition to build Chrysler cars in Mysore with a licence. The Mysore government would buy shares to the value of Rs 150 lakhs, almost two-thirds of the needed capital for the factory. With war on the anvil, values of commodities were very high, and the state was already experiencing food shortages. JCW perhaps felt the time was not right given Mysore's war-related expenses or simply might not have seen much potential in the project. During Nalvadi Krishnaraja Wadiyar's reign, the Mirza-Vishveshwaraiah duo had led many capital-intensive projects such as the Krishnaraja Sagara dam, a multipurpose irrigation-hydroelectric project. The KRS dam took 1,034 crore rupees in 1938, almost US$ equivalent of 140,000 then, and the story goes that the royal family had to pawn their jewellery to finish the project, with the Mysore exchequer empty with other spendings. JCW's approach to the development of modern Mysore seems to have been very different from his uncle's on the nature of projects. The torrid images of death during the Mysore famine and the ghastly famine stories from all over the subcontinent were abundant reminders of the pitfalls of mismanagement in resource restricted princely states. As a student of history and political science, he perhaps understood that those who do not learn from history are doomed to repeat it. His approach to the development of Mysore was clear. A fiscally conservative World War–based economy centred on low-capital, small-scale projects of far-reaching impact. His mandate was definitely irrigation, education and culture.

As early as 1912, Alfred Chatterton, the first director of Mysore's Department of Industries and Commerce, was appointed to envision Mysore's industrial growth. As opposed to Sir M. Vishveshwaraiah, his recommendations were less bombastic, but more relevant in using Mysore's indigenous resources such as sandalwood and skilled labour to produce commodities for the global market. The Mysore Sandalwood oil factory, the experimental weaving factory and the very first factory to manufacture artificial fertilizers in Mysore were set up with this approach to industrialization. The administrative approach of the Maharaja was closer to Chatterton's model than the big-project dreamers. Soon after coronation, this approach of the young Maharaja created a lot of tension with the 'old horses' of Nalvadi Krishnaraja Wadiyar's reign. In the case of the car factory, the Maharaja was under great pressure from the likes of Sir M. Vishweshwaraiah, the architect of modern Mysore's industrialization, who said, 'It is a positive ignominy for a country like ours to be without such a factory.' JCW declined to meet him or further any discussions on this matter either with Mirza or him. This added a great amount of tension between JCW and Mirza. The Maharaja is said to have sent feelers that Mirza should resign as he had acted autonomously and given his word for the automobile project without his consent. Mirza resigned on 9 May 1941, due to mounting tensions. This firm stance by JCW must have come as a shock to many veteran civil servants of Mysore, who perhaps were expecting a more conformist 21-year-old Maharaja. He showed them early on that he was no yes-man. JCW's ideology and approach to Mysore administration is perhaps the least understood or hailed. His larger than life personality, versatility of talents, and his musical genius capture much attention in most of his biographical memoirs.

Soon after his coronation, the young Maharaja toured his state extensively, to rousing welcomes and long pleas for development of infrastructure. In about five years, as documented in the piles of correspondences between Municipal Councils, District Boards, Private Trusts and common people, he travelled to over 150 towns in his state for research and follow-up on development-related activities. While keeping a tight control over food, grains, and commodities, and with a very limited budget, many big headways were made in his reign. Hospitals for women, a middle school for remote communities, water supply and drainage services to villages, electricity for small-scale industries—Mysore grew inside-out and sustainably. Nalvadi Krishnaraja Wadiyar's legacy is documented in history for the king who took up large industrial undertakings—the Sivanasamudram hydroelectric project, the Krishnaraja Sagara Dam and a railroad from Mysore to Bengaluru. JCW's administrative legacy lives on as the stable hum of grass-root level development, historic nonetheless for the communities that benefited from them. While these stories don't make for the astounding images that portrayed Mysore as an industrialized state, nevertheless they were staggeringly significant.

The speeches he gave at the inaugural events of such developmental activities are interesting. He is quite clear that certain projects will have to either wait or will need active community enterprise; some he declines with a firm no and justifies his denial. In many cases, he encourages well-positioned proposals for infrastructure development. The correspondences sing in only one tonic, that kingship sat extremely well on his young shoulders. While his own dreams of being a concert pianist and studying with Rachimanoff, were interrupted by the drone of official duties, the correspondences sing the song of a very engaged king. Of what use is difficulty, if it does not reveal a man's character? He ruled with the same passion with which he perhaps composed.

Reply to addressees presented by the District Board, Hassan, the Town Municipal Council, Sakleshpur, and Colonel W.L. Crawford, on the occasion of the laying of the foundation stone of the Crawford Hospital at Sakleshpur, 19 February 1941:

In European countries there are many people busying themselves at the present time with considering what shall be the elements of the new order that is to be set up when the war is over. I venture to think that the most profitable approach to this problem is to consider rather what are the elements of the old order that have to be abolished. In England, for instance, it is generally agreed that the one thing essential is to abolish unemployment, and from that pro-position there follow a whole series of others which reach into every part of the body politic. The corresponding problem in India is to improve the standard of living; that means to improve the standard of vitality, the standard of desire, the standard of possession, the standard of thrift, the standard of co-operation, and so on ad infinitum. I hope today that you are making a start, in Saklespur at least, with a beginning of this upward path, by this hospital, which will help to remove disease, and by the child welfare centre, which will help to reduce the appalling maternal and infantile mortality. We shall make life much more worth living, and therefore worth working harder for, and so replace the vicious circle in which we have so long been involved, with what I hope, will prove to be a circle of a different kind.[2]

Reply to an address presented by the District Board, Kadur, on the occasion of laying the foundation stone of the bridge across the Bhadra river near Kalasa, 18 February 1941:

Mr Sarabhoja, Mr President and Members of the Kadur District Board,—I am very glad that it has been my good fortune, so early in my reign, to be able to pay a visit to a portion of the State which has the reputation of being so difficult of access as Kalasa, and still more so, to be able to take part in an extensive programme of undertakings for removing from this part of the State the reproach of inaccessibility. The bridge of which I am laying the foundation stone today will form one of a chain of works which will connect Kalasa with the network of roads running to Koppa and Narasimharajapura on the one hand, and to Mudigere and Chickmagalur on the other, and I hope that the time may come when, with the assistance of our neighbours across the border, we may be able to extend the connection on the other side towards the coast.

Similarly in the matter of schools. As you are aware, my Government have recently taken elementary education under their direct control and have embarked on a scheme for establishing 1,000 new schools in the next four years. When that scheme is completed, your district will, it is hoped, have one school for every village of 300 inhabitants and upwards, which I think you will find fully to meet your difficulties in the matter.[3]

Reply to an address presented by the town Municipal Council, Kunigal, 9 July 1942:

I am very gratified to know that the construction of a reservoir across the Shimsha at Marconahalli is already bearing fruit by bringing large tracts of land under irrigation and improving visibly the economic condition of the people in this taluk, I need hardly remind you of the policy of my Government in undertaking irrigation projects. The prosperity of the peasantry is the highest return which they expect from the promotion of such schemes.

It affords me genuine pleasure to acknowledge your expressions of gratitude in connection with the construction of this important work of irrigation. You have sought the assistance of my Government in the improvement of your water supply scheme and in the speedy execution of the drainage scheme which has been drawn up for your town. You have also referred to the need for adopting special anti-malaria measures. I am glad to inform you that your proposals in regard to water supply and drainage have been sanctioned, and I hope it will be possible for my Government to view your other requests with sympathy.[4]

BRIDGE OVER JAYAMANGALI RIVER

His Highness the Maharaja, replying to the Address presented by the President and Members of the District Board, Tumkur, on the occasion of laying the Foundation-stone of the Bridge across the Jayamangali River near Puravara, on 30th July 1949, said :—

This is the second bridge, the foundation-stone of which I have the privilege of laying, in my tour in your District on this occasion. I am glad to know that through your efforts and with the help of my Government, a long-felt want in this part of the State will be fulfilled by the construction of this bridge. Better means of communication, better facilities for educational advancement, more opportunities for occupational studies, and further medical facilities are all requred, particularly in these rural areas.

With limited finances at the disposal as much of local bodies as of the Government, it seems to me that the most important decision to be taken is the decision regarding priorities. An improvement in the economic position of the villager leads to an improvement in the financial position of the State. The best method of improving that economic position seems to lie in affording proper health conditions to the population and developing communications, so that the result of their efforts in production may find adequate compensation. Educational progress will be more easily possible if the economic position of the raiyat and thereby the financial position of your Board and of the Government improves.

I am glad to note that my Government has completed the electrification of Koratagere and Madhugiri and I understand that the present Budget provides for the completion of the electrification of Sira and Pavagada Taluks. I hope that with these facilities, there will be a perceptible improvement in the life of the people of this area. You have referred to various industrial schemes which, you feel, can be undertaken in this part of the State. I have no doubt that my Government will consider these proposals very carefully and that such schemes as are feasible will be undertaken either directly by the Government or through assistance to private industrialists.

I have great pleasure in laying the foundation-stone of this bridge across the Jayamangali river.

Official reply to the address presented on the occasion of inauguration of bridges across the River Jayamangali

BRIDGE ACROSS THE NAGINI RIVER

HIS HIGHNESS LAYS FOUNDATION-STONE.

His Highness the Maharaja of Mysore, replying to the Address presented by the President and Members of the District Board, Tumkur, on the occasion of laying the foundation-stone of the Bridge across the Nagini river at Keggere, on 29th July 1949, said :–

The purpose of my visit this evening to this part of your District is to lay the foundation-stone of a bridge across the Nagini river, which will make this District Board road an all-weather road, connected to the main Bangalore-Mangalore road. I have had the privilege, during the past few years, of either laying foundation-stones for or opening bridges across many rivers in the State.

Connecting the Gulf

Such bridges are symbolic; they not merely give facilities for easy travel for persons but they also help in the carriage of freight. More than that they bridge the gulf that exists between the rural population and the urban, the gulf in economic development and in social progress. The importance of such linking up of rural areas with the main marketing centres can easily be realised and forms one of the main methods of improving rural economy

Progress made by the District Board

It is with some concern that I learn that the Marconahalli reservoir, whose foundation-stone was laid by my late revered uncle, has not fulfilled the high expectations which it held forth at its inception. Your suggestions for providing more water to the wet lands under that reservoir will, I have no doubt, receive the careful consideration of my Government.

I am glad to learn of the progress that your Board has made in several directions and of all the responsibilities that you have undertaken in maintaining roads and opening fresh roads, in providing hospitals for villages and in increasing the number of maternity homes and veterinary hospitals.

Strengthening Finances

Finance has always been and will continue to be a problem for every administration from the highest to the smallest. I am therefore not surprised to learn from your Address that your finances need strengthening; but may I point out that it is not always from the Government that that strengthening can come and that it is equally a duty cast on you to devise ways and means by which you can augment your income? I trust that with the co-operation of the Government and the District Boards, measures may be devised for strengthening these local institutions.

I have great pleasure in laying the foundation-stone of this Bridge and trust that great prosperity will attend all the areas which are served by this road which will now be a permanent and all-weather proof highway to the main centres of trade and commerce.

Official reply to the address presented on the occasion of inauguration of bridges across the River Nagini

Mysore in War

World War II stirred great patriotism in him. A defeat of the Allies and occupation of India by the Axis forces would have unleashed the unthinkable on India. He appealed:

> At this hour of grave national crisis, when the enemy is at the gates of India, I appeal to my people to rally to the defence of our motherland, and forgetting all religions, political and class differences, present a united national front. The object of the National War Front movement is to strengthen the war effort of the people and to consolidate the national will to offer united resistance to Nazism and Fascism in every form and shape.[5]

Managing Mysore and public sentiments in a complicated polity required much honest leadership. Why should Mysore fight with its oppressors? The Indian National Congress–backed freedom fighters perhaps saw this appeal in a very different light. Maintaining internal security during this time was no joke; emotions ran high, much like prices of commodities. Mysore contributed men, money, resources, and many years of economic frugality to the war. There was a dearth of hope amidst testing times; JCW had to manage public sentiment:

> Apart from these tangible contributions to the war effort, there are numerous other ways in which we can strengthen the home front and bring victory nearer. The most important of these is to cultivate the will to victory. A spirit of cheerful optimism, and readiness to put up with the numerous little sacrifices and inconveniences occasioned by the war, namely, the soaring prices, scarcity and consequent rationing of foodstuffs and necessaries, lack of the little luxuries we have been accustomed to, shortage of petrol, and discomforts of travel, will very much help us in building up the will to victory.

JCW hosted the All-India War Services Exhibition in Bangalore on 10 June 1943, a meeting ground for innovators, scientists, governments and the civil servants:

> For the first time in Bangalore, you will see assembled together the various types of armaments with which the fighting forces of the United Nations and the brave sons of India, who are employed in the Naval, Military and Air Forces, are equipped. You will be shown specimens of anti-aircraft guns, machine guns, tanks, armoured vehicles, air-planes and models of warships and submarines, with which this relentless war against Axis tyranny and oppression is being waged. You will also be shown specimens of captured German, Italian and Japanese equipment. There will also be exhibits depicting the humanitarian activities of the Red Cross Society and the St. John Ambulance Association. You will, in short, be given an idea of what this world-conflict implies, which might help every one of you to realise the imminent need for playing your own part in bringing it to a speedy and victorious conclusion.[6]

The wounds of war were far too many. It was no mere battle of ideologies, but a battle of brutality, bodies, blood and bane. The dead bodies came and along came the pain of fighting a war that seemed to rage on and on. To order your men to fight an enemy on turfs that they are alien to them, under commanders who may see them just as hands that wield the gun, is definitely difficult. Yet, it needed to be done, and it was. Mysore's bravehearts fought well and hard, many victories were secured like the famed story of the Battle of Haifa in Israel in World War I. A memorial to these gallant men stands in Mysore. Like any war memorial, it makes one ponder about the fragility of life. It takes many loving years for a mother to raise a baby, and all it takes is a stray bullet to undo all that in a second. Only the names of the dead recorded in grim prose, no sounds of the jingling bangles that once lulled them to sleep, or the lullabies they heard.

Speech at the farewell parade of the First Battalion, Mysore Infantry, 4 November 1940:

Captain Mir Sarfaraz Hussain, Officers and Men of the First Battalion, Mysore Infantry, You are leaving the State that has been your home in order to play your part in the gigantic battle that is being waged in many quarters of the world by the forces that are maintaining truth, right, honour and justice against those that have been massed to impose a brutal tyranny upon the world. The task is one which will need all your strength, your courage, your patience and your energy.

I shall follow your movements with the deepest interest and I shall look to you to maintain, wherever you may be sent, the Mysore tradition of discipline and courage and of courtesy and kindness to the peoples of the countries in which your lot is cast. I pray God to bless you and guard you and to give you success in all your undertakings.[7]

MYSORE INFORMATION BULLETIN

Vol. IX Bangalore, November 30, 1946 No. 11

APPRECIATION OF MYSORE'S WAR EFFORT

SALUTING GUN PRESENTED TO HIS HIGHNESS THE MAHARAJA

Lt.-General Sir Rob Lockhart, G O. C, Southern Command, on behalf of His Excellency Field Marshal Sir Claude Auchinleck, the Commander-in Chief in India, presented a Saluting Gun to His Highness the Maharaja of Mysore at a Special Parade held at Bangalore on 7th November 1946 "In commemoration of the comradeship which existed between the Indian Army and the units of His Highness' forces which served under the Crown, and in appreciation of the contribution of these units to the common effort during the late war." In accepting the Saluting Gun, His Highness the Maharaja said : "We shall value it as a token of His Excellency's appreciation of the part the State of Mysore and its force have played in this war."

Excerpt from *The Mysore Bulletin*, 1946. JCW was presented with a saluting gun at a special parade held on 7 November 1946, in appreciation of his contributions to war efforts

A Mysore war fund was created out of fundraising from various stakeholders to help provide many amenities to the soldiers and the families. A Women's Auxiliary Committee was created to aid such war-based services to Indian troops. A civilian welfare committee was created to provide canteen services for the Indian Air Force. A happy reminder of this still stands as the Victory Hall in Cubbon Park in Bengaluru today, where the state government organizes social and cultural events.

Speech on the occasion of the laying of the foundation stone of the Canteen for Indian troops, Cubbon Park, Bengaluru, 19 June 1944:

> I have now great pleasure in laying the foundation stone of the Victory Flail, which I hope will be one of the many fitting memorials of the final and complete victory of the Allies, which cannot be distant. In the years to come, the Victory Hall will recall to the minds of men the sacrifice and hardship undergone by the Indian soldiers in fighting for the cause of freedom and righteousness.[8]

Land Reforms

In the end, it all boils down to land. Under JCW's rule, on the anvil of the war, the political equations between the Crown and the princes were quite opposite to what they were at the time of the coronation of his grandfather. Impoverished by wars and mounting political strife in Great Britain, the emergence of the Labour Party and public sentiments which consistently questioned the 'usefulness' of a pedigree queen, the Crown saw allies in the princes. By 1940, Mysore's subsidy to the Crown had decreased, thanks to some shrewd diplomacy on the part of Mysore. Mysore had greater autonomy on its governance, had established back-channels to lobby for its growing independence from the Crown on internal matters. During Nalvadi Krishnaraja Wadiyar's reign, and before World War I, given the restrictions imposed, Mysore's wiggle room towards financial abundance was almost nil. In his book, Björn Hettne, Professor of Economic History at the University of Goteburg, Sweden, argues that given the need to pay a large subsidy, stagnant land revenue incomes, frequent famines, food shortages and the dominance of Madrasi administrators, Mysore was content at a royalty of two crores in 1911. By 1940, when JCW assumed the throne, Mysore needed to break out of its oldest trap: stagnant land revenue incomes. He was to try to solve this tangle at a time when the nation was at war, food was low, and political instability the highest.[9]

The Mysore land revenue system was inherited from the system of the Vijayanagara empire, which is best described as a layered system of semi-autonomous provinces headed by the Palegar/Inamdar/Amildar, who liaisoned with village level units. Every village used to have a village accountant cum tax inspector–type of government 'hand', who maintained records and reported to the provincial head—usually called the Shanbhoga. The local chieftain, usually a large landlord Gowda/Patel would wield political clout in managing the landlords, tenants and the local politics of such a system.[10] Mysore's dominant taxation system was the Ryotwari system[11] where the landlord was allowed to cultivate land if taxes were paid as ordained. The taxes collected were in kind if the land was classified as wetland (like paddy and sugarcane fields), money was the mode of payment for dryland crops.[12] Land tenancy was complicated, due to famines, food shortages, slim irrigational facilities and unpredictable monsoons. Under the rule of Nalvadi Krishnaraja Wadiyar, Mysore had already diversified from seeking revenue from agrarian avenues to seeking monies from industrial and export incomes. Under JCW's leadership, a major revamp of the taxation system was first studied in extensive detail. His own research acumen came in handy. A detailed questionnaire was drafted and inputs were collected from all stakeholders about the issues with the current land revenue system. The idea was to revise the classification of lands into dry, wet and garden, to prevent fragmentation of lands below cultivable limits and to draft a tenancy law along the lines of the Bombay Tenancy law.

Table 7.1: Occupation Patterns of Selected Livelihoods in the Mysore Princely State							
Year	Population	Shepherds Herdsmen	Cultivating Owners	Non-Cultivating Owners	Tenants	Agri Labourers	Cotton Weavers
1891	41.1 Lakhs	24737	29.55 Lakhs	65374	1.89 L.akhs	50,000	89759
1901	55.4 Lakhs	72000	27 Lakhs	342231	5.15 Lakhs	3.52 Lakhs	82000
1911	58.06 Lakhs	27000	31.5 Lakhs	171549	6.63 Lakhs	1.77 Lakhs	34000
1921	59.78 Lakhs	27000	37.21 Lakhs	177170	2.86 Lakhs	5.17 Lakhs	55000
1931	65.57 Lakhs	30000	37 Lakhs	54366	4.5 Lakhs	7 Lakhs	44000
1941	73.28 Lakhs	Not Available	42.99 Lakhs	55300	3.09 Lakhs	3.92 Lakhs	Not Available
1951	90.74 Lakhs	Not Available	50.33 Lakhs	262305	4.32 Lakhs	6.15 Lakhs	Not Available

A comparative table of occupation patterns in Mysore from 1891-1951, showing significant increase in land owners and agricultural labour in Mysore from 1941-1951

This was a move to protect and preserve a rich agrarian economy in the Kaveri Delta belt—which had suffered from absentee landlordism, mortgaged lands, and heavy levies on farmers. Under his leadership, several land reforms had begun as early as 1942, and the statistics of landlords and tenants in princely Mysore during his tenure shows an increase in non-cultivating owners, an increase in agricultural labour, and the steady decrease of absentee landlordism (Table 7.1). The study of land issues in Mysore led to The Mysore Tenancy Act, 1952 (Mysore Act XIII of 1952), and it continues to serve the land reform acts, which came much later after Indian Independence: The Mysore Village Offices Abolition Act, 1961 (Mysore Act XIV of 1961) and The Mysore Land Reforms Act, 1961 (Mysore Act X of 1962).

The Diwan of Mysore while addressing the Dasara session of the Mysore Representative Assembly in 1946 reports the various successes of the many land reforms initiated. 'The land revenue demand for the year was 1,43,75,554 including arrears, the collections including remissions amounted to 1,27,32,054 representing 88% of demand as against 94 per cent in the previous year.' The system of Record of Rights scheme, which records details such as the name of the landholder, the number and size of the plot area, and revenue rate (for agricultural land), was reported to have been completed in all taluks, except Yelandur, Devanahalli and Heggadadevanakote. The Diwan reports that debt cancellation schemes were concurrently introduced in twenty-three taluks to facilitate this transition. He also notes that a large number of pending legal proceedings and interventions were made as well. He notes that 11,945 darkhasts or pleas out of a staggering 16,129 darkhasts pertaining to land-related legal complications were cleared in record time to make way for change and progress.

Hobli Multipurpose Societies

Another great success of the JCW administration was the innovative idea of multipurpose societies of Mysore that provided small amounts of timely loans for agricultural entrepreneurs. This innovation made it possible for them to weather financial crises better. It was the Mysorean version of the modern microfinancing model. Under Nalvadi Krishnaraja Wadiyar's reign, Karnataka was yet again at the forefront of the cooperative movement in India. The Mysore Co-operative Control Act of 1905 was ahead of the national act at that time, and allowed for cooperatives in urban and rural areas. A number of cooperative banks mushroomed in Mysore and Bangalore, several of which are active even today. JCW's administration put a spin on the idea of such cooperative societies, and experimented with the idea of using this 'cooperative' idea in a rural reconstruction context. The multi-purpose societies were thus created all across Mysore with the goal of increasing the scope of the cooperation to include collective farming, animal husbandry, access to local fair price markets, to create facilities for grain storage and such. The idea was to create villages as self-sufficient entities that did not depend on urban centres for either finance, produce sale or providing employment. This concept of the 'Hobli Multipurpose Societies' was in sync with Gandhi's call to strengthen India's villages, along the ideals of swadeshi and swavalambana.

The Mysorean Future—Five Years at a Time

As early as 1946, Mysore under JCW's direction was looking at five-year plans in various departments as a way to reshape its future. Joseph Stalin is credited with having applied this method of planning economic growth in chunks of five years, with his first Five-Year Plan (1928–32), which concentrated on a roadmap for bolstering heavy industry and defragmenting land ownership for agriculture by increasing state-controlled farms. Upon analysis, JCW seems to have applied the idea to create a sustainable future for Mysore's natural resources. In 1946, a Five-Year Plan for 28 irrigation projects at an estimated two crores of rupees were drawn up to wet cultivate about 93,000 acres of lands. This was almost a decade before the first Five-Year Plan was announced by the Nehru government for India. Owing to his pioneering research on irrigation, agroecology and conservation, a drive was taken up to restore 10,000 of the 20,000 minor water reservoirs in the state, which harboured macro and micro ecosystems. A Five-Year Plan was drawn to conserve the mineral wealth of Mysore while prudently exploiting its resources for mining and industrially relevant activity. In an innovative approach to decrease deforestation, over 10,000 acres of land were designated as 'fuel-forests'—a zone to cultivate trees in abundance to meet the needs of the growing timber industry without losing large amounts of green cover. A silviculture research station, a first-of-its-kind study centre with a focus on such scientific forestry, was envisioned. The institute would advice on limits and zones for harvesting forest produce, regeneration of deforested tracts and preventing soil erosion.

Another ambitious Five-Year Plan to promote and make sericulture a thriving rural industry in Mysore was drawn up. Over 2,00,000 families were engaged in sericulture, making it the largest cottage industry in Mysore—with over 3,000 villages involved. It was also the largest subsidiary industry practiced by many agriculture-based families, often offsetting the unpredictable profits with mainstream agriculture. A research institute was planned at Chennapatna, with the goal of conducting research into issues, the factors that could lead to the success of the sericulture industry, and to advocate proper measures for sericulture. A mammoth Rs 3,189 lakhs of non-recurring investment into this sericulture business was made over five years with a recurring expenditure of about Rs 300 lakhs. The modus operandi was clear—sustainable growth, planned modules for development and conservation of natural resources, and a grass-root up approach to developing Mysore.

It is not that ambition was lacking in the motives of the Mysore Government, when it came to various infrastructure developmental projects. For example, the Honnemaradu project headed by K.T. Bhashyam, the Minister for Electricity, (yes, there was a dedicated portfolio for that!) sought to further exploit the fierce waters of Sharavathi river for a massive half a million kilowatt hydroelectric project. The Lakkavalli reservoir-dam on the Bhadra river, 150 miles from Bangalore was sanctioned at a cost of Rs 9 crore! JCW's government through the war-torn years between 1942–1946 nursed the dream of the ambitious Krishna Rajendra hydro-electric project at Jog falls. The power station operated with 120 MW capacity, one of the largest hydroelectric stations in India at that time. The power station was previously named Krishna Rajendra hydro-electric project and was renamed as the Mahatma Gandhi hydro-electric project and inaugurated in 1948, during JCW's tenure. Aware of the ecological costs of such large projects, given that the Sharavathi river valley houses rich biodiversity, the idea was to balance development with reduced brunt of displaced communities, lands, animals, flora and fauna.

The interesting fact is that JCW does not seem to have been so sold romantically on the idea of an industrial Mysore, with big dams, large expenditures and rampant industrialization. Sustainability was at the core of all of such infrastructure development initiatives. This was a stark contrast to the attitudes of developing Mysore during the stint of Sir M. Vishweshwaraiah as Diwan and mixed economy approaches of Mirza Ismail under Nalvadi Krishnaraja Wadiyar's rule. JCW had an almost opposite approach—to strengthen the rural infrastructures, to irrigate sustainably, to industralize with guard and to reform with purpose.

ARCHIVAL EXCERPTS

HOBLI MULTI-PURPOSE SOCIETIES

CATERING FOR DAILY NEEDS OF VILLAGERS

It is proposed to organise a society for each village or group of villages on a limited liability basis with a view to make co-operation a live force in the economic regeneration of the masses. It will be a Consumers' Society to cater to the daily needs of the villagers such as kerosene, salt, betel-nut, matches, pulses, etc. These societies shall be affiliated to Hobli Multi-purpose Societies which in turn be affiliated to Taluk Multi-purpose Societies.

Functions of the Hobli Multi-purpose Societies

1. To encourage thrift and savings and to promote self-help and co-operation among the members. Small Hundi boxes would be distributed among the villagers so as to be of immense use in helping the villagers to save money and the amounts so collected in Hundies will be credited to their accounts to be opened in Multi-purpose Societies.

2. To arrange for supplying farmers' needs for production such as seeds, manure and agricultural implements: to take interest in the preparation of compost manure.

3. To supply domestic requirements to its members like cloth, yarn, kerosene, salt, matches, pulses, etc., on the basis of established needs at the cheapest possible prices.

4. To encourage subsidiary activities such as poultry-farming, bee-keeping, mat-weaving, basket-making, brassware, manufacture of sandal sticks, coir and rope industry, pottery, promoting hand-loom weaving, paper-making, etc.

5. To arrange for sale of agricultural produce of the raiyat in the nearest marketing organisation so that the questionable practices like unfair commission and false weights may disappear.

6. To finance loans to members for several purposes such as to purchase ploughs, cattle, agricultural implements, etc.

7. To be Fodder Storage Societies, the object being to stock fodder and be of use to the members at the time of Fodder shortage.

8. To maintain stud bulls and buffaloes for the improvement of cattle breed.

9. To serve as Milk Collecting Centres or Milk Co-operative Societies for supply of milk.

10. To take interest in Co-operative farming and bring into cultivation the waste lands on scientific lines; to be practically land improvement societies aiming at increasing the area under cultivation and also to increase the sources of irrigation; to raise topes, gardens and to plant trees, etc.

11. To undertake the construction of houses for the rural people; to secure plots for the members and to advance loans for building purposes.

12. To take interest in primary education and in starting adult education schools to eradicate illiteracy.

13. To provide medical facilities and public health amenities by adopting health programmes on house and home hygiene.

14. To introduce better measures to stop waste of expenditure and litigation.

15. To arrange for liquidation of prior debts of the members of the society and to recommend grant of loans to Land Mortgage Bank.

Constitution of Hobli Multi-purpose Societies

The Chairman of important Village Panchayets in the Hobli may be nominated as Directors of Hobli Multi-purpose Societies. Important non-official men of the locality will also be eligible to the Directorate, in addition to the Presidents and Directors of the Primary Societies in the Hobli.

Finance of Hobli Multi-purpose Societies

1. The Village Panchayets comprised in the Hobli may be permitted by the Deputy Commissioners as provided in the Village Panchayets Act to take shares in Hobli Multi-purpose societies. They may also be asked to keep deposits in societies.

2. To collect shares from every individual important person residing in Hobli.

3. To sanction grants from the Taluk Development Committee for specific purposes, such as starting of cottage industries, etc.

4. To obtain loans from the Apex Bank whenever necessary

Important features of Hobli Multi-purpose Societies

The Multi-purpose society is the only efficient institution to promote rural reconstruction. Important people of Village Panchayets and leading efficient persons are welded together into a community for the rural uplift. Rapid expansion of activities in villages will check the tendency of the people leaving villages for towns. The Panchayets raise the civic consciousness while the multi-purpose societies will raise definitely the economic conditions of the people.

General

The present credit societies in villages will be converted into village multi-purpose societies wherever possible.

It is no doubt true that there is difficulty in securing good secretaries on account of general illiteracy in the villages. It is also true that societies with small working capital are unable to bear overhead charges. The Revenue Inspector or the Development Inspector of each Hobli may be entrusted with the work of writing of accounts, etc., and effective supervision of these societies as the number of villages in each Hobli has been reduced very recently.

A FIVE-YEAR PLAN TO DEVELOP MYSORE FORESTS

10,000 ACRES TO BE BROUGHT UNDER FUEL PLANTATION

With an increase in population and growth of industries the demand on the States forest resources is increasing day by day. Some of the major industries such as the Mysore paper Mulls, the Mysore Plywood Corporation, the Wood Distillation and Preservation Plant, the Laq and Paint Works, the Sandal Oil Factories, the Match Factories, besides a large number of saw mills in the State, are the direct outcome of exploitation and utilisation of the forest resources. The five-year programme for development of the forest resources is drawn up in order to attain self-sufficiency in respect of raw materials needed for the various industries and the fuel needs of the State.

Scarcity of fuel supply to maidan tracts is being acutely felt. Unless vigorous measures are taken from now, the problem of fuel supply to urban areas in these tracts will assume serious proportions. To meet the requirements, it is proposed to raise fuel plantations on 40,000 acres of land in maidan regions, 25 per cent of the area being stocked by Government agency in 40 taluks in Bangalore, Kolai Tumkui, Mandya and Chitaldrug districts at the rate of 2,000 acres annually during the next five years. These plantations are expected to yield on maturity 250,000 tons of fuel of the value of Rs 12,50,000 at the end of ten years for an outlay of about Rs 7½ lakhs spread over 8 years.

One lakh and fifty thousand tons of fuel are being exploited every year to meet the requirements of the Mysore Iron and Steel Works at Bhadravati.

MYSORE INFORMATION BULLETIN, APRIL 1946

WATER RESOURCES

Twenty-eight Irrigation Projects at an estimated cost of Rs. 2 Crores

Development of Irrigation as a means to realise economic self-sufficiency in the matter of food production in the State has always received prior consideration of the Government. Mysore is one of the best endowed States in India in the matter of potential water wealth. A five-year programme of Irrigational projects, designed to bring under wet cultivation about 93,000 acres has been drawn up, involving an estimated outlay of Rs. 2 crores.

Major irrigation works, of which some are already under way, include (1) construction of Tunga anicut costing roughly Rs. 57 lakhs to irrigate 27,000 acres, (2) construction of a pick-up weir costing roughly Rs. 11 lakhs to irrigate 6,500 acres, (3) construction of Dandavathi reservoir costing roughly Rs. 11 lakhs to irrigate 8,000 acres, (4) Bhadra left bank channel costing Rs. 10 lakhs to irrigate 8,000 acres, (5) a tank at Devarabelekere in Harihar taluk costing Rs 17 lakhs to irrigate 5,750 acres, (6) a reservoir at Antigola costing Rs. 9½ lakhs to irrigate 7,000 acres, (7) a tank at Suvarnamukhi costing Rs. 9 lakhs to irrigate 3,000 acres, (8) an anicut across Vedavati near Naranapur costing Rs 1·85 lakhs to irrigate 2,200 acres, and (9) extension of Turuganur Branch of Irwin Canal costing Rs. 3·65 lakhs to irrigate 5,000 acres. The others are relatively small projects, each of them is expected to irrigate 500 to 1,000 acres. When these projects are completed and the lands under them are brought into cultivation, the production of food grains in the State will considerably increase.

10,000 Minor tanks to be restored

Out of 20,803 minor tanks in the State, 5,585 have been restored. Of the balance, about 10,000 tanks may be assumed to require restoration. These tanks, if restored, will ensure steady supply of water to the lands under them and contribute to the increase in the production of food crops. It is programmed to complete the restoration of these (10,000 tanks) within a period of 20 years at the rate of 500 tanks each year at an estimated outlay of Rs. 10 lakhs per year.

A Five-Year Programme envisaged

A five-year programme for the further exploitation of the State's mineral resources has been drawn up by the Geological Department. It includes the prospecting of the gold-bearing reef deposits at Bellara in Tumkur District, a plan to develop large-scale mining and levitation of china-clay from kaolin deposits at Bageshpura in Hassan District, schemes for the manufacture of cement and cement asbestos products and production of hydrated lime and lime products at Banasandra.

A FIVE-YEAR PLAN FOR SERICULTURAL DEVELOPMENT

ITS IMPORTANCE IN RURAL ECONOMY

The Sericulture Industry in Mysore plays an importatn role in rural economy as the largest and most important cottage industry practised largely as a subsidiary means of livelihood by small agriculturists. It is estimated that over 200,000 families are engaged in the various branches of the industry in over 3,000 villages in the State. The schemes of development aim at improving the quality and increasing the quantity of output, reducing the cost of production and stabilising the industry on a satisfactory and efficient basis so as to face external competition.

Excerpts from the *Mysore Bulletin* delineating the various Five-Year Plans of the Mysore Government during JCW's reign

MYSORE INFORMATION BULLETIN

Vol. XII] Bangalore, March 31, 1949 [No. 3

HIS HIGHNESS THE MAHARAJA'S GRACIOUS MESSAGE.

—:0:—

THE FOLLOWING MESSAGE OF HIS HIGHNESS THE MAHARAJA OF MYSORE WAS READ ON THE OCCASION OF THE INAUGURATION OF THE NEW RURAL DEVELOPMENT SCHEME ON 6th MARCH 1949.

I am happy to learn that my Government have decided on a new scheme of Rural Development and that the scheme is being inaugurated to-day in all Districts by the different Ministers of my Government. The importance of the village in the economy of the State has long been recognised by the Government and for over a generation, attempts have been made to build up the village economy which was fast disintegrating under the pressure of modern conditions and the demands of modern life. It is a truism, oft repeated but not fully appreciated, that the life of the country is in the villages and that in the prosperity of the rural people lies both the strength and the security of the State itself. Autonomous village communities which served all the needs of the villagers have disintegrated. The requirements of the village are not met to-day from within and the migration to urban areas is steadily creating in its wake many problems, economic, social and moral.

The attempt of the new Rural Development scheme is to revivify the activities in the village and to make the villager feel less discontented with his lot and more prosperous. To promote better conditions of agriculture, to place at the disposal of the agriculturist those facilities which make for better cultivation and yield better results, is one of the objects of this scheme. To remove the pressure on the land, to diversify the occupations of the villagers, to interest them, or rather to re-interest them, in those village industries which they were practising in the past and to introduce new village industries, is an equally important phase of the work of the Rural Development Committees.

The village must once more be a unit as much of culture as of prosperity and happiness. The villager must come back to his own All this requires essentially the co-operation of the people. Differences should be laid aside; partisan spirit should be eschewed; a healthy spirit of rivalry must exist where faction once prevailed. I fully hope and trust that the new Committees, composed essentially of leaders of non-official opinion, which have been given independent powers to promote the good of the village may bring prosperity to the villages and rejuvenate the life of the villagers. My Government are determined to advance the economic conditions and promote healthy prosperous life among the rural areas I wish the scheme all success and I am certain that the Presidents and members of the Rural Development Committees, helped and assisted by all officers of the State, will inspire confidence in the villagers and in a short period bring about a welcome change in the economic and social conditions of rural areas.

JCW's message on the occasion of inaugurating the Rural Development Scheme published in the *Mysore Information Bulletin* 1949

BRINGING FERTILITY TO DRY AREAS

LAKKAVALLI IRRIGATION PROJECT—TO COST ABOUT Rs. 9 CRORES

Government have sanctioned the starting of the construction of a large reservoir, costing about Rs. 9 crores at Lakkavalli on Bhadra River about 150 miles from Bangalore. In this connection it may be added that two engineers are to be deputed to study the latest practices in U. S. A., with particular reference to T. V. A. The following note gives some details in regard to the project which will be of the greatest utility in the dry taluks of Shimoga, Honnali, Channagiri, Davangere and Harihar and to the arid tracts of Chitaldrug District.—

DEVELOPMENT OF HYDRO-ELECTRIC WORKS IN MYSORE. HONNEMARADU PROJECT.

INSTALLATION OF HALF A MILLION KILOWATT POWER PLANT.

Sri K. T. Bhashyam, Minister for Electricity, accompanied by the Chief Electrical Engineer, the Superintending Engineer and other officers of the State, visited the Honnemaradu Valley to fix the dam site for impounding the waters of the Sharavati, with a view to generate power to the extent of over half-a-million kilowatts.

Honnemaradu is about five miles up the Sharavati, from the Jog Generating Station now known as "The Mahatma Gandhi Hydro-Electric Works". These works were opened by His Highness the Maharaja of Mysore, during February 1948. The station is built on the banks of the river at a narrow space cut out of rocks. It has an installed capacity of 120,000 kilowatts. The first stage consisting of four generators each of 12,000 K.W. capacity have been installed and the second stage of four generators each of 18,000 K.W. capacity is under execution. Two transmission lines of 110 K.V. have been constructed between Bhadravati and Jog as part of the first stage of the scheme. The construction of the other two transmission lines of 110 K.V. between Jog and Bhadravati will be taken up during the course of next year. All the power generated is transmitted to Bhadravati, from where it is transmitted onwards to various parts of the State at different voltages.

At present, the Sivasamudram system and the Jog system are tied at Bhadravati through two frequency changer sets. The aim is to extend the 50 cycle system to the entire State in due course, except the Kolar Gold Fields area, which will be fed by Sivasamudram on the 25 cycle system.

A reservoir has been constructed, known as the Hirebhaskar dam. It impounds 25,000 million cubic feet of water. It is intended to supplement the natural flow of the river during the dry season to meet the demand of the station for a generation of a firm power of 102,000 kilowatts at 75 per cent load factor.

Sharavati is a rapid and voluminous river. The rainfall in the catchment area is heavy and the average annual yield in the river is in the neighbourhood of 150,000 million cubic feet. As all the waters of the river go over the falls and reach the sea, it is considered necessary that a reservoir, capable of impounding the maximum quantity of water, should be constructed and all the water thus impounded utilised to supplement the natural flow of the river during the summer season for generation of power. After a detailed survey of the place, it has been considered desirable that a reservoir should be built at the place known as Honnemaradu, about three miles down the river from Hirebhaskar dam. It is a narrow valley flanked on either side by hills and the river-bed is rocky. A reservoir at the place constructed to a height of about 165 feet is calculated to impound over 100,000 million cubic feet.

The water from the reservoir to the extent required by the present generating station is proposed to be diverted into the existing power channel by the Karagal Anecut constructed for the purpose.

Excerpt from the *Mysore Bulletin*, March 1949, outlining the proposal to develop a half-a-million kilowatt hydroelectric project at Honnemaradu across the Sharavathi river

8
AN INSTRUMENT OF FREEDOM

'Dhana Dhanya Soubhagya Daayini Dharma Sansthapini
Durgam Adyanta Srividya Dharani Paala naratam
Matimnah Prachodayallalitaam'

(The source of prosperity
The domiciliate of dharma
Elevate my perception, oh! Durga symbolized in the Srividya.)

—An excerpt from the Carnatic kriti, *'Chintayami Jagadamba'*

On 15 August 1947, it was actually only the princely states that were free on 'paper' to choose the Dominions of India or Pakistan.[1] Even this would be somewhat factually wrong, as by then most states and their kings or princes were coaxed, cajoled, romanced, mollycoddled or cornered into signing the Instrument of Accession—a document by which they 'outsourced' certain powers to the dominion of India.[2] Upon close examination of the events leading to the declaration of Indian Independence, the truth that emerges is that interestingly, the princely states were free to function as states of the Indian dominion until they joined the Republic of India on 26 January 1950. India was officially only a Union of India, a Commonwealth country until it asserted its sovereign, democratic, republic status on 26 January 1950. The fate of the large British provinces with an estimated population of over 300,000,000 in the subcontinent was already sealed by Lord Mountbatten and Sir Radcliffe; the areas were bartered between East and West Pakistan or India. Mysore, in this scenario, went from colonial 'dyarchy' of sorts during colonial rule, to independent statehood between 15 August 1947 and 25 January 1950, and finally became a constitutionally recognized territory of the Republic of India in 1950. This makes JCW, technically, the only sovereign king after many generations of the Wadiyar dynasty to be free from indirect rule during this period. On 9 August 1947, the Instrument of Accession was signed between JCW and the Governor-General Lord Mountbatten, asserting his rights of sovereignty over his state, and expressing his wilful intention to join the Dominion of India as per the inclusions, provisions and framework delineated in the Government of India Act of 1935. With this, he had for the first time sovereignty over Mysore like never before, not as a vassal of the British government of India. This is a much misrepresented fact, many chronicles of Mysore erroneously quote that Mysore melded with the Republic of India in 1947 and that JCW ceased to be a sovereign in 1947. However, this freedom perhaps felt more suffocating than before, as the nation organized itself to dethrone most of its imperialists and hereditary monarchs—the word 'Maharaja' would soon be a vestigial adornment to many.

Up until the turn of events that forced Lord Mountbatten to split the subcontinent into India and Pakistan through the Indian Independence Act, the multilayered diplomacy between the representatives of the British Crown, the parliament and the princely states was moving towards a confederate-model, where the princely states would centralize external affairs, defence, communications, and keep several key portfolios central to their region. States could have their own constitution, somewhat along the lines of what is prevalent in the United States of America, where states have independent voice in matters of religious policies, civic liberties, judicial nuances and so forth. Such diplomacy had begun as early as 1920, where a royal proclamation of the King-Emperor George V established a Chamber of Princes (Narendra Mandal). The goal was to create a forum for open dialogue and direct communication with the colonial government of British India, bypassing influential political agents of the time.[3] The Chamber of Princes remained quite active up until the individual Instruments of Accession were negotiated. A Chamber resolution by Narendra Mandal clarified their engagement with the emerging apparatus of democracy for India:

> The Chamber of Princes, while welcoming the attainment by India of its due place among the dominions of the British Commonwealth under the British Crown, records its emphatic and firm view that, in any future constitution for India, the essential guarantees and safeguards for the preservation of the sovereignty and autonomy of the States and for the protection of their rights and interests arising from treaties, and engagements and Sanads or otherwise, should be effectively provided and that any unit should not be placed in a position to dominate the others or to interfere with the rights and safeguards guaranteed to them, and that all parties must be ensured their due share and fair play; and that, in any negotiations for formulating a constitution for India, whether independently of the Government of India Act 1935, or by revision of that Act, representatives of the States and of this Chamber should have a voice proportionate to their importance and historical position.[4]

Mirza Ismail, Diwan of Mysore, had attended the three Round Table Conferences in London between 1930 and 1932 aimed at creating consensus on how India would come to be politically organized without the 'crowning' presence of British administrators. The conferences were largely unsuccessful in creating a complete consensus but were moving towards drafting of the constitutional reforms needed to push India towards Dominion status. Winston Churchill spewed disgust at the Socialist party's agenda to favour the creation of independent India, and remarked, 'The whole conference was manipulated and manoeuvred by the Socialist Party, to achieve the result they had set before themselves from the beginning, namely the conferring of responsible government at the centre upon Indians.'[5] Following the Round Table Conferences, when the scheme of a federation was proposed in the Government of India Act in 1935, the princely states were on board, near consensus was reached, except the world broke out into war yet again in 1939, playing the ultimate spoilsport to the confederate model and changing the destinies of over 500 kingdoms in India.[6]

On the Anvil of War

It was in this political chaos that JCW was thrust on the throne, due to the untimely demise of his uncle, Nalvadi Krishnaraja Wadiyar, and his father, Yuvaraja Narasimharaja Wadiyar. In 1940, when JCW assumed the crown, all efforts for a smooth transfer of power to a confederate India somewhat were outseated by the need to enter British India into war; hence the paramountcy on provinces and the various British treaties with princely states continued. In many ways, it was clear to JCW as it was to many contemporaries that once the clouds of war would clear, the princely states would have an opportunity to meld into a union where their sovereignty could continue minus colonial overtures. However, that was not to be. With the Government of India Act of 1935, and the increasing strength of the Narendra Mandal, an opposite wave started. A stir-up of socialist sentiments regionally and nationally brewed, with the rise of political leaders, who were very clearly anti-royalty or anti-prince order. The Indian National Congress, in these years, stepped up its affairs with labour unions and socialist political associations in princely states to counteract a king-run state model.[7]

In many ways, Mysore was already functioning as a constitutional monarchy of sorts. Our current President, Ram Nath Kovind, in his speech at the Centenary Celebrations of JCW, affirmed the constitutional framework of Mysore that JCW led: 'As we remember Maharaja Wadiyar here today, he can best be described as the most eminent monarch-democrat.' At the inaugural speech made to Mysore Legislature on 9 June 1941, JCW said, 'The torch of constitutional progress has been handed down to me as a family heritage. It is my ambition, as I am sure it is yours, to ensure that its light does not grow dim but will burn ever brighter with the passage of time.' As compared to other states of India, Mysore had established a bicameral legislature since the time of Nalvadi Krishnaraja Wadiyar, and was publishing a civil list that gave clear accounts on expenditures, assets, properties and financial profile of the royal family versus the administration. There was better transparency in administration than seen in most other princely states, some of whom were run like a small family business. Mysore kings were truly ahead of the curve when it came to introducing the policies, proceedings and structures of a neo-constitutional democracy in Mysore before many other states in colonial India. In many ways, this explains the composure of JCW during a time when many other princes shrank at the thought of decentralized power of any kind.

By August 1940, the British government had accepted the demand to create a Constituent Assembly entrusted with the job of possibly drafting India's future constitution, which came into being under the Cabinet Mission Plan on 16 May 1946. Through the facilitation of the Cabinet Mission Plan of 1946, elections were held for the first time for the Constituent Assembly. The results of the elections threw a wrench in many manicured manoeuvres made by the four major stakeholders: the Indian National Congress, the Muslim League, the Narendra Mandal and its sympathizers in India and Britain, and the Mountbatten–Nehru–Sardar Patel–V.P. Menon coalition. The members were elected by provincial assemblies by a single transferable vote system out of 389 seats, 292 were representatives of the states, 93 representatives from princely states, and 4 from chief commissioners' provinces of Delhi, Ajmer, Coorg, and interestingly, British Baluchistan. The design of the Constituent Assembly shook the stakeholders up real hard. Rosita Forbes, an English travelogue-writer and who travelled to India and met many of these princes, wrote in *India of the Princes* notes on the many vested interests that operated at the time:

> The India Act of 1935 is presumably based on the assumption in case of the Federation of the States would introduce a strong conservative element to counter balance the untested socialism of the Congress party. While conferring complete autonomy on the 11 provinces of British India, subject to the reasonable but much criticised safeguards, it gave to the Princes representation in the Central Legislature far in excess of what could be claimed on a basis of population. For while the peoples of the States number only 80,000,000 compared to 270,000,000 of British India, the Princes can send 104 members out of the 250 to the Upper House (the Council of State) and 125 out of the 375 to the Federal Assembly. At present the Congress hold office in seven of the 11 provinces of British India, and their Hindu leaders appear to regard Federation as a conspiracy between Britain and the Princes to put an end to any hope of Indian unity and freedom.[8]

The Nightmare of Freedom

It was not until the Muslim League's insistence for a separate dominion and the widespread communal riots soon after the constituent assembly elections, that both Lord Mountbatten and Indian Congress leaders woke up to the dangers of letting princely states go scot-free—to either assert independence, or allege loyalty to either Pakistan and India. The scary vision of a 'Balkan India' with hostile territories, like a giant jigsaw puzzle super-imposed on the

Indian map, in many ways spurred efforts to unify India into a union. While Lord Mountbatten worked closely with Congress leaders and was getting increasingly weak-kneed by the Muslim League's assertion for a Muslim State, there were back-end negotiations of the princes with the Crown directly through one crafty Sir Conrad Corfield. He was surreptitiously working against the Mountbatten and Nehruvian coalition of a unified India by opening up channels for the princes to speak directly with members of the British parliament and their sympathizers in England. The Nawab of Bhopal, for instance, was hoping to stay independent and showing all political leanings of perhaps joining the Dominion of Pakistan:

> I feel necessary to repudiate, in language which will not permit of doubt or ambiguity, the insidious suggestions made by certain quarters in India, which misrepresent the Indian Princes as opponents of India's Constitutional freedom and as impediments to her progress to that end. Never was there a greater distortion of the truth. We yield to none in patriotism and love for our own country. We wish to see her great and honoured, filling in her own right a position in the comity of the world to which her history and the achievements of her people entitle her. To assist in securing this end, we are ready to make what contribution we can. But the sanctity of covenants is the foundation of all civilised life, and no party which respects sanctity of covenants can blame us for urging that any constitutional arrangements for India must ensure due fulfilment of the established rights of the States and that these rights should not be unilaterally modified.

A secret memorandum, for instance, circulated in the Narendra Mandal in April–May 1945, clearly gives away their sense that they would remain big stakeholders in the new central government: 'The Indian States will be glad as always in the interest of their Motherland, to make their contribution, in every reasonable manner compatible with the sovereignty and integrity of the States, towards the framing of the new Constitution of India.' This was, however, unacceptable to Lord Mountbatten, the Congress, which was already in power in the provinces, and to the vision of how British parliament at large, thought of a stable and independent India. A fractured map of discontinuous territories, big and small kingdoms, all grappling with delusions of secure independence seemed rather irksome at the time to them. It was not an environment of great trust and unity of any sort but a mangled mass of narrow-sighted greed, falsity of national spirit, fear of extremist socialist ideas, a need to grab power, and a resistance to give it up. Freedom was suddenly a nightmare, not a dream.

In the years leading to the Declaration of Indian Independence, it is noted that Mysore and several larger states remained aloof to the machinations of the game, until V.P. Menon and Sardar Vallabhbhai Patel devised a 'gulpable' pill in the form of an Instrument of Accession, which allowed them to accede to Indian Union on defence, external affairs, and communications. Patel and Menon also secured Lord Mountbatten's assent to negotiate with the princes individually in July 1947.

Sensing the changing tides and in synergy with the vision of a united India, JCW was one of the first few kings to sign the Instrument of Accession in August 1947. It is reported that in July 1947, JCW along with Arcot Ramaswamy met a delegation of rulers and ministers of Patiala, Gwalior, Bikaner and Nawanagar—convincing them to join the Indian Union and thereby kick-starting the landslide of getting kingdoms to sign the Instrument of Accession. In many ways, this swerved the needle towards the making of the Indian Union. JCW and Mysore, yet again, showing the way it's done with grace!

9
THE SAGA OF THE SCEPTRE

'My Crown is in my heart, not on my head:
Not deck'd with Diamonds, and Indian stones:
Nor to be seen: my Crown is call'd Content,
A Crown it is, that seldom Kings enjoy.'
—William Shakespeare, *King Henry VI, Part 3*

The period between 1945 and 1952 was perhaps among the most politically turbulent phases for not just Mysore but for the whole of India. It was one that saw many transformations of power in independent India—new power structures emerged, showing many sceptred dreams of self-governance and of a new order of centralized power. Like any structure, be it monarchy or a republic, it was fraught with the same issues of legitimacy, unequal distribution of power and a disconnect between the willed and the executed. The fate of many small and big princes and princely states were decided by a complex turn of political events, repercussions of which are felt even today, as litigations between their state governments and the members of royal families continue to be bitterly fought in India's courts.

Interestingly, this journey of power transformations between 1940 and 1950, saw JCW relinquish his sovereignty and find his way into a life of significance. The journey of decreasing authority over his Mysore, from the Maharaja of Mysore in British India, to the Maharaja in the Dominion of India, to a Rajapramukh in Greater Mysore to later, the Governor of Mysore must have been rather difficult. Many perceptions of his relinquishment of the throne exist in anecdotal and documented accounts. There are rather celluloid-like stories of how he gave up his kingdom in a go, and overreaching accounts of his saintliness in having done so. Some ill-informed naysayers quip that he had no power anyway, so, he must have reconciled rather quickly! However, upon examination, he seemed to have approached this with a sense of equanimity—a sense of detachment from the outcomes but a firm interest in administering the state and his interests to its best futures. In his lecture, 'Avadhuta—Reason and Reverence', he quotes a simile to explain how an Avadhuta shakes off such ephemeral attachments, having observed the moon, one of his preceptors:

> The moon waxes and wanes but this is no indication of any diminution of her luminosity. It is the result of a partial reflection of the rays of the sun. Similarly the vicissitudes of birth, existence, growth, youth, senility, and death are states of the body and leave the *Atman* unclouded by them.

One finds that during this difficult time, he held his own, kept his options open, used his sense of judgement, leveraged his national stature well and accepted the inevitable. As the Rajapramukh of Mysore, and later as the Governor of Mysore and Madras, he reigned in a different power dynamic altogether. Paradoxically again, this loss of administrative power over Mysore, interestingly, made space for his other avatars to hold stage in his life. It is not very often that the afterlives of deposed kings can fill many pages of their biography either! In fact, the chapters of his life gather more steam, as he lived out a life of significance in the years to come.

A Mysore Constitute

At the time of signing the Instrument of Accession, the general thought was that each princely state would remain independent as a federal state as outlined in the Government of India Act of 1935. The idea of a republic gained ground towards the end of drafting the constitution with Indian National Congress-dominated state constituent assemblies in most princely states voting to adopt the Indian constitution. This sealed the fate of the princely states, and they merged with the Indian Republic on 25 January 1950, with the assurance of a privy purse and privileges as enjoyed by them on 15 August 1947, by constitutional guarantees. Articles 294, 362, 363 and 366 were incorporated to serve this.

Earlier, on 3 June 1947, when Lord Mountbatten, made a public declaration about the Partition of India into two independent dominions, it rattled many. The then Diwan of Mysore, Arcot Ramaswamy Mudaliar convened a press meet and announced that the Mysore Maharaja and the government had decided to accede to the new Dominion of India and to send representatives to the Indian Constituent assembly. This was followed by the Indian Independence Act which received Royal Assent on 18 July 1947. Through this Act, two independent dominions were created on 15 August 1947, whose democratic and other destinies remained moderately unsorted nonetheless. While this act released the 560-odd Indian princely states from the paramountcy of the British government, the dominant idea was that the states would be free on matters other than the ones acceded to the federal government. The Instrument of Accession, when proposed, merely mandated that princes externalize on three subjects of Defence, Communication, and External affairs to the Dominion, not to the Indian Union, as there was no such entity yet. With the proclamation that Mysore indeed had signed the Instrument of Accession and that a Constituent Assembly of Mysore would come into action, towards drafting a constitution for Mysore, JCW, like many of his peers, was working towards a new constitute for

Mysore. On 24 September 1947, he gave his assent to the setting up of a new structure of Mysore government and on 29 October 1947, Mr K.C. Reddy became the first Chief Minister with a cabinet of nine ministers. The goal of this ministry was to set up a Constituent Assembly composed of elected representatives of the people, and frame a constitution bill for the state of Mysore.

Voices of Dissent

If one reviews popular press articles of the time, it is erroneously portrayed that socialist movements and demands for 'responsible government' erupted after signing the Instrument of Accession. At the time of Independence, Mysore already had a legislative assembly and legislative council that ideated and passed legislations, except for on certain reserved subjects, which were entrusted to the Diwan and the Maharaja. The Maharaja and the Diwan enjoyed veto powers and powers to bring in laws valid for short terms, in cases of calamity and hostile legislative conditions. The demands for 'responsible government' for Mysore actually were masked demands for complete autonomy for people's representatives, like in a Republic. As early as during the reign of Nalvadi Krishnaraja Wadiyar, political lobbies called 'Praja Mandals' derived from the non-brahmin movements seeking caste-based reservations in the government apparatus had become active. By 1917, they had organized themselves into Praja Paksha, a proper political outfit operating with a mandate. By 1938, before JCW came to power, these parties were working towards an alternative power structure, one that borrowed momentum from the ideological struggles of social justice and upliftment of backward communities, but at the end of the day, like most political parties, they too were seeking autonomy and power. Even before JCW's ascent to the throne, such animosities with the Diwan-led Mysore government had resulted in many ugly casualties, one of which is touted to be the exit of Sir M. Vishweshwaraiah, the architect of Mysore's modern and engineering marvels. Sir M. Vishweshwaraiah as the Diwan was of the firm belief that merit be the only basis for job appointments and promotions, and not caste. The non-brahmin lobby felt that since the backward communities had poor access to education and exposure required to qualify for such positions, a reservation-based system served the cause of social justice. Sir Mirza Ismail is said to have raised the quota of such reservations to almost 75 per cent, swinging the dominance of non-brahmin presence in the government to a great extent. Progressive lobbies countered such developments, ones that were fiercely promoted by the intellectuals of Mysore, and sympathized by even Yuvaraja Narasimharaja Wadiyar, the father of JCW. During the second convention of the Praja Mithra Mandali, held in 1929, chaired by the future Diwan of Mysore, Arcot Ramaswamy Mudaliar, a call to the backward communities was given to organize their thoughts and hearts, and establish their identity towards the development of the society.[1]

The Mysore Praja Samyukta Paksha (United Organization of Mysore People) was formed to demand responsible government in Mysore—it demanded equal opportunity to all and sought a backdoor means to implement the various agendas of the nascent socialist voices. A first conference of this united front was held at Hassan in January 1935. Despite its name as a 'Samyukta Praja Paksha', like any party trying to come together as a cohesive unit with multiple organizational and personal agendas, the party was marred by differences of opinion, vested interests and personal agendas. In 1935, K.C. Reddy from this party won the maximum seats in the Representative assembly and in the legislative council, so in many ways, a 'responsible government' with people's voices was already in place before JCW came to power! Interestingly, the members of this party wielded more power than the Mysore Congress, which was criticized for its pro-brahmin and pro-monarchy attitudes and not being able to gain a people base. In many ways, the Samyuktha Praja Paksha became the eyesore of the Congress. To counter it, Congress leaders upped their game. Anti-monarchy rhetoric had begun. K.T. Bhashyam Iyyanger and others, after whom the Bhashyam circle in

Bangalore is named, were arrested after a very provocative speech against monarchy and creating a ruckus.[2]

After a significant Mysore Congress board meeting in February 1938, the Congress decided to step up activities in Mysore, which resulted in noted public agitations such as the Shivapura flag hoisting session, the Vidurashwatha incident and the Issur rebellion[3]. The visit of Mahatma Gandhi in 5 January 1934 gave Congress both visibility and a national status like never before. Diplomatic negotiations with the Diwan by National Congress leaders led to a symbolic hoisting of the Indian national flag along with the Mysore flag, but the stalemate between the Praja Paksha, Congress and the Mysore government continued during the time of Nalvadi Krishnaraja Wadiyar's death and JCW's coronation. Many political outcries and demonstrations erupted in Mysore, notably headed by T. Siddalingaiah, H.C. Dasappa, S. Siddayya, K.C. Reddy, H.K. Veeranna Gowda, K.T. Bhashyam, T. Subramanyam, K. Hanumanthaiah, S. Nijalingappa, M.N. Jois, and others. Such movements in Hyderabad were also initiated, with the Hyderabad Congress launched in 1938, and making its demand for a responsible government. The Quit India Movement further intensified ideas of Swaraj and self-rule, which was interpreted by local leaders as demanding complete political control of Mysore without the Diwan and the Maharaja's hold on the bicameral legislature. The Mysore government was alarmed at the growing incidence of such public agitations and declared them illegal—many were arrested and released in 1944.

The War of Rights

In many ways, these anti-monarchy sentiments reflected the developments in the globe at large. After World War I, global movements for overthrowing monarchs, interestingly, led to putting dictators in power, who threw the world into another World War—Hitler, Mussolini, Stalin. It was much like in the times of Julius Caesar, who used the machinations of republican legalities to consolidate power as a legal dictator. Juan Carlos, the last king of Spain was ousted in 1931 with the declaration of the Second Spanish Republic. Wilhelm II, the last German Emperor and the King of Prussia, abdicated in 1918, just before the end of World War I and Germany's defeat. Nikolai II Alexandrovich Romanov, a saint-king, also known as the 'Passion Bearer' was forced to abdicate in 1917.

Interestingly, the British paramountcy, post World War required princely presence to assert its dominance over India. It also was desperate for the co-operation, support and contribution of the wealthy Indian princely states to the war efforts. World War II (1939–1945), saw Mysore and JCW's administrative focus dedicate most of its logistical and political energies in supporting the British government in war. V. P. Menon, in his definitive book, *Integration of Princely States*, documents the assurances given to princes to solicit their support and the power of their monies, without which Britain's dwindling chances in the war would further be weakened.[4] At the annual session of the Chamber of Princes held on 17 January 1946, he notes that the Viceroy Lord Wavell assured the gathering of 'no changes in their relationship or the rights guaranteed by treaties without their consent'. They were encouraged to continue deliberations 'to fulfil the three fundamental criteria of good government: political stability, adequate financial resources, and effective association of the people with the administration'.

Mysore supported war efforts by bolstering research and development in the aviation and war-based industries. Mysore and other princely states provided military manpower and resources to the war. Educational institutes such as IISc focussed on applied research in manufacturing items for military and industrial use. Sir M. Vishweshwaraiah, who was the President of IISc's Court from 1938 to 1947, saw the war as an opportunity to do just that. 'Our failure to take advantage of the present opportunity to give a fillip to industries will mean a tragic waste of a chance which occurs only once in several generations.' After a visit by JCW to the Department of Electrical Technology, and following diplomatic efforts, grants to IISc were increased from the Mysore government and the governments of Bombay, Hyderabad, and even the British government of India. IISc's Department of Aeronautical Engineering was set up in 1942 during such a war-time mandate, and worked with Hindustan Aircraft Limited to repair and maintain British and American war planes. IISc's pedagogical repertoire grew to include aeronautical engineering and internal combustion, engineering, mechanical engineering, electrical engineering, and new fields such as metallurgy.

With the war coming to an end, and the Labour Party forming the government in 1945, and its leader Clement Attlee firmly announcing the party's intent to turnover the administration to Indians, elections were held in India before independence. Elections for the 296 seats assigned to the British Indian provinces were completed by August 1946. The big-five and smaller princely states were occupied with controlling internal security and negotiations at a national level on the nature of sovereignty they would all come to experience. As the states reorganized their thoughts in a new milieu, vested interests saw this as an opportunity to stake a claim for 'responsible government' again. What the demand was actually for was to eliminate the Diwan and the Maharaja from any administrative or veto powers. As expected, the Indian National Congress kept up its role as the friendly neighbourhood watchdog of democracy, amplifying counterpoints within Mysore. False campaigns and rumours were aplenty—that the Maharaja was refusing to accede to the 'Indian Republic', which did not exist then in the first place, and was now going to strip the legislature further of its powers. The subdued celebrations of Indian freedom by the Mysore government in August 1947 and the lack of symbolic gestures, like not flying the tricolour flag at key locations, gave fuel to anti-monarchy rhetoric, which the Congress was only too happy to ferment.

Like Mysore, many other states like Travancore and Hyderabad did not spell out their new administrative apparatus soon after the signing of the Instrument of Accession. This further fuelled tensions. The Maharaja of Mysore had earlier messaged the people on 8 January 1947. He had instructed the Diwan to take steps towards further constitutional reforms in consultation with leaders of various parties in the state. But the Congress leader, K.C. Reddy was not appeased.[5]

In September 1947, barely a month after signing the Instrument of Accession, a large class of workers and students across Mysore and Bangalore went on agitations collectively called the 'Mysore Chalo Movement'. As some of them turned violent, protesters attacked the Mysore palace leading to civilian-police encounters. On 24 September 1947, JCW gave his assent to setting up of a new structure of Mysore government, and on 29 October 1947, K.C. Reddy became the first Chief Minister with a cabinet of nine ministers. The goal of this ministry was to set up a Constituent Assembly composed of elected representatives of the people, and frame a constitution bill for the state of Mysore. In this quasi-constitutional monarchy set up, the Diwan remained, as a power segue between the Maharaja and the government. Not satisfied, local Congress leaders renewed their demand for a so-called 'responsible government'—it was a surrogate demand for full autonomy. The skirmishes continued.

The Mysore in India

Soon after the drafting of the Indian constitution, nationally the way forward was clear. India was to reimagine itself as a Republic. After much furore and deliberations in the Constituent Assembly, the majority of members opined that instead of a separate constitute for Mysore, the Constitution of India being framed should be the taken up. In other words, the republican watershed moment had come for Mysore—this was, in many ways, that moment when the Mysore Gaddi was rested as an artifact. The Mysore Constituent Assembly passed a resolution that the Constituent Assembly of India should be made applicable to Mysore state. The Maharaja issued a proclamation on 25 November 1949; consequently, the Representative Assembly and the Legislative Council were dissolved on 16 December 1949; the Constituent Assembly, which was constituted in 1947, became the provisional Assembly of Mysore until the elections could be held under the new constitution. With this, the powerful post of Diwan of Mysore, the power segue between monarch and his people was also abolished, fully disinvesting the power mantle further. JCW continued as Rajapramukh of Mysore from 26 January 1950, to 1 November 1956, an administrative title held by many other princes such as His Exalted Highness Mir Osman Ali Khan of Hyderabad, Maharaja of Travencore Sir Bala Rama Varma II. Re-election for the first assembly of Mysore under the new constitution was completed in 1952, with ninety-nine elected members and one nominated member. After the reorganization of states on linguistic basis, four districts from Bombay state, three from Hyderabad, a district from the Old Madras State, the state of Coorg and the princely state of Mysore were enmeshed into a 'greater Mysore', which was renamed as Karnataka in 1973. JCW took over as the first governor of the reorganized Mysore state, from 1 November 1956 to 4 May 1964, and was the Governor of Madras from 4 May 1964 to 28 June 1966.

Portrait of Chamarajendra Wadiyar X, grandfather of JCW, by Raja Ravi Varma

Portrait of Krishnaraja Wadiyar IV, uncle of JCW

Portrait of Yuvaraja Narasimharaja Wadiyar, father of JCW

JCW with his mother Yuvarani Kempu Cheluvaja Ammanni

JCW with father, uncle and grandmother Maharani Kempa Nanjammani Vani Vilasa Sannidhana

Painting of JCW after his Upanayana

In a traditional turban

While on a foreign tour

JCW with Krishnaraja Wadiyar IV during a religious ceremony

JCW with his family en route to a tour of Europe

JCW on a hunting expedition

JCW on a wildlife photography tour

JCW with his first wife Maharani Satya Prema Kumari

JCW with his second wife Maharani Tripura Sundari Ammani Avaru and first daughter Gayatri Devi

Childen of JCW: Meenakshi Devi, Srikantadatta Narasimharaja Wadiyar, Kamakshi Devi, Indrakshi Devi

JCW's wife, mother and sister Thakurani Sahiba of Sanand, Sujaya Kantha Ammani, with children of the family

JCW with his children, including his last child Vishalakshi Devi (far right)

Children of JCW with heir-apparent Srikantadatta Narasimharaja Wadiyar

Children of JCW with their mother Maharani Tripura Sundari Ammani

JCW with his second daughter Meenakshi Devi

With his wife, Maharani Tripura Sundari Ammani, and pet dog at his residence

JCW on a tour of Europe

JCW being welcomed back by family after his USA and Europe tours

Final goodbye from the people of Mysore to JCW, after his death on 23 September 1974

ARCHIVAL EXCERPTS

MYSORE INFORMATION BULLETIN

Vol. XII] Bangalore, April 30, 1949 [No. 4

RESPECT THE MYSORE NATIONAL ANTHEM.

The Cinema Theatres in the State are bound by one of the terms of their licenses to exhibit an approved Mysore National Anthem film at the close of each cinema show. It has come to the notice of Government that when the National Anthem is being played, the respect due to the same has unfortunately been not shown by some of the persons visiting the theatres. There will usually be a rush to the exits to be out of the theatre as early as possible. This behaviour would amount to showing disrespect to the National Anthem, although there may not be the slightest intention on the part of the spectators to do so.

The Government, therefore, appeal to all the cinema-going public to remain standing as a mark of respect, and not to leave their places in the auditorium, while the Mysore National Anthem film is exhibited at the close of each show. It is all the more necessary, in the present state of Independence, that all of us behave in a disciplined manner and show the respect due to National symbols like the National Flag and the National Anthem.

109

A message from JCW urging Mysoreans to show the same respect to the Mysore Anthem as to national symbols such as the National Flag. Excerpted from the *Mysore Bulletin*, 30 April 1949

MYSORE INFORMATION BULLETIN

Vol. XII] Bangalore, November—December 1949 [Nos. 11 & 12

Proclamation

OF

HIS HIGHNESS MAHARAJA

SRI JAYACHAMARAJENDRA WADIYAR BAHADUR OF MYSORE

THIS TWENTY-FIFTH DAY OF NOVEMBER, ONE THOUSAND NINE HUNDRED AND FORTY-NINE, IN THE TENTH YEAR OF MY RULE.

Whereas BY A PROCLAMATION DATED THE 29TH OCTOBER, 1947, I ORDAINED THAT MY MINISTRY SHOULD SET UP A CONSTITUENT ASSEMBLY COMPOSED OF ELECTED REPRESENTATIVES OF THE PEOPLE AND ENTRUST IT WITH THE TASK OF FRAMING OF A CONSTITUTION BILL FOR THE STATE OF MYSORE,

And whereas THE CONSTITUENT ASSEMBLY SO SET UP HAS RECOMMENDED THAT IN THE CONSTITUTION OF INDIA NOW BEING FRAMED BY THE CONSTITUENT ASSEMBLY OF INDIA WHICH INCLUDES DULY APPOINTED REPRESENTATIVES OF THIS STATE, THERE SHOULD BE INCORPORATED SUCH CONSTITUTIONAL PROVISIONS AS ARE APPROVED BY THAT BODY FOR, AND IN RELATION TO, THE GOVERNANCE OF THIS STATE, AND THAT THE CONSTITUTION SO FRAMED SHOULD BE ADOPTED BY THIS STATE;

I now hereby ordain

THAT the Constitution of India shortly to be adopted by the Constituent Assembly of India shall be the Constitution for the State of Mysore as for the other parts of India and shall be enforced as such by me, my heirs and successors in accordance with the tenor of its provisions;

That the provisions of the said Constitution shall, as from the date of its commencement, supersede and abrogate all other constitutional provisions inconsistent therewith which are at present in force in this State;

That both Houses of the Legislature of Mysore as at present constituted shall be dissolved on the fifteenth day of December, 1949;

That thereafter, and until such time as the House or Houses of the Legislature of Mysore has or have been duly constituted and summoned to meet for the first session under the provisions of the Constitution of India, there shall be only one House of the Legislature to be known as the Legislative Assembly of Mysore;

That the constitution of the said Legislative Assembly of Mysore shall in all respects be the same as the constitution of the Constituent Assembly of Mysore, all members of which shall, on the sixteenth day of December, 1949, become members of the said Legislative Assembly of Mysore.

JAYA CHAMARAJA WADIYAR.

(Seal.)

Landmark proclamation by JCW on 25 November 1949, ordaining that the Constitution of India be adopted as the Constitution of Mysore. With this proclamation, the Legislative Assembly of Mysore was reabsorbed into the new constitutional structure as of 16 December 1949. This is a historic proclamation as it clearly states how and when Mysore joined the Indian Republic-to-be

WHY THE TWO HOUSES OF LEGISLATURE WERE DISSOLVED

The question of what should be the Legislature during the interim period between now and the elections which are to be held as per the constitution framed for the States in India had been a subject-matter of deep thought to His Highness the Maharaja and his Government. The two alternatives were, either to continue the Mysore Representative Assembly and the Mysore Legislative Council as they were till the elections were held under the new constitution or to convert the Mysore Constituent Assembly into the House of Legislature, as has been done in Travancore, Sourashtra and the Centre. In this connection, there were discussions between the Government of India and the Mysore Government and it was as a result of these discussions that the Mysore Ministry tendered the advice to His Highness the Maharaja to convert the Constituent Assembly of Mysore into the House of Legislature for this interim period. The fact that the present Houses of Legislature had been elected as early as 1945, two years before India got her freedom, was a point which could not easily be got over, especially when there was a body more recently chosen by the people and when there were such strong precedents as stated above and when the Government of India also felt strongly that the Legislature should be in keeping with the new set-up. His Highness the Maharaja and the Ministry are deeply conscious of the fact that the Representative Assembly, which was inaugurated by His Highness' grandfather and was the earliest representative institution of the kind in India, has had a long and unique record of service and so had the Legislative Council, though of a comparatively shorter duration. It was only after deep and anxious consideration both at the Provincial and the Central level that the inevitable decision was taken.

AVOID ADDRESSES OR ELABORATE RECEPTIONS

In connection with the tours of Ministers in the State, instructions have been issued from time to time, emphasising the desirability of avoiding formal reception or elaborate social functions on such occasions, so as to allow Ministers of Government more time to attend to important business.

2. The attention of Deputy Commissioners and other officers concerned has been drawn separately to these instructions for strict observance in letter and spirit.

3. Government wish to make it known that members of local organisations and other leading citizens are always welcome to meet and exchange views on local problems with Ministers during their tours ; but they do not wish to accept any formal addresses or elaborate receptions involving any expenditure.

4. The Public are hereby requested to co-operate with the Government in the prompt and efficient discharge of their duties by not drawing unnecessarily on the time of the Ministers during their tours.

Public awareness statement on why the two houses of Legislature were dissolved during the transition of Mysore as a princely constitute to the Republic of India. Excerpted from the *Mysore Information Bulletin*, November 1949

10
THE DEMOCRAT IN THE DURBAR

Soon after his coronation, the first undertaking of JCW was to oversee elections and put in place a reformed structure of Mysore's Legislative Council and Representative Assembly. In a speech delivered to a Joint Session of the two houses of the legislature and while inaugurating the reformed constitution for Mysore on 9 June 1941, he vests this new responsibility on the people's representatives with great candour:

> Members of the Representative Assembly and the Legislative Council—It affords me sincere pleasure to welcome you to this joint inaugural meeting of the two Houses of our Legislature and to give you this message of goodwill on the eve of your entering upon the new responsibilities which will be yours hereafter.

The tone and tenor of the speech resonate with just one message: great integrity of will must precede great power. In March 1881, JCW's grandfather had gifted the state with Mysore's own Magna Carta. Soon after assuming powers of the state, His Highness Chamarajendra Wadiyar X inaugurated the Mysore Representative

Assembly in the same year, with much murmur and grumpiness from the British administrators. The Maharaja remembers the political will of his grandfather on this occasion:

> In order to realise the magnitude of this advance, you have only to recall the fact that the Representative Assembly was first brought into existence in order, in the words of its authors, that the views and objects of the measures adopted by the government might be 'better known and appreciated by the people for whose benefit they were intended' and that 'the action of the government should be brought into greater harmony with the wishes and interests of the people'.

Sir J.D. Gordon, who was the Chief Commissioner of Mysore in 1879, prior to the transfer of power, had recommended that such an assembly be part of the Mysore governance under the Maharaja. The Government of India did not like the introduction of another voice in the already dual-administrative setup. Gordon, who was the tutor for Chamaraja Wadiyar in civic matters, had envisioned an assembly of retired civic servants, representatives of various demographics and communities. After Chamaraja Wadiyar X's coronation, Diwan Rangacharulu convened such a deliberative assembly comprising prominent ryots, merchants, and thinkers of the state to exchange views on public matters on 29 March 1881. The official order for the constitution of the Assembly was issued by the Maharaja on 25 August 1881, soon after, much against the larger British think tank, which felt that it was 'premature to introduce in the beginning an institution which had not yet been tried in British India'. Yet Chamaraja Wadiyar X had his way, and Mysore created history. The fact that Gordon was appointed the Resident of Mysore after his coronation helped the Maharaja in working the British diplomatic machinery well. Gordon had previously served as Private Secretary to the Viceroy and Governor-General of India from 1866 to 1873, and he aided the Maharaja on this mission.

The assembly was deemed a statutory body, not initially invested with any recognized powers or privileges. They were free to advice, counsel, rebut, criticize, suggest and recommend to the Diwan—on matters of public interest. They were also the people who gave grounds-up knowledge to the Diwan on the workings and efficacy of administrative actions. The range of subjects to be discussed was not restricted. It was a live Right-To-Information session, where anything could be questioned, from the expenditures, dam constructions, educational infrastructure to internal security. From its first meeting on 7 October 1881, to 1916 with 144 nominated members, the assembly grew into an elected body capped at 250 (the government was given the right to increase the size to 275 to provide representation to certain sections). The Diwan remained the ex-officio President of the Assembly and the members of the Cabinet were ex-officio vice-presidents and the term was three years. Another important development was that the assembly now participated in law-making, rather than hearing a report from the Diwan on the previous year's successes and failures. The whole of India watched this development with great curiosity, the nationalist weekly, *The Mahratta*, remarked that 'the British government might do well to take a lesson from the enlightened Maharaja of Mysore'. Some were sceptical. Sir K. Seshadri Iyer recounts the tone and earnestness of such sessions: 'The continued interest which the members evinced in public affairs and the practical common sense, which characterised the discussions, had served to refute the assumption that the institute was in advance of the times'. JCW confirms his trust in the apparatus that his forefathers had curated thus: 'a spirit of co-operation and a sense of responsibility have rarely been absent'.

The strength of democratic voices grew steadily in Mysore. Upon recommendation by the Mysore Assembly, a Legislative Council of non-officials was constituted in 1907 by Nalvadi Krishnaraja Wadiyar as the first Legislative Council of Mysore. This council was to assist in law-making with a term of two years and an initial strength of ten, which by 1919 grew to thirty. Soon the Council also became an elected body, with eight elected representatives matched against eighteen non-officials and twelve officials mostly retired from service. By Regulation XIX of 1923, the Council grew powerful, could vote on grants, move motions and discard them, and grew to fifty members. Another protocol was initiated—a Bill had to pass the Assembly before it was reviewed by the Council, which was headed by the Diwan. The Maharaja sat atop this well-curated, democratic machinery, with certain exclusive rights to rule on reserved subjects. In another historic move, in 1929, Mysore allowed women to stand for Legislative Assembly and Council elections. The two bodies were independent, not bicameral like Karnataka's current legislature, and had defined functions of their own. Further reforms to refine the current structure were undertaken and found their way into the Government of Mysore Act of 1940. The Maharaja was coronated at this important juncture in Mysore's legislative politics. JWC announced:

> The Government of Mysore Act, 1940, may well be regarded as the culmination of a policy initiated by my revered grandfather, and developed in the light of his own political insight and rare experience, by His late Highness, in order to ensure increased association of the representatives of the people with the government of the State. I feel that in addressing this joint meeting of the Houses today I am bearing to a further stage, the torch of constitutional progress, which has been handed down to me as a family heritage. It is my ambition, as I am sure it is yours, to ensure that its light does not grow dim but will burn ever brighter with the passage of time.

The major reforms were a substantial increase in strength of both houses, greater representation for minority communities, and women by direct election, wider people's franchise in both houses. The Legislative Council could have an unofficial President and a Deputy, and the Representative Assembly was given greater control over legislations and control of expenditure of Mysore's revenue. To top this all, in a stroke of true democratic intent, he allowed freedom of speech and immunity against arrest during proceedings of the Assembly. This was a rather bold move, given the country was in the throes of both nationalist and pretentiously nationalist movements, with a good sprinkling of leaders who could use this freedom to create nuisance. Addressing the joint session of the two Houses, the Maharaja said, 'For my part I am convinced that a variety of experience on the part of my ministers can only add to the weight and value of the advice that I receive from my council. It is now for us all working together with the welfare of our State as our united objective, to take steps to ensure that our future is worthy of our part.' Another reform was to assign portfolios to his ministers in the cabinet. The ministers were: K.V. Anantharaman as the Minister of Finance and Revenue, J. Mohammed Imam as Minister of Education, and H. B. Gundappa Gowda as his Minister of Public Health.

JCW addressing his legislative assembly as Maharaja of Mysore

The creation of portfolios was meant to cover the blind spots in the previous structure by entrusting power to do good and serve well:

> Above all, I am sure you will appreciate the decision to give a place to the elected representatives of the people in my Executive Council, and entrust them with regular portfolios of the administration. The antithesis that is sometimes set up between official and non-official points of view may often lack substance in the conditions of public life prevailing in our State. Nevertheless, the appointment of non-official ministers is rightly regarded as a reform of a far-reaching character.

JCW at the Legislative Assembly

Prophetically predicting the instability of governments to come in the people's Republic of India, he offers a word of caution to his legislature: 'As popularly elected bodies, you are embarking on new responsibilities at a remarkable moment of history. Today many parts of the world are strewn with the wrecks of popular institutions. Some have been destroyed by external aggressors; some have collapsed of their own weakness.'

In a short while, it was apparent to all involved that the Maharaja had his own administrative vision and was unafraid to use his power, while empowering a constitutional apparatus to assist him. In addition, he was getting the reputation of being quite hands-on, often to the discomfort of people who had served for years under his uncle and suddenly felt under the lens. During the elections for Mysore in 1941, the Maharaja was livid that the acceptance of nomination papers were 'influenced' and that several candidates were rejected on flimsy grounds—alluding to foul play. He spoke to the Mysore Resident, who documented his increasing loss of confidence in the Diwan Mirza Ismail's handling of the elections. The Resident reported this to the Viceroy's office. 'He told me frankly that the hands of the government were not clean in this matter and that he has lost the confidence in Dewan.' Mirza Ismail and the young Maharaja had quite opposite views on governance—Mirza often exhibited highhandedness, much to the Maharaja's ire. Mirza was known for his suppressive labour policies, and when a strike broke out at Kolar Gold Fields, the Maharaja sought a copy of the labour legislation from Mirza Ismail—who is supposed to have denied it, in the name of 'interference'. It was clear to JCW that the Diwan–Maharaja dynamic had to be redrawn in his tenure. The case of the automobile factory was the final nail in the coffin for the Mirza–JCW duo in office. Mirza resigned soon after. JCW was quick to see the connection between rigging of election procedures and motives to create a hostile government—a structure he was vesting more and more power with! Despite such hurdles, he went ahead with the reforms, putting great belief in the power of democracy. He said:

> It may well be asked whether this is a time to embark on a large experiment in the expansion of democratic institutions. My answer to such a question would be that I am a convinced believer in the virtues of democracy and in the qualities of the people of Mysore. I do not, for a moment, disguise from

JCW with his Diwan, N. Madhav Rao

> myself that the successful conduct of democratic institutions, especially at a time like the present, is a very difficult task, that it will require all the best that is in us, and especially that tolerance and consideration for others which are the leading qualities of a truly civilised man.

To an observer such moves could have seemed counter-productive to a monarch who wants to stay in power. Such an empowering of the legislature was not however without foresight and deep insight into local and global politics. His own deep study of political science from the time he was a student at Maharaja's College indeed came to be of great use. During this period, imperialism was waning; the British government needed the princely states more than they needed the British hand in ruling their states. It was a clever stroke to give access to populist demands and yet ride the administrative machinery than be an autocrat, which he could perhaps never have been in the first place. This was smart diplomacy in an era of great turbulence.

JCW was aware of how other princely states had harnessed their administrative machinery to develop their states. He had read about the successful team of veteran V.P. Madhava Rao and a young king Ayilyam Thirunal, who had turned around the fortunes of Travencore between 1860 and 1870. The duo's schemes to reform the land revenue system and industrialize Travencore with a good lid on labour legislations had been successful. So, the Maharaja appointed yet another Madhava Rao (strange coincidence that!), as the Diwan of Mysore on 31 March 1941. His choice in N. Madhava Rao as Diwan was to create a team where there was good synergy between him and his main wingman.

It is in good faith of his own capabilities and the demonstrated success of democratic machineries that he had set up, that he decided to completely transfer power to the people of Mysore in 1950. Yet it took only very little time for the democratic apparatus to show signs of fracture—a fracture that has gotten only bigger over time. Till date, only 3 chief ministers have completed full-terms since the inception of the state in 1956. The drama of Karnataka politics has filled many pages of tabloids, newspapers, books and there are many dissertations on Karnataka's history of treacherous politics. JCW's tryst with Congress politics in independent India was at best described as double-edged. His friendship with Nehru, Patel and the higher commands of Congress remained intact, while his relationship with Mysore Congress was hot-and-cold. He had many adversaries, who were vocal about their irritation to his continued presence as Rajapramukh and later Governor. The Maharaja was no mute spectator to the Congress politics in Mysore either—he used his national stature and connections well enough to influence events for Mysore.

In May 1958, B.D. Jatti succeeded S. Nijalingappa as the Chief Minister of the State. Prior to the state elections in 1962, there were two factions in the Mysore Congress, one headed by Nijalingappa, and the other by B.D. Jatti. Nijalingappa's hold over the party was stronger then and he was able to doctor the fielded candidates list to favour him, thus becoming the future Chief Minister. There was great bitterness inside and outside on the streets of Mysore. The Maharaja was indeed witnessing the eloquent demonstrations of a 'very responsible government', which was taking the chase to power quite irresponsibly. His previous advice to his ministers was definitely 'well-taken':

> Most of you represent particular areas of the State; some of you represent special communities or interests; and some may have come here to promote particular policies. I urge you, while faithfully representing your own constituents, never to forget that in all things the State must come first, and that if our reforms are to be a success, each of the many castes, creeds and communities of which the State is composed, must feel that its rights are protected and its interests promoted so far as they are consistent with the good of the State as a whole.

Such an ideal was never realized, in fact, the political developments were pulling away the fate of Mysore far from it.

At this juncture, he is said to have written many reports to Nehru, after deliberating on them with care. On 28 November 1961, Nehru appends a note to Neelam Sanjiva Reddy:

To,
N. Sanjiva Reddy: Jayachamaraja Wodeyar's Report on Mysore Congress
November 28, 1961

My dear Sanjiva Reddy,
I enclose a note, which I have just dictated after seeing the Maharaja of Mysore. I am giving a copy of it to Indira. I am not sending it to anyone else.

Yours sincerely,
Jawaharlal Nehru

Jayachamaraja Wodeyar on the Congress in Mysore:

1. The Maharaja of Mysore came to see me this evening. He said he particularly wanted to tell me his reactions to what was going on in Mysore in regard to the choice of candidates for election. He was rather worried about this, more particularly because of the different pulls of the Ministerialist party on the other side and the Congress organisation there on the other. The result of this has been apart from a fairly small number of agreed seats, the others have panels or at least two names for each seat representing the groups. If these kind of things continued, the result may well be harmful to the interests of the Congress.
2. If there was a united approach from the Congress there was every chance of the Congress winning 75 to 80 per cent of the seats. Otherwise the Congress may not get more than 50 to

55 per cent and the rest would go to many Independents and some people from other Parties, and the result would be lack of stability. That would be bad for any work to be done there.

3. What he was anxious about was a suitable and progressive government and therefore he would welcome these two major groups in the Congress in Mysore pulling together, which would ensure a substantial and stable majority.
4. He said that it would be a good thing if our Central Election Committee could indicate in some way whom they wanted to be the Chief Minister and then broadly support him so that he could have a firm position.
5. He told me that the public in Mysore state, or at any rate, many people of note, had come to him and expressed their disappointment at the kind of persons that were being included in the list of candidates from Mysore. A number of good people were being left out; a number of people who were not good were included. He said that he had been touring recently in the areas of Mysore state, which had been recently added and many people came to see him there and expressed this opinion. Generally speaking, he seemed to imply that there was much sympathy for the present Chief Minister Jatti and a feeling that he should continue as Chief Minister as he had done well during his term. Although he did not say so positively, it was clear that he himself favoured the continuance of Shri Jatti as Chief Minister.
6. He told me that some prominent persons had gone to Shri Nijalingappa and suggested to him that he should play the role of an elder statesman and keep above these group conflicts and not be himself a candidate for any post like that of Chief Minister. Some others had suggested that Nijalingappa should come to Parliament or be made a Governor. All this meant that they wanted Nijalingappa to leave the state politics and only advise from a distance.

7. The Maharaja also said that the fact that the Election Committee had nominated themselves for seats in the election had been much criticised.
8. The Maharaja repeatedly expressed his unhappiness about this situation and hoped that some way out of this difficulty would be found so that the major groups there in the Congress should pull together. For his part, although he did not say so definitely, it was clear that he favoured the continuance of the present Chief Minister Jatti as Chief Minister, and wanted him to be strengthened.

Nehru took cognizance of this and the importance of presenting a united front during the elections, as advised by the Maharaja. Interestingly, Nehru notes that the Maharaja had much sympathy for the then current Chief Minister B.D. Jatti, who in his view had fared well, and urged the High Command to strengthen him. JCW, incidentally, was the first President of Basava Samithi, founded by B.D. Jatti in 1964, suggesting cordial relationship between the two. He also advises Nehru to postpone the party reorganization to after the state elections, so that the party may focus on winning, which Nehru did. Several attempts to reconcile differences were made by the 'High Command', and B.D. Jatti's ministry expanded to include men from the Nijalingappa faction. Yet differences continued with the highly 'responsible men seeking responsible government', angling for power and internal politics than on empowering people's voices. By 1962, one can safely say that the Maharaja's idealistic vision of returning power to the people had ended in a huff. The paradox was that new democracy in Mysore was perfectly demonstrating how fragile democracy can be and what a bane decentralized power structures can be. When Mirza Ismail was reported to have interfered with elections and fielded candidates, the Maharaja could intervene and take action. Here he could not do much but watch the drama. A decade ago, any self-preserving actions as a monarch were dubbed as power hungry, vain and greedy. But, the very men who screamed

'Mysore Chalo' for self-governance could not even govern their greed, a couple years into 'responsible governance'—something that they so wanted for Mysore. The political tomfoolery continued for a few more years, much to JCW's frustration. On 21 June 1962, S. Nijalingappa came back to power, in a stunning political manoeuvre. After losing assembly elections in Chitradurga, he installed his aide S. N. Kanthi temporarily, as he won the by-election to come back into the assembly to become the chief minister—yet again. In many ways, such a mockery of the democratic apparatus must have infuriated the Maharaja and he was determined to leave soon after.

The Deputy Minister of External Affairs, Lakshmi N. Menon, who was an Indian freedom fighter and politician, reports to Jawaharlal Nehru about her discussion with the Maharaja:

> A few days ago, I was in Bangalore on my way to the Tibetan Refugee Camp in Mysore. As I was the guest of the Governor, Mr Pakvasa [Governor during JCW's absence], I had some discussions with him regarding certain matters, and at his request, I am placing the following matters before you:
>
> (i) The Maharaja of Mysore returned from his foreign tour three weeks before the scheduled time for want of foreign exchange, and I was told that he would not like to continue as Governor because he has no work and also the Ministers do not consult him on anything.
>
> (ii) He is a man of diverse interests and has written many books on philosophy. Upanishads, Africa, river systems, etc. and therefore he would like to be considered for some other work either in India or abroad. As his resources are sufficient, he would not like to accept any remuneration for any assignment he might be given.

Nehru soon wrote to Lal Bahadur Shastri, in a letter with a rather direct subject: 'Jayachamaraja Wodeyar Wants to Go'

Forest Rest House, Manali

June 18, 1961

My dear Lal Bahadur,

My Deputy Minister, Lakshmi Menon, has sent me a report. I am sending this to you as it may interest you, more particularly what the Maharaja of Mysore is reported to have said to her and her talk with Jatti. It is clear that Maharaja of Mysore cannot continue for long. His term apparently expires in November. He could, perhaps, be asked to continue for a month or two more, but there is no particular advantage in making this request to him. Therefore, we should think in terms of his retiring in November. What Jatti says is interesting. But it is a bit too much to expect us to pull out six or seven persons from Mysore and provide for them elsewhere.

Yours affectionately,
Jawaharlal Nehru

The letter indicates that he had an ally in B.D. Jatti. The Maharaja was unhappy with 6 to 7 politicians/ministers who may have disrespected him at that time. The Maharaja was critical of several Congress leaders and his relationship with them is perhaps best described as intolerant. He actively participated in the workings of the Government, and was not afraid to show the stick when needed. The fact that he had declined to accept any salary during the whole of his Governorship of Mysore gave him an air of moral authority as well.

Soon Mr Nehru also wrote to Dr S. Radhakrishnan, Vice President at that time:

Find a job for 'Jayachamaraja Wodeyar'

June 20, 1961

My dear VP,

You know perhaps that the Maharaja of Mysore is not at all happy in his post as Governor. He has made it clear that he does not want to continue in it after the expiry of the present term, that is, about October or November next. Evidently, he wants us to suggest some other kind of work for him. I do not quite know what we can do for him. He likes going abroad and he can sometimes be sent on some deputations. I do not think that it would suit him to be made an Ambassador. We can hardly send him to a small and relatively unimportant post abroad, and I would rather hesitate to send him to one of our more important and difficult posts. Pakvasa, no doubt at the Maharaja's instance, has sent me a paper containing 'subjects of interest' to the Maharaja. I enclose this paper. Can you suggest what we could do to him?

Jawaharlal Nehru

After much deliberation, he was requested to assume office as the Governor of Madras, and Nehru wrote to K. Kamaraj, CM of Madras at that time (1954–1963):

To K. Kamaraj,

Jayachamaraja Wodeyar as Next Governor

March 18, 1962

My dear Kamaraj,

Your present Governor, Shri Bisnuram Medhi, will end his term of office on the January 21, 1963. That is still far off. But I wanted to find out from you what you think about a suggestion that has been made to us regarding Medhi's successor as Governor of Madras. It has been suggested that the Maharaja of Mysore, who is now Governor of Mysore, might be made Governor of Madras. I do not think it will be desirable to continue him in Mysore for too long. But he is a quiet, scholarly and dignified person who might do well as Governor of Madras.

I should like your reaction to this suggestion. Of course, the changeover will only come at the end of Shri Medhi's term.

Yours Sincerely

Jawaharlal Nehru

K. Kamaraj agreed, and ultimately, Maharaja agreed to shift to Madras on 4 May 1964, just before Pandit Nehru's death on 27 May 1964. By the time, Tamil Nadu also saw K. Kamaraj being replaced by M. Bhaktavatsalam as CM. In this new political environment, the Maharaja writes a letter to Shringeri Jagadguru. In the book, *The Multifaceted Jivanmukta,* on the life of His Holiness Jagadguru Sri Abhinava Vidyathirtha Mahasvamin of Shringeri, there is a reference to a letter by the Maharaja.The following is an English translation of his letter in Kannada dated 6 August 1964, and penned in Mysore:

Humble prostrations to the exquisite lotus feet of Śrī Sringeri Jagadguru, Śrīmad Abhinava Vidyātīrtha Mahāsvāmin by me, who am a recipient of Your Holiness's grace. Mahāsvāmin! If it be Your Holiness's will, please consider and plainly advise me what I should do in the future—whether I should stay on in Madras (as Governor) or go abroad (to a Western country) and work or enter politics. Of these options, which one does Your Holiness advice? [...] I am sending this missive through A. G. Ramachandra Rao in a confidential manner. It would be sufficient if Your Holiness were to convey Your Holiness's opinion through him. Though I do not wish to trouble Your Holiness, I am compelled to write this letter as I have no other option. The extremely obedient server of Your Holiness's feet,

Sd/- Jayachamaraja Wodeyar.[1]

JCW with Shringeri Jagadguru Bharathi Teertha Swamy in Shringeri

The letter was sent to him merely three months after the start of his tenure as Governor of Madras on 4 May 1964. The above letter was written on 6 August 1964. The move out of Mysore must have been rather difficult. Adapting to the new political circles in Madras, that displayed the same games of power play and mongering, must have been exhausting to a scholar and free spirit at heart. Often administrative positions are antagonistic to the life and methods of an artist, a thinker and a scholar. The fact that he had to reconfigure his life several times after relinquishing the throne must have been exhausting as well. The brunt of legal battles with the Mysore government on his properties, endless legal communications must have put a dent in his spirit too. Even though there is every reason to believe that K. Kamaraj did his best to make him feel welcome, this letter exposes his inner turbulence. The decision to leave Mysore itself must have been very painful in the first place. The Guru must have advised him to stay put at Madras through A.G. Ramachandra Rao, and eventually, he stayed on as Governor of Madras till 28 June 1966. He turned in his resignation citing worsening health. After the death of Nehru, with his strongest ally in the Indian National Congress gone, he decided to come back to Mysore, for better or worse. With this return to Mysore, he was fully divorced from the idea of being part of any democratic setup in the years to come.

The democrat had finally rested in his own durbar.

Photographs of JCW with Political Leaders of His Time

JCW (centre, seated) with Pandit Jawaharlal Nehru (fourth from left, seated), Chief Minister B.D. Jatti and members of his Cabinet

JCW (fifth from the left) with Chief Minister S. Nijalingappa and members of his Cabinet

JCW (second from left) with President of India Dr Sarvepalli Radhakrishnan (third from left), Chief Minister Kengal Hanumanthaiah (fifth from left) and others

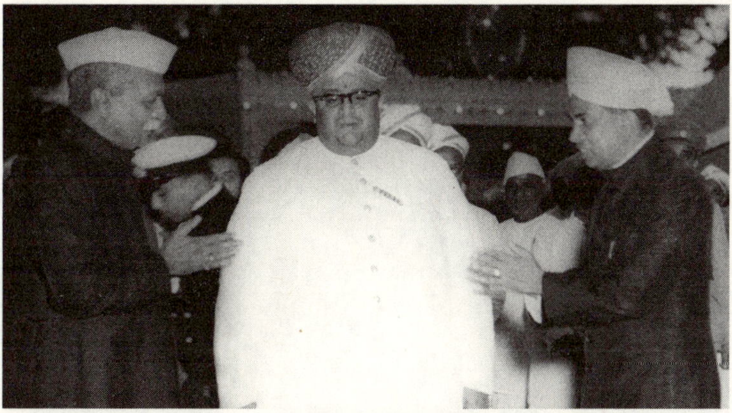

President of India Dr Rajendra Prasad (left) and Shri Kengal Hanumanthaiah (right) felicitate JCW at a ceremony

Greeting the public at a ceremony in Bangalore's Ravindra Kalakshetra

Addressing a meeting of the Legislative Council as Governor of Mysore

JCW reviewing the construction of Vidhana Soudha, the current home of the Karnataka Legislature in Bangalore

JCW being welcomed to the joint session of the Legislative Assembly with Chief Minister S.R. Kanthi

Chief Minister K. Hanumanthaiah showcases the overall plan for the Vidhan Sabha to JCW

JCW addresses the joint session of the Legislative Assembly of Mysore

Addressing a joint session of Legislature at Puttannachetty Town Hall, Bangalore

JCW being welcomed to address the Mysore Legislature at Puttannachetty Town Hall, Bangalore

Addressing a joint session of the legislature at the Puttannachetty Town Hall

Receiving the police Guard of Honour at the Puttannachetty Town Hall as Governor of Mysore

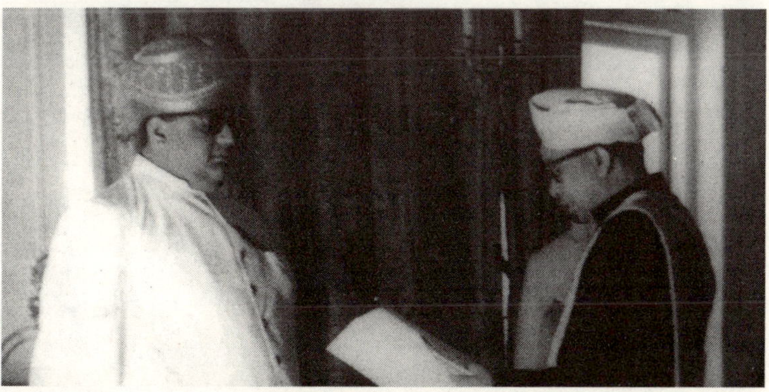

Swearing in Chief Minister K. Hanumanthaiah in the capacity of Rajapramukh of Mysore in 1952

Swearing in Shri S.R. Kanthi as the Chief Minister in the capacity of Governor of Mysore in 1962

Speaking to Chief Minister Kadidal Manjappa after his swearing-in ceremony in 1956

At the swearing-in ceremony of S. Nijalingappa in the capacity of Rajapramukh of Mysore in 1956

Swearing in Shri B.D. Jatti as the Chief Minister of Mysore in the capacity of Governor of Mysore in 1958

At the swearing-in ceremony of Smt Yashodamma Dasappa, leading politician and activist of her time, into the Cabinet of S.R. Kanthi in 1962

With members of the S.R. Kanthi cabinet in front of the Bangalore Palace

JCW on his last visit to Shringeri prior to his demise in 1974

11
SOVEREIGN SOUVENIRS

Hindustan Aircraft Limited: The Mysorean Legacy in India's Aerospace

It takes a fierce nationalist and a shrewd visionary to capture several vested interests into one that benefits the country. William Douglas Pawley was a US ambassador, noted businessman, and part of the First American Volunteer Group (AVG) of the Chinese Air Force deployed to bomb Japan and defend China. Assembling aircrafts for combat in World War II, and edged out of the Japanese occupation of China, he was looking for a home base in India. In a parallel universe, Walchand Hirachand, an entrepreneur was looking to expand his company's offerings. The just-coronated 21-year-old JCW saw this opportunity to lay the runway for a public sector enterprise that would pioneer aerospace research and manufacturing in India. Hindustan Aircraft Limited (HAL) was thus born in 1940, interestingly conspired mid-air on a flight back from America!

HAL was started as a private company with a whopping capital of Rs 4 crore—with Walchand Hirachand; two private investors, Tulsidas Kilachand and DM Khatau; and the Mysore government as investors, and with work assurances from the Government of India. It was incorporated on 23 December 1940, as Hindustan

Aircraft Limited and lives on as India's largest defence and aerospace company: The Hindustan Aeronautics Limited. Mounting Japanese attacks and preparations for an imminent war made the British government acquire one-third of Hindustan Aircraft Limited in 1941, and later nationalize it in 1942. The Mysore government refused to hand over its stake in the company, but agreed to give the British government of India control of its operations. Thus, HAL started assembling aircrafts in collaboration with several companies in the USA, until its transfer to the new government of India in 1947; it was later placed under the Ministry of Defence in 1951. Post-war, HAL has concentrated on bringing out indigenous aircrafts, the first of which was the HT-2 Trainer, the first indigenous aircraft, under the guidance of aeronautical engineer Dr V. M. Ghatage in 1951. HAL's legacy is entwined with the growth of India's defence and aeronautical industry. HAL continues to make its mark, quietly but steadily, contributing to India's space missions even. It recently delivered the 'Orbiter Craft Module Structure' of Chandrayaan-2, India's second lunar exploration mission. From the HT-2 trainers to the Kirans to Sukhois, HAL continues to fly high, taking its Mysorean legacy to the skies.

The old timers of Mysore recollect, with great pride, the true majesty of JCW's 'Mysore Dakota', which was always 'flying high' after India's Independence! After the end of World War II, surplus Dakota DC-3 planes were available for sale in India. The Hindustan Aircraft Company, co-owned by the Mysore government was servicing these 'workhorses of the air'—as they were called. These were converted into civilian aircrafts, 21-seater passenger planes, one of which was acquired by JCW as his first magic carpet in 1946. The beauty was called Mysore Dakota VT-AXX. The Mysore Dakota was extensively used during the nation-building efforts by Sardar Vallabhbhai Patel, Pandit Nehru and other Indian leaders. It was piloted by one Capt. V. Sundaram, who was a civilian pilot for Tata Airlines, and his co-pilot and wife Usha. The Maharaja had left the plane at the disposal of Sardar Patel, so much so that Captain

Sundaram was referred to often as the personal pilot of the Deputy Prime Minister of India!

JCW receiving Sardar Patel at Mysore. The Mysore Dakota aircraft with the Gandabherunda symbol can be seen behind them

An interesting titbit from that era is that Sardar Patel is supposed to have clocked over 1,00,000 miles on the Mysore Dakota, before he decided to set foot in Mysore, which he finally did in February 1949. A delegation of dignitaries, including his daughter Maniben Patel and his Secretary V. Shankar among others, visited Mysore and received the typical Mysorean hospitality. A warm telegram promptly reached JCW soon after:

> I should like to send Your Highness, your government and the people of Mysore my sincere gratitude for the magnificent reception they gave me and for the generous hospitality and affection extended to me during my short visit to Mysore. It was a real pleasure to me to renew my acquaintance and contact with Your Highness and your State after twelve years and to find that under Your Highness' aegis the people of Mysore have attained fulfilment of their aspirations and are making such excellent progress on the road to happiness and prosperity. Mysore's role as the prominent progressive State is being worthily maintained by Your Highness and

> your government. I shall be most grateful if Your Highness will kindly convey to all concerned my warm thanks for the excellent arrangements made for my visit. In particular, I should like to say a special word about the Police. Their arrangements left nothing to be desired and the orderly and smooth execution of the programme was largely due to the zeal and keen sense of duty displayed by them. Finally, I should like to assure Your Highness that we are carrying with us most happy recollections of our visit and deeply appreciate the consideration and kindness extended to us by Your Highness personally.

This visit was the highlight of the Mandakalli Aerodrome (now the Mysore Airport), which was later overshadowed by the growth of HAL Airport and the Jakkur base. The Mysore government established this aerodrome on 290 acres of land, which was later transferred to the Ministry of Civil Aviation, Government of India. In 1948, JCW bought 200 acres of land to build the sprawling Jakkur Aerodrome, which started full operations in 1948. Today, Jakkur serves as a base for many private aviation enterprises, and is a niche microlight flying airfield. JCW transferred this to the Government of Karnataka with the condition that only a flying school would be established. The Government Flying Training School (GFTS) thus came into being on 26 March 1949. The school today struggles with the sloth of a bureaucratic apparatus left to manage it, but offers tenured programs leading to the issue of the Commercial Pilot License (CPL) and the Private Pilot License (PPL). The school has facilities for flight training, has hangars for private owners and offers low-key maintenance services. Pandit Nehru, who inaugurated the Flying School, flew on the Mysore Dakota to Mysore, and received his Honorary Degree of Doctor of Science from the University of Mysore at a special convocation held on 28 December 1948!

The HAL main gate, 1942

Vultee Bomber assembly line, 1945

HAL Airport Control Tower and Tarmac, 9 July 1947

The first flight of Harlow Aircraft, July 1941

The Walrus aircraft after overhauling, 1944

Founder's Day function: (L-R) HH The Maharaja of Mysore, Shri Hanumanthaiah, CM Dr M. Visveswaraya and Sir Mirza Ismail, Dewan, 10 February 1954

Members of Mysore Legislature on a visit to HAL, 30 May 1950

Visit of H.H. the Maharaja of Mysore to HAL, 3 July 1948

HH the Maharaja of Mysore with HT-2 Aircraft, 29 June 1952

Some Food for Thought: The Central Food Technological Research Institute, Mysore

In a note on 'Ecological Surveys to Precede Large Irrigation Projects', JCW is honest and critical of the large irrigation projects taken up in the past. He argues for a more holistic approach to irrigation, one that takes into account terrain, watersheds, natural and ecological relationships:

> For instance, the Krishnaraja Sagara Lake has failed to come up to expectations four times since 1945, including the present year in respect of the inflow of water at expected periods. The Mettur Dam has not satisfied the requirements of irrigation and hydroelectric power for the past seven or eight years.

Nalvadi Krishnaraja Wadiyar's rule and the approach to irrigational infrastructure for Mysore was indeed ambitious. Large dams at the cost of crores of rupees were erected in the fervent hope that such engineering marvels would prevent Mysore from falling into the throes of famine and food shortage yet again. JCW explains: 'One explanation seems to be that when these earlier irrigation projects were proposed, the several natural factors bearing on the rainfall and run-off water and other circumstances, which are directly related to the proper functioning of the valley, have not been considered thoroughly and scientifically.' It is this research into the successes and failures of the past that informed his more holistic irrigational strategy for Mysore: 'The object of this note is to emphasise that even in respect of the smaller irrigation works undertaken by the state government, it must be the invariable rule that there should be a detailed scientific survey of all the natural resources and other features in the drainage area of the valleys.' During his tenure, he focused on forest conservation near catchment areas, replanting and re-afforestation of such critical areas, assessment of geological wealth and rare plant and animal life conservation. A mind that understood musical harmony as a law, perhaps saw that harmony with nature and animals must be conserved if man was to thrive.

The significance of his administrative foresight is best understood in the backdrop of famines and severe food shortages in India. Overall, India was facing famine after famine, the Great Bengal famine being the worst recorded in the history of India. The Viceroy of India minced no words to indicate what a mammoth crisis it was—a tight control of food resources for Mysore was absolutely essential. In the period between 1940 and 1947, one of the critical successes of his rule was to manage the food shortage in Mysore and put in place administrative policies to prevent a large-scale famine, like in Bengal.

The *Mysore Bulletin* was a monthly communication brought out by the Mysore government every month for the ten years of his rule. An interesting mix of messages from the King, some personal messages and Mann-ki-Baat, reports of schemes, rebuttals to rumours, published prices for commodities, some titbits and trivia. The *Mysore Bulletins* of this time tell the grim tale of how torrid everyday life was. Free kitchens were opened. Irrigation wells sank dry. Subsidies were announced. The armchair politicians cried foul, no relief was good enough. The Mysore Food Order was passed, no extravagant festivals, no more than 40 persons at marriages, and 20 persons at religious festivities. Everyday life was well-regulated by the government, the wants were banished as needs nudged, and survival got harder and harder. This reality can, in many ways, explain the Mysorean urge to escape reality through dreamy, artistic journeys with music and art! For the creative juice can offer immunity to pain in ways no analgesic can.

"INDIA IS FACED WITH A SERIOUS SHORTAGE OF FOOD"

H E. THE VICEROY'S CALL FOR SACRIFICE

Broadcast Speech by His Excellency the Viceroy at New Delhi on 16th February 1946.

SCARCITY OF JAGGERY

In view of the acute scarcity for jaggery and the high prices prevailing in the State since a few months, it is considered necessary to make certain modifications in the Jaggery Control Order, 1945. A Revised Jaggery Control Order, 1946, incorporating the required modifications has been issued.

The main provisions of the revised order are as follows :—

(1) No person shall carry on business as a dealer in jaggery in Mysore State after 1st December 1946 except under and in accordance with a license issued by the licensing authority.

(2) No jaggery can be exported outside the State except under permits granted by the Controller.

(3) The Controller may in case of necessity prohibit or restrict the export of sugarcane to any place outside any area, direct canegrowers to deliver sugarcane to a specified Sugar Factory and restrict the manufacture of jaggery.

FRESH MILK.

Owing to various reasons stringency is being experienced all over the State, especially in the larger Urban areas, in regard to supplies of good fresh milk available to the public. As this is an essential article of diet on which the health of the community depends, especially in the case of pregnant women, nursing mothers and children, it is necessary to make larger supplies of it available to the general public by the prohibition of its use by hotels, restaurants and other such institutions, in the manufacture of such luxuries as, badam kheer, milk syrup, cream cakes and other sweetmeats. With this object in view, Government have promulgated an order called "The Mysore Milk (Use in the Catering Establishments) Control Order, 1946, which will take affect from the 15th March 1946 in the Cities of Bangalore and Mysore in the first instance.

RICE AND MILLETS

The stock position of millets in the State has run very low and complaints are being received that certain rural areas have not been getting even the minimum supplies of millets. It has, therefore, become necessary to substitute rice for millets wherever possible, and to make available the millets thus released to rural areas where they are urgently required.

The Director of Food Supplies has, therefore, issued instructions that with effect from the 1st January 1946 the second and third grade varieties of rice be issued in substitution for millets to ration card holders in Bangalore City, Mysore City and Civil and Military Station. It may be noted that the sale price of the varieties of rice so substituted will remain unaffected.

VEGETABLE OIL PRODUCTS

With a view to better regulating the manufacture, movement, sale and distribution of vegetable oil products in the Mysore State, the Vegetable Oil Products Control Order, 1945, issued under Notification No. SD. 382—C. 229-44-7, dated 20th July 1945, has been amended and re-issued as the "Vegetable Oil Products Control Order, 1946", according to which —

1. The Vegetable Oil Products Controller in Mysore may prohibit or restrict the manufacture, stock or sale of any variety or quality of Vegetable Oil Product.

2. Every person in Mysore dealing in such products is required to display a price list showing the current selling prices.

3. The restriction against the export of the products without a permit except by *bona fide* travellers to the extent of 5 seers as part of one's personal luggage and except under military credit notes, continues. (Press note dated 5th August 1946).

Excerpts from *Mysore Bulletins*, including a call from the Viceroy urging citizens to cooperate in the management of extreme food shortage in India and Mysore and reports on relief efforts made by Mysore Government by to wipe out food grain deficits in Mysore

FREE KITCHENS FOR THE POOR AND THE DESTITUTE

Ever since the food situation in the State became difficult, Government have been particularly concerned about the needs of the poorest and the destitute among the population. Some ameliorative measures in this direction have already been taken. Following the inspiring and gracious lead of His Highness the Maharaja in providing for the free feeding of the poor in Mysore City, free kitchens have been opened in other places in the State where simple cooked food is supplied free to the poorest inhabitants. It is the desire of Government that this work should be expanded, especially in areas where the food situation is causing anxiety. The Director of Food Supplies in Mysore, Bangalore, has accordingly issued instructions that very early steps be taken by the Deputy Commissioners to open such free kitchens in their Districts wherever necessary including rural areas. The following instructions will be observed in the administration of these free kitchens :—

(1) The selection of persons entitled to be fed at these places will be made by the Deputy Commissioner or other local authority empowered by him and wherever possible the assistance of the local food council will be enlisted in this behalf. Special identity cards will be issued to such persons and the rations, if any, allotted to them at the Government Depot will be cancelled ;

(2) Only cooked ragi or jola with vegetable soup will be provided. Potatoes and groundnuts may be used in the soup to supplement vegetables ;

(3) Ragi and Jola for this purpose may be issued from the Government Depot, if supplies of cooked food cannot be arranged for by local philanthropists ;

(4) A definite number of persons will be allotted to each kitchen.

(5) No able-bodied person and no person who has the means of eking out his or her livelihood will be fed at such kitchens.

Local philanthropy is to be enlisted in this behalf as far as possible, so as to keep down the cost to Government.

98 MYSORE INFORMATION BULLETIN, January—March 1946

7. General.

With a view to conserving the available stocks of foodgrains and making them last for as long a period as possible, the "Mysore Food (Restrictions of service of Meals by Catering Establishments and others) Order, 1946, has been brought into force with effect from the 30th March 1946, whereby rations for "Jutras", car festivals or functions of any description connected with religious institutions beyond the sanctioned scales under the Muzrai Regulations are not granted. The hours of business in catering establishments are restricted and the preparation for sale by them of any articles of food involving the use of cereals or milk or milk powder or cream or sugar or any rationed commodity is banned. The Order also prohibits, the serving of cooked or prepared food for more than 40 persons at marriages and 20 persons at other religious functions.

In order to increase the quantity of fresh milk available for consumption, the "Milk Control" Order, 1946 was promulgated which makes it an offence to use milk for purposes other than those contemplated in the Order.

(Contd.) Excerpt from *Mysore Bulletins*, including a call from the Viceroy urging citizens to cooperate in the management of extreme food shortage in India and Mysore and reports on relief efforts made by Mysore Government by to wipe out food grain deficits in Mysore

Building Bridges: Irrigating Mysore

In JCW's reign, irrigation remained an area of active research, governmental passion and thrust. Mysore continued to have water supply issues because of failed monsoons or crop-schedule issues. J.M. Imam, one of JCW's cabinet ministers in the reformed Mysore government said:

> Many progressive measures were undertaken during the short reign of the young Maharaja (actually 10 years!), specially in the field of irrigation, electrification and education. Many irrigation projects such as Bhadra reservoir, Thunga anicut, Nugu, Kabini and scores of minor tanks came into being. Electric power was made available in rural parts to enable ryots to install irrigation pumps.

Bridges were built, much research was done to strategically develop the small towns of Mysore state, to enable human and natural resources and to maximize industrial and overall growth. Decade-long pending projects were finished. The energy of a young king, who went out to get first-hand reports, who travelled to the sites and spots of sinking wells and drying fields made a difference.

> **Reply to an address presented by the Shimoga District Board, on the occasion of the laying of the foundation stone of the bridge over the Bhadra River, near Hole-Honnur, Shimoga District, 10 March 1944:**
>
> It is with great pleasure that I participate in the ceremony of laying the foundation stone of the bridge to be built over the Bhadra river, as it affords me another opportunity of seeing something of the work that the Shimoga District Board is doing in various directions, and particularly in improving the means of communication in this district. I recall that three years ago I laid the corner stone of the bridge over the Tunga River at Tirthahalli, which has since been completed and opened for traffic. These two projects had been pending for several

decades, and it must be a matter of great satisfaction to the District Board that one of them has been brought to completion and the fruition of another is in sight.[1]

Reply to addressees presented by the Chamarajanagar Municipal Council and the Mysore District Board, on the occasion of the opening of the Sri Jayachamarajendra bridge over the Suvarnavati River, 21 December 1943:

The bridge over the Suvarnavati River, which I am about to open, meets a long-felt want. It connects the surrounding villages with Chamarajanagar, providing facilities for travel and for the transport of agricultural and forest produce to important centres. I understand that a scheme for the supply of drinking water from the Suvarnavati River has been prepared by the Sanitary Engineering Department, but it has had to be deferred owing to the difficulty, in the present conditions, of procuring the materials required to put the scheme through.[2]

Reply to an address presented by the District Board, Kadur, on the occasion of the laying of the foundation stone of the bridge across the Bhadra River near Kalasa, 18 February 1941:

The bridge of which I am laying the foundation stone today will form one of a chain of works which will connect Kalasa with the network of roads running to Koppa and Narasimharajapura on the one hand, and to Mudigere and Chickmagalur on the other, and I hope that the time may come when, with the assistance of our neighbours across the border, we may be able to extend the connection on the other side towards the coast.[3]

The Cheluvamba Mansion: The Central Food Technology Research Institute's (CFTRI) Gift to the Nation

This battle for food perhaps triggered the idea of starting a research centre that could look into saving, preserving, packaging, and storing grain samples for posterity. Thus the Central Food Technology Research Institute (CFTRI) was born in Mysore. The facility that houses this unique research initiative is indeed a mansion. JCW donated the very charming Cheluvamba Mansion, originally constructed by Krishnaraja Wadiyar IV for the third princess of Mysore—Cheluvajammanni—to this cause. It was inaugurated on 21 October 1950, by the Hon'ble Sri C. Rajagopalachari and the Maharaja presided over the ceremony. The opening of the Institute added one more national laboratory to Dr Shanti Swarup Bhatnagar's[4] phenomenal run at adding over 12 national laboratories during his tenure.

JCW and former Governor-General of India C. Rajagopalachari at the inauguration of the Central Food Technology and Research Institute (CFTRI), Mysore

In his speech, JCW highlights the significance of food research:

This Institute is one amongst the many enterprises that are evidence of the innate constructive genius of our nation. Our Government, since the advent of Swaraj, has been trying to liquidate the arrears of centuries in the matter of scientific, industrial and material progress. Think of the many research laboratories it has organised; of the many dams and reservoirs it has planned for the conservation of waters needed in our dry and droughty land; of the many power stations that are in the stage of planning or actually under construction for the improvement of the economic condition of our people; of the encouragement it has given to ship building; and of the many research laboratories—pure and applied: it is establishing all over the country and the stimulus and support it has given to research and creative activities.

In his message on this occasion, Pandit Jawaharlal Nehru, the Prime Minister of India, underscored the national importance of such an institute for India:

> We have given top priority to the production of food grains or subsidiary foods. It is obvious that food is of the first importance and its value cannot be judged merely in money terms. We cannot depend on imports for our food and, therefore, we have laid down a target for food sufficiency. How can science help in this? The primary responsibility is of our Department of Agriculture. However, science can help in this greatly. It can also help in various other processes. It is particularly with these other processes that this Institute will be concerned. I hope the work done in this Institute will bear fruit not in developments on paper and in scientific journals but in terms of human values and in increase of suitable food for our people.

For over six decades since then, the CFTRI has been pioneering research and technology in the food industry, making food science an interdisciplinary subject with immense translational value.

The Raman Research Institute: The Raman Legacy in Bangalore

The journey of Sir C.V. Raman, especially after his groundbreaking research leading to the Nobel Prize, is a bittersweet tale of the savant against the system. Sometimes the aftermath of success is worse than the aftermath of failure. Soon after his appointment at IISc, his irritations with the overall culture of Indian science research began and continued to deepen with every passing year. He nursed a dream of being in a research body that was free of disciplinary boxes, bureaucratic interference and gave creative freedom. Long before the idea of the Raman Instititute was perhaps crystallized in his own mind, he had approached the Mysore Government for a space for the Indian Academy of Sciences, along the lines of the American model of National Academy of Sciences. In a display of the spirit of true Mysorean hospitality for such ideas, a 10-acre plot was promptly sanctioned for the same in 1934. It also came with a clause that if the land was not utilized for seven years, it could be taken back. In 1941, when JCW had just been coronated, a proposal was made to use the land for the Raman Research Institute instead. The land was thus sanctioned for the Raman Research Institute and the process of bringing the institution to life was set in motion. It is said that Raman had dreamt of walking out of IISc and into his own research utopia with glee—something he did in 1948, thanks to the will of the Maharaja. Speaking on the occasion of the special convocation of the University of Mysore held at Crawford Hall, Mysore, in 1962, his words sum up how he felt about the JCW legacy and Mysore:

> I would begin by saying that we recognise in His Highness a true son of Mother India whose voice is the authentic voice of our ancient land. This is not surprising when we consider his antecedents. For over five centuries, the ancestors of His Highness were the rulers of Mysore. Anyone who has seen the countryside of the State would be familiar with the remarkable manner in which its former rulers had transformed an arid and thirsty highland into a flourishing countryside by the construction of an immense number of barrages built of stone and earth across every dip in the land which could be used for

JCW with Nobel Laureate Sir C. V. Raman, receiving an Honorary Doctorate–Doctor of Law--from the University of Mysore in 1962

a set purpose, namely that of conserving the precious gift of water falling as rain and storing it for use as and when needed. These sparkling sheets of water which we see everywhere in the State are like the eyes in a human face. They lend both beauty and animation to the landscape. Indeed, as I have said often, and say it once again, Mysore is one of the loveliest places on the earth.

JCW with Sir C.V. Raman and regents of Indian Institute of Science

National Tuberculosis Institute

The Prime Minister of India, Pandit Jawaharlal Nehru, reached 'Avalon' at 8.30 a.m. It is difficult to articulate the enthusiasm that pervaded the atmosphere. It was as if the best people had gathered to dedicate themselves to fight the dreaded menace called tuberculosis. The Indian National Flag fluttered on top of Avalon, symbolising that India, through this Institute, would give it a hard try. The entire premises was tastefully decorated for the Inauguration.

This is how the Annals of the National Tuberculosis Institute (NTI) describe the starting of the landmark research institute in

India at Avalon. Avalon was originally the residence of JCW's sister, given away to the nation for a much deserving cause. The report also quips that despite Dr P.V. Benjamin, Director General of Health Services (DGHS) and Adviser in Tuberculosis (TB) for the Government of India being eager to acquire it and JCW's eagerness to relinquish Avalon to the TB crusade, the starting of the NTI took quite some time since the idea was approved on paper. The National Tuberculosis Institute serves as a premiere research institute under the Directorate General of Health Services, Ministry of Health and Family Welfare, Government of India. In 1955–58, the Indian Council for Medical Research (ICMR) conducted a survey that showed a high incidence of pulmonary tuberculosis across the country. Acting upon the impending medical burden, the government decided to initiate actions that would finally culminate in a TB control programme. A centre was required to study and analyse the issue from clinical, epidemiological and sociological approaches, while capacity-building on human resource and knowledge curation aspects too needed to be focussed on. The technical assistance was provided by the World Health Organization and the UNICEF funded most of the support initially.

S. Ramaswamy, an officer present at the inaugural ceremony observes:

> Avalon, surrounded by vast evergreen, wore a bridal look. The atmosphere of the assemblage was serene and silent as if in a chapel, just before the prayer. It seemed that the select gathering of doctors, technical people and interested workers in the field had come here to take a new message, digest it and carry it to the masses with the zeal of one who had discovered the truth. It was not a mela (fair), not a social gathering, not even the opening of a building, but the inauguration of a bold new idea and a radical venture to fight one of the deadliest enemies of the human race.

In 1945, the Asiatic Society of Bengal, whose mandate was to enhance and further the cause of research, submitted a proposal to establish a National Cultural Trust consisting of three academies: an Academy of Music, Dance, and Drama, an Academy of Letters, and an Academy of Art and Architecture. Post Independence, the idea was furthered and with a resolution by the (then) Ministry of Education, Government of India, dated 31 May 1952, notified in the Gazette of India of June 1952; three national academies: an Academy of Music, Dance, and Drama (Sangeet Natak Akademi; SNA), an Academy of Letters (Sahitya Akademi), and an Academy of Art (Lalit Kala Akademi) were created. It was the first national academy of the arts gifted to the new Republic. The Sangeet Natak Akademi was imagined as 'the apex body of the performing arts' in the country dedicated to 'preserving and promoting the vast intangible heritage of India's diverse culture expressed in the forms of music, dance and drama'.

As one of the founding members of the Academy and the Executive Board, JCW was invited to craft the mandate for the SNA, in a nation which was also regrouping its energies in culture. Not only does this belie his national stature but also the trust reposed by his peers in his ability for cultural leadership towards the nation. As someone who was widely travelled and had understood the inner workings of institutions of national and international importance, he was later invited to take up the post of the chairman of SNA from September 1961 to November 1965. In 1966, he was elected Ratnasadsya of the Academy, a national honour received by only the most celebrated of musicians and scholars of the country.

The citation reads thus:

Jaya Chamaraja Wadiyar

I present to you, Sir, His Highness the Maharaja of Mysore, Shri Jaya Chamaraja Wadiyar. Born in an ancient ruling family which has always been patron of arts, Maharaja Jaya

The current campus of the National Tuberculosis Institute, Bangalore

Prime Minister Pandit Jawaharlal Nehru at the opening of the National Tuberculosis Insitute at Avalon mansion donated by JCW

The banner and board at the entrance of the National Tuberculosis Institute campus in Bangalore

Prime Minister Jawaharlal Nehru being received by the Karnataka legislator and JCW at Bangalore airport

Chamaraja Wadiyar is not only a composer of Karnatak music but also a distinguished scholar in the fields of music, aesthetics, Sanskrit literature and philosophy. He has many a publication to his credit, and universities at home and abroad have bestowed honour on him. In his Court were, as with his predecessors, some of the most distinguished musicians of our country. The Maharaja's Catholic taste is revealed by his deep interest in Western music. The Trinity College of Music in London has elected him an Honorary Fellow. Appointed by the Government of India, he distinguished himself in guiding the Sangeet Natak Akademi as its Chairman for four years. For his eminence as a scholar in the field of arts and a patron of music, the Akademi has elected Maharaja Jaya Chamaraja Wadiyar as a Fellow.

The Indian Wildlife Board

Much like the homo sapiens of India, the animals of the subcontinent were impacted by the policies of what can be called environmental and ecological imperialism. In the words of Madhav Gadgil and Ramachandra Guha, authors of *This Fissured Land*, India was caught between two major interests, the Indian settler-cultivator modalities and the European industrial development–backed resource management.[5]

From time immemorial, agrarian societies have appropriated land for 'societal' use, thus bringing in the age-old problem of demarcating what belongs to humans and what belongs to the kingdom of animals, natural flora and fauna. We quite do not believe in the 'we are all part of the Kingdom of God' philosophy when thinking about such matters. Every king or lord has to deal with the matter of how much of a naturalist or conservationist he can afford to be, given that his major revenue comes from cultivable land snatched away from its natural occupants. Every kind of power structure—from local chieftains to Maharajas—has been conscientiously forced to think of how this land 'debt' is paid off to our animal kinsmen.

The Mysore governments, like in other aspects, made notable strides in conservation policies. Timber operations were separated from wildlife conserves, like at the Venugopal Wildlife Park within Bandipur from 1940 onwards. Hunting animals as game was banned as early as 1931, putting an end to an imperial sport dear to many princely families. From Chamaraja Wadiyar's small menagerie, the 157-acre Mysore Zoo, officially named Sri Chamarajendra Zoological Gardens, came into being. The Mysore Zoo was and is world famous, boasting state-of-the-art facilities, research faculties and animals that have made Mysore their home for generations. The African giraffe, green anaconda, baboons, zebras, and rhinoceros are happy occupants of this enterprise. One of the oldest zoos in the country, the Mysore zoo has a veritable success in pioneering conservation education, captive breeding techniques, research, documentation, rehabilitation, and outreach as well.

Owing to such a great track record, JCW was appointed as the Chairman of the Mysore and Central Board for Wildlife in 1952, which was renamed as Indian Board for Wildlife later. Speaking on the occasion of the birth centenary of JCW in Mysore in 2019, Mr Jairam Ramesh, economist and politician, welcomed the recent Supreme Court decision to reinduct cheetahs into the Indian wildlife ecosystem. He noted that back in 1952, as the Chairman of the Board, JCW had indeed identified the cheetah as being on the verge of extinction. On the matter of JCW's selection to the Board, Jairam Ramesh says, 'I think one reason why JCW was selected was because unlike a number of other royals, he was not trigger-happy or trophy crazy. Moreover, he belonged to a state which had notable conservation records.' JCW hosted the inaugural meeting of the Indian Wildlife Board between 24 November and 1 December 1952, at Lalitha Mahal Palace. With his active participation and leadership, four committees brainstormed on the policies that shaped the history of wildlife conservation in India. National parks were identified, legislative policies and separation of power between state and Centre were deliberated, and a tiered-list of animals needing various types of protection was recommended. JCW himself chaired all committees and played host to the hilt. JCW's personal interest in the Asiatic lion was evident in the valedictory address at the same conference, and a case for 'Project Lion' was made to protect the magnificent creature that adorns India's Ashoka Pillar and the emblem of the Republic of India. His idea propelled the creation of a second sanctuary for lions near Varanasi—the Chandraprabha Wildlife Sanctuary, after Gir Sanctuary in Gujarat. Under his leadership, the committees made a strong recommendation that a national directive be in play, because until then, the matter of conservation was left to the individual states. JCW was vociferous about one issue, that the natural resources—wild life and forests should be managed by the union government and not left to the states. Before the recommendations and directives were formally recognized as a legal Act, many, many issues had to be dealt with. Clearly many lobbies and vested interests were focussed on the formulation of this landmark Act regulating access to India's vast natural resources. It was in 1972 that this landmark Wildlife Protection Act was literally pushed through the parliament by 'the only man in the Indian Cabinet'—Smt. Indira Gandhi—almost twenty years after JCW's team had envisioned such a law. This landmark Act protected a list of animals, birds and plants, and also established ecologically-significant, protected areas in the country, such as wildlife sanctuaries, national parks, etc.

Birds from all over the world made Mysore their nesting home, much like the Mysore court, which housed the famous songbirds of

India—such as Abdul Karim Khan, Gauhar Jan, and others. Between 1645 and 1648, when Kanteerava Narasimharaja Wadiyar created an embankment on the River Kaveri to form the islets of Ranganatittu, little did he know that his man-made island would be home to chirpy avian citizens of Mysore. Situated about 19 kilometres from Mysore, and spread over 40 acres, the islands are named after Ranganatha Swamy, an avatar of Lord Vishnu, the protector of all worlds. Noted ornithologist Dr Salim Ali's seminal work on the birds that came to Ranganatittu and its significance made way for a kingly order in 1940, and the sanctuary was established in 1943, under JCW's rule. The irony of this was that as these birds were being invited into Ranganatittu sanctuary, the world was at war, and Mysore's men were being sent out of their sanctuary to fight a battle for British India!

All India Speech and Hearing Institute

The idea of establishing a research institute, which would focus on speech and hearing concerns of Mysore's population, led to a grant of 20 acres of land at Kurubarahalli, at the foot of Chamundi Hill, to develop the very first All India Institute for Speech and Hearing. This land was, however, later exchanged with the University of Mysore's Manasagangotri Campus, where the current campus stands. Dr Radhakrishnan, President of India, inaugurated this institute after establishment in 1966, and hailed the vision and benefaction of JCW—yet another gift to the nation from Mysore. This autonomous institute is now fully funded by the Ministry of Health and Family Welfare, Government of India, and has continued to serve the needs of the hearing impaired, and people with communication and language disorders.

THE PRESERVATION OF WILD LIFE IN INDIA

A COMPILATION

Published with the Financial Assistance

OF

His Highness

Sir Sri JAYACHAMARAJA WADIYAR BAHADUR, G.C.I.E

MAHARAJA OF MYSORE

Cover page of the first-ever data compilation on Indian wildlife, *The Preservation of Wildlife in India*, written by Lt Col R.W. Burton, published with the financial assistance of JCW. This publication went on to inform several wildlife protection and advocacy acts for India

A Universe of Learning in Mysore and Mysore University

The Mysore University was more than a passion for His Highness. As someone whose identity was firmly established as a student, as a sadhaka, as an upasaka, there was great resonance between his own values and the ideals of the university. The Mysore University was founded in 1916, as the culmination of much noteworthy advancement in social justice and access to education under the reign of Krishnaraja Wadiyar IV.

The Wadiyars were avid patrons of learning. In their own lives, they had experienced the joy of life-long learning through deep engagements with both indigenous knowledge systems of India and Westernized education. To understand the educational innovation behind the very idea of the Mysore University, one must understand the realities of education in pre and post-colonial India. The idea of public instruction and general education was not prevalent even in pre-colonial India. The business of textual, cultural and philosophical knowledge was somewhat relegated to centres of religious learning. The knowledge of money matters, merchandise, import-export, and industrial business was concentrated with the merchant and trader classes. The agrarian knowledge of growing food and animal husbandry was with the peasant class. The sculptors taught their sons and daughters the art of sculpting, and the goldsmith perpetuated the art of smithery to his kin. Knowledge was not generalized and definitely not regulated by a central authority on such matters. During colonial rule, the idea of centralized education came to India, with the larger intent of creating literate men to serve a British administrative setup. The royalty and the wealthy classes sent their children to schools for English education, which now was a prerequisite to function in a new world. Private tutors, royal schools, missionary schools all catered to this new milieu of literacy, basic and higher education—a model of education that was grafted into India.

In this context, Mysore took a dual approach to education—it welcomed centralized and higher education as it recommitted to Indian knowledge systems. Under the leadership of Diwan K. Seshadri Iyer (1883–1901) the Oriental Research Institute and the Department of Archaeology were initiated. Research and rejuvenation of traditional knowledge became a priority. The Kannada Sahitya Parishat was founded in 1915 to develop Kannada language and culture. In the 1930s and '40s, several Hindi language promotion organizations were started—Dakshina Bharatha Hindi Prachar Sabha and the Hindu Prachara Samiti. In 1943, the Mysore Hindi Prachara Parishat was started. Sanskrit colleges, Veda-schools came to being, such as the Mysore Sanskrit College and Jayachamarajendra Veda School in Bangalore, and Siddaganga Sanskrit School at Tumkur. The patronage to Indic knowledge systems and education grew under JCW's rule, and by 1944 over a hundred institutions were actively teaching Sanskrit as a major subject.

In 1918, primary education was made compulsory, and Sir M. Vishweshwaraiah as the Diwan, introduced schemes and scholarships for backward classes and untouchables to access this education system. He was a fierce advocate of technical and vocational training, industrial training, social education and business organizational training. He donated his award money to start a one-of-a-kind Jayachamarajendra Polytechnic at Bangalore. Situated on a sprawling 14-acre campus, it is the largest polytechnic college in South East Asia and it continues to offer value-based technical education. The Medical College at Mysore also came into being, and is still one of the oldest and well-reputed medical schools in the country. Simultaneously, equal importance was given to resuscitate Indian healing systems of medicine; the Jayachamarajendra Institute of Indian Medicine was inaugurated in 1943. On this occasion the Maharaja said:

> It gives me great pleasure to preside over the function of this evening. It has been the policy of my government not to undervalue the efficacy of Ayurvedic and Unani systems of treatment. I have watched with interest the research made in this country from time to time in the indigenous

> systems of medicine. For want of facilities or owing to other circumstances, they do not seem to have been conducted on modern recognised lines. It is only exhaustive investigation based on scientific methods in a well-equipped laboratory that will help the achievement value. This will be a centre for organised research on modern scientific lines into the actions and uses of our indigenous drugs and herbs. It has been said that no two practitioners of Ayurveda or Unani prepare their medicines according to the same formula. There is great scope for improvement in this respect; and the standardisation of indigenous medicines may very well be another object deserving of consideration in this Institute.[6]

When Mysore University was founded, it was a part of a grand vision to bring the philosophies of liberal arts to the educational tone in Mysore. Various scholars headed by the educationist, C. R. Reddy, compiled the educational goals and objectives of this university and sculpted the grand mission of the university for over five years. Original research, dissemination of knowledge, and programmes that prepared students for public, political, administrative and social life, were drawn up as core mandates for this university. The vision of several international universities were studied, particularly that of Universities of Chicago and Wisconsin–Madison, and Oxford University. Sir M. Vishweshwaraiah, who was responsible more than anyone else for the birth of the university describes the ideals thus:

> The general object in the broadest sense is to encourage learning, to promote higher education, to create a centre of culture, to light a torch that would dispel the gloom of ignorance from the remotest corners of the country. The specific aim in Mysore should be to develop the intellectual ability and executive power of our citizens.

The Mysore University was thus a labour of great love and foresight, and was also the first university in any princely state of India.

Prime Minister Jawaharlal Nehru at the Mysore University convocation where he received his Honorary Doctorate

At his commemorative speech delivered at the special convocation of Mysore University's Silver Jubilee, the academic romantic in him peeps out, as he speaks about the intended purpose of the university as a youthful intellectual hub:

> Informal discussions of a few friends about all things in heaven and earth up to all hours of the night and morning, wherever the argument is followed; the clash of minds between the youthful historian, medical student, chemist, theologian and engineer with the resulting recognition of the existence of different points of view, and of all things this exhilarating sense of intellectual daring and adventure...

These were his dreams for the student experiences at the Mysore University.

Several departments of the university and programmes were started by his personal initiative, either through personal donation of funds or allocation of buildings. Dr B.L. Manjunath, Vice-Chancellor of Mysore University between 1950 and 1954, says:

> His Highness took keen interest in the development of the university and its various departments. He was very anxious to establish a Chair in Indology at the least that could be done by us to perpetuate the culture bequeathed to us by our ancestors. He was a voracious reader and had an excellent personal library to which he continuously made additions selected from reviews in current journals. He was anxious that this collection should be made available to the University of Mysore. But before he could finalise the arrangements, he was snatched away from us.

As the Chancellor, he was most involved with the university's functioning and its upliftment. Dr B.L. Manjunath recollects, 'When he was Chancellor of the University of Mysore, I had the privilege of serving him for some years as the Vice-Chancellor. I recall with great pleasure my meeting with him in connection with university affairs in which he was keenly interested.' In 1950, JCW created an endowment chair in Indology and appointed Prof. H.N. Raghavendra Char, Professor of Philosophy, as its head. The department has now been renamed as the 'Department of Ancient History and Archaeology' and has conducted major excavations at Megalithic and Neolithic sites in Karnataka. This was a landmark move to start the study of India and its majesty from an inside-out perspective, to create a structure that would perpetuate scholars who would study India with no ethnic or anthropocentric bias. Even today, Indology remains the hand-puppet of European and American scholars, who have dominated writings and popular discourse about India.

The University of Mysore with the keen support and guidance of JCW also started the first-of-its-kind post graduate course in geography, another feather in its cap. A School of Music was also started. Noted musicologist and scholar, late R. Sathyanarayana recollects how the School of Music was started with a generous donation from JCW:

> It was JCW who conceived the idea of starting a music college at the University of Mysore. When efforts were put in that direction for the first time, it had to be shelved because of the mutual jealousy of some musicians. Later, JCW left a large sum of money as a donation to the Mysore University. That was the seed money with which this great institution was started. There is a special relation between Mysore University and the Maharaja. It was indeed here where His Highness attended classes just like a commoner, and got his degree.

Speaking on an occasion at the Mysore University, JCW's passion for his alma mater is clear:

> Vice-Chancellors and Delegates of the Universities of India, Ladies and Gentlemen,—We are met together to celebrate what I may perhaps describe as the coming of age of the Mysore University, and on such an occasion it is a great pleasure to me to welcome the representatives of so many sister universities and learned bodies from all parts of India. It is a familiar tale how it was decided, more than a century ago, to introduce Western learning into the schools and colleges of India, how this pouring of new wine into old bottles was followed by the creation of the first three universities on the model of the London University, how they and the colleges affiliated to them were responsible for supplying India with the body of men, who have conducted the bulk of its administration, its education, and much of its public life during the past half-century and more.

Examining the trajectory of how Mysore University was indeed imagined as a teaching and not an examining agency, reaffirms the purpose with which it was actually opened:

> It is also a matter of common knowledge that at a very early stage in their history, the defects of the examining and affiliating universities made themselves felt; in particular, the separation of teaching from examination, the minor part played by the teachers in administration, and the lack of corporate life among the students. The Indian Universities Act of 1904 sought to remedy these defects, and in 1913 the Government of India declared themselves in favour of unitary teaching universities. The first university of the new type to be incorporated was the Hindu University of Benares, in 1915, and the second was our own, created by the Mysore University Regulation of 1916.

Ever candid, he points to the gap in intent and execution till date and emphasizes on a paradigm shift in how the university imagines itself in India's development:

> The present position is that we have now something like 1,37,000 students in the 18 universities of India, of whom 4,700 are in Mysore, the great majority of them struggling to find their way into the professions of government service, medicine, teaching, and the law. I take first a quotation from Sir Brajendranath Seal, a wise vice-chancellor, who combined a keen sense of statesmanship with profound scholarship. The quotation deals not so much with the objectives of the university as with those to be aimed at in the general scheme of education and development of the country. Writing on the project for a technological institute, Dr. Seal said that the only possible remedy for the low physical vitality and productive capacity of our Indian peoples lay in an organisation of our industries (including agriculture as the staple industry of the country) in such a way as will help us to work our own

> abundant resources to meet our own primary wants. We have vast resources to develop. We have an ambitious agricultural and industrial policy and programme. We have a great and growing stream of ardent youth asking to be shown how to take their part in the development. What we have to do is to train and direct that stream into the places where it will yield the greatest results.

Mysore University continues to work towards the ideals laid down by the many visionaries including JCW. The motto of the university is symbolized by its emblem: the Gandabherunda flanked by the Sharabha on either sides. It is as if the spirit of the Rigveda: *Nahi Jnanena Sadrisham Pavithramiha Vidyate* (Nothing is as purifying as knowledge) on one side complements the other motto '*Satyamevodhaharamuaham*' (I always uphold the truth). Notable faculty of the university include former President of India Sarvepalli Radhakrishnan, Royal Medal laureate Sivaramakrishna Chandrasekhar, and Jnanpith awardee and Kannada litterateur Kuvempu. Notable alumni of the university include Bharat Ratna awardee Dr C.N.R. Rao, cartoonist R.K. Laxman, founder of Infosys N.R. Narayana Murthy and former Chief Justice of India M.N. Venkatachaliah. Pandit Nehru was honoured with an honorary doctorate by the Mysore University, and JCW, in his address as the Chancellor of Mysore University, said:

> Pandit Jawaharlal Nehru has not been content with work only in the political field. He is a man of letters and his works have been widely read all over the world and appreciated as much for their literary flavour as for their grave and sublime thoughts. His connection with the scientific world, the encouragement he has given to scientists and among his numerous duties, the time and attention that he has been devoting to the promotion of scientific and industrial research is testimony to both, his interest and his unalloyed devotion to the country in every direction.

12
A MYSOREAN PHILHARMONIA IN LONDON

Richard Osborne: *Legge really stabilised the Philharmonia's finances and was able to engage you permanently with the orchestra in 1949 as a result of money from the Maharaja of Mysore. Did you ever meet him?*

Herbert Von Karajan: *No, but I was fascinated by this man because he wanted above all things for us to record the Bartok Music for Strings, Percussion, and Celesta. There was no recording at that time, and it was a very difficult piece for the orchestra to bring off but I was determined to do it. In a way, the very roots of music are touched on in this work.*

This is how Karajan, the legendary Austrian conductor, described the enigmatic young Maharaja, whom he had never met. Yet he remembers his experience of recording the unique pieces of music that the Maharaja selected as ones through which the very 'roots of music are touched'. In a series of interviews with Richard Osborne, one of Britain's most respected broadcaster and writers, which he recorded for his biography, *Herbert Von Karajan: A Life in Music*, he describes the experience of conducting and recording the eclectic fare

JCW commissioned. Never before recorded in the world of Western classical music, thanks to a kindred soul from Mysore, whom he never met.

Ironically, this Herculean effort to give new life to the Philharmonia Society in Britain was done despite mounting financial woes and litigative tussles with his own government. As the dwindling civil list allowance shrank and frustrated correspondences with Mysore government grew, he found great redemption in playing knight in shining armour to Western classical music. Walter Legge travelled to Mysore in 1947–48, in the hope of resuscitating the dream of a Philharmonic Orchestra—an orchestra that believed in an intellectual revitalization of the symphonic dream in Western classical music. About the visit he said:

> The visit to Mysore was a fantastic experience. The Maharajah was a young man, not yet thirty. In one of his palaces he had a record library containing every imaginable recording of serious music, a large range of loudspeakers, and several concert grand pianos. He had intended to be a concert pianist and had been accepted by Rachimanoff as a pupil when both has father and his uncle died and he succeeded the throne—which meant giving up all ideas of a musical career and returning home at once. In the weeks I stayed there, the Maharajah had not only agreed to paying for the recordings of the Medtner piano concertos, an album of his songs, and some of his chamber music; he also agreed to give me a subvention of £10,000 a year for three years to enable me to put both the Philharmonia Orchestra and the Philharmonia Concert Society on a firm basis.[1]

Legge records that the Maharaja had not only thoroughly researched the EMI Catalogue and its offerings but had views which were 'trenchant as they were refreshingly unpredictable'.

'He was thrilled to Karajan's Vienna Philharmonic recording of Beethoven's Fifth Symphony ("as Beethoven wished it to be"), held Furtwangler's recording of the Fourth Symphony in high esteem, and was disappointed by Galliera's account of the Seventh Symphony, which he would have preferred Karajan to record.'[2] The Maharaja, for the next five years, invested great time, care and passion in ensuring the world gets to hear a repertoire unheard of in music history—much like himself, sophisticated yet eclectic in taste. Yet very few today are aware that JCW quietly revolutionized European art music's path in that time. Above all, he expressed serious doubts about Toscanini's recordings. 'The speed and energy are those of a demon,' he wrote to Legge, 'not an angel or superman as one would ardently hope for.' One of the reasons he so admired Furtwangler's Beethoven was that it was 'such a tonic after Toscanini's highly stung, vicious performances'. Reports Walter Legge in his letter: 'Because of his vision and support, in collaboration with EMI, many beautiful works breathed a new life: Balakirev's First Symphony, Roussel's Fourth Symphony—pieces considered conducting and performing 'nightmares' such as the Music for Strings, Percussion, and Celeste by Bartok.' Along with the fortunes of the Philharmonic Orchestra, the musical vision of the Maharaja pretty much installed Herbert von Karajan (1908–1989) firmly as one of the most celebrated artists of the 20th century. International fame hit him like never before, for the music he now performed and conducted was new, intriguing, and strikingly fresh. In a post-World War economy, and through the production enterprise of Legge, he emerged as a versatile presence across old and new mediums—from television, vinyl to CDs.

The *Gramophone* magazine reports on this unique benefactor from India: 'It was his intention over a long period to make possible recordings of neglected works of outstanding interest and of those acknowledged masterpieces of music which for one reason or another had not been recorded or had not been adequately performed on records.'[3] The first spate of recordings were:

BALAKIREV: *Symphony No. 1 in C.*
Philharmonia Orchestra
Conducted by Herbert von Karajan.
BALAKIREV: *Pianoforte Sonata.*
Louis Kentner.
BARTOK: *Music for Strings and Percussion.*
Philharmonia Orchestra
Conducted by Herbert von Karajan.
LIAPOUNOV: *Twelve Studies. Louis Kentner.*
ROUSSEL : *Symphony No. 4.*
Philharmonia Orchestra
Conducted by Herbert von Karajan.
SCRIABIN: *Pianoforte Sonata No. 3;*
Pianoforte Sonata No. 4.
Friedrich Wührer.
SCRIABIN: *Pianoforte Concerto.*
Solomon and the Philharmonia Orchestra
Conducted by Issay Dobrowen.

The Maharaja did not merely invest money, which in itself was no mean contribution, but also, ensured that a greater amount of musical thought, love, and passion was poured in at every stage. What is even more heartening is the fact that such an offering of money and passion was gifted to kick-start a musical enterprise in the country that was colonizing India! I guess true passion knows no geographical boundaries. The effort on part of JCW was a significant exertion of time, endless correspondences, petitions to procure foreign exchange, planning, executing and chaperoning these bold new forays in music. JCW created a musical foundation governed by a committee, and had in place a five-year recording plan for the orchestra (he clearly liked the idea of Five-Year Plans!), and after consultation with eminent musicians in several countries, a comprehensive list of works was drawn up. 'The only condition was that there should be a committee of distinguished personalities in British musical life—excluding performers. I returned to London happy about everything except the prospect of a committee to advice on programmes. As things turned out, it was only in the first year that the generous subvention would be paid in full,' notes Walter Legge.

If the Philharmonic Orchestra continues to be 'at the top of its league as a concert-giving and recording orchestra since its inception' as they claim to be, the vision for its continued success was definitely laid out by JCW with Walter Legge. 'The Maharajah's generosity bridged the period until the royalties from the Philharmonia's record sales were sufficient to maintain the orchestra without subvention,' credits Walter Legge.

Yet, their website today, does not credit the timely intellectual and significant monetary contribution of the Maharaja, perhaps because it's a part of a comfortable amnesia, which all successful structures choose to harbour, so that their uncomfortable beginnings are masked.

To make sure that the decisions of such an ambitious project were not guided only by the intellectually 'elite' minds but also by the hearts of the listeners, a first-ever international consumer psychology survey was done. This makes perfect sense in today's world, where every product is placed in the market with thorough exploratory testing, market segmentation and research. But it was the research acumen of the Maharaja, which thought of this, and that's how the world's perhaps first musical plebiscite was held. 'It is His Highness' wish to be guided in the final choice of works by the desires of the music-loving and record-buying public,' and for this purpose, *Gramophone* magazine and the Philharmonia Concert Society sponsored a two-pronged competition.

In the first competition, participants selected from a given list of 20 works, the order of personal choice, giving an indication of the overall 'sellability' of every piece per participant. The second competition in psychological experimental parlance: a control study. The participants would then select from the same list of 20 works, what they would prefer. The first competition tested personal valences and the second ascribed preferences. It was decided that the entries would be judged by a committee consisting of His Highness the Maharaja of Mysore, Compton Mackenzie, Christopher Stone, Alec Robertson, Professor Gerald Abraham, Dr William Walton, the Hon. Elisabeth Scott-Montagu, Rudolf Gamsjager, Walter Legge, and His Highness' personal agent, Capt. S. T. Binstead.

JCW's thought leadership infused new thinking in the arena. A remote Indian prince had visualized a global psychosocial experiment to scientifically analyse people's preferences and valences for classical music! If the difference or mismatch between the personal choice and what he believed was better in the 'field' was steep, then it would indicate how perceptions of the individual and the collective were different. It would separate actual desirability of each piece of music and the perceived desirability. The genius of the competition was that it simultaneously measured the public awareness of such pieces. Thus the producers could score how great the difference was between a reader's own choice and what they believed others would deem good. It would also yield data on which geographical areas could be targeted for recorded pieces, to increase sales.

LIST OF WORKS INCLUDED IN COMPETITION

BACH: *Christmas Oratorio.*
BALAKIREV: *Incidental Music to Shakespeare's King Lear.*
Pianoforte Concerto.
Symphony No. 2. En Boherne.
BARTOK: *Pianoforte Concerto No. 1.*
Pianoforte Concerto No. 2.
Pianoforte Concerto No. 3.
Rhapsody No. for Pianoforte and Orchestra.
Viola Suite.
Suite for Orchestra, No. 1.
Suite for Orchestra, No. 2.

Divertimento.
BEETHOVEN: *Fidelio (complete).*
Choral Fantasie
ALBAN BERG: *Violin Concerto.*
Lyric Suite.
Der Wein.
Pianoforte Sonata.
BERLIOZ: *An album of selected passages from Les Troyens and La Prise de Troie.*
BRUCKNER: *Symphony No. I.*
Symphony No. 2.
Symphony No. 3.
Symphony No. 4.
Symphony No. 5.
Symphony No. 6.
Symphony No. 7.
Symphony No. 8.
Symphony No. 9.
BUSONI: *Pianoforte Concerto.*
Rondo Arlen hinesco.
Fantasia Contrappuntistica
Cortege (Doktor Faust).
Indian Fantasie.
CASALLA: *II Couvento Veneziano.*
CORNELIUS: *The Barber of Baghdad —an album of representative excerpts.*
DVORAK: *Stabat Mater.*
FIELD: *Pianoforte Concerto No. 7.*
GLAZOUNOV: *Symphony No. 4.*
Symphony No. 5.
Symphony No. 6.
GLINKA: *An album of representative orchestral works*
HANDEL: *An album of arias from the Italian Operas*
JANACEK: *From the diary of one who disappeared.*

Mass.
KABALEVSKY: *Pianoforte Concerto No. 2.*
Pianoforte Sonata No.2.
KODALY: *Psalmus Hungaricus.*
KOECHLIN: *Sonata for Horn and Pianoforte.*
Paysages et Marines.
Five Pianoforte Sonatinas
LIADOV: *Birulki.*
LIAPOUNOV: *Pianoforte Concerto No. 1.*
Ukranian Fantasie for Pianoforte and Orchestra.
Pianoforte Sonata.
LISZT : *Fantasia on Meyerbeer's Robert le Diable.*
Fantasia on Mozart's Don Giovanni.
Fantasia on Mozart's Le Nozze di Figaro.
Fantasia on Donizetti's Lucia di Lammermoor and Paris.
Tarantella (Dargomwijsky) transcription.
MAHLER: *Symphony No. 2.*
Symphony No. 3.
Symphony No. 6.
Symphony No. 7.
Symphony No. 8.
MARTINU: *Ricercari.*
Symphony No. 1.
Symphony No. 2.
Symphony No. 3.
Symphony No. 4.
Symphony No. 5.
MONTEVERDI-REDLICH: *Vesperae.*
MOUSSORGSKY: *Boris Goudonov (complete)*
(a) Original Version.
(b) Edited by Rimsky-Korsakov.
MOZART: *Die Entfiihrung aus dem. Serail.*
NIELSON: *Symphony No. 4.*

Symphony No. 5.
Symphony No. 6.
PANOUFNIK: *Nocturne.*
PROKOFIEV: *Pianoforte Sonatas No. 6.*
Pianoforte Sonatas No. 8.
Pianoforte Concerto No. 2.
Pianoforte Concerto No. 4.
Pianoforte Concerto No. 5.
Violoncello Concerto.
RACHMANINOV: *Violoncello Sonata.*
Corelli Variations.
Pianoforte Sonata No. 1.
Pianoforte Sonata No. 2.
ROUSSEL: Symphony No. 1.
Bacchus et Ariane.
Suite, Op. 14.
Rhapsodic Flamand,.
Pianoforte Concerto.
Trio, Op. 58.
Suite, Op. 33.
Sonata for Violin and Pianoforte.
SAINT SAENS: *Variations, Op. III.*
SALOS: *Canzones Castilianas.*
SCHMIDT: *Symphony No. 3*
Symphony No. 4
Variations on a Hussar Song.
Variations on a theme of Beethoven.
SCHONBERG: *Quartet No. 2.*
Kammersinfonie No. 1
Kammersinfonie No. 2
Five Orchestral Pieces.
Pianoforte Concerto.
Violin Concerto.

SCRIABIN: *Preludes for Pianoforte.*
SCHUMANN: Complete unrecorded pianoforte works.
STRAUSS, R.: *Salome (complete).*
Elektra (complete).
SZYMANOWSKI: *Harnasie Ballet Music.*
Symphonic Ballet Music.
TCHAIKOVSKY: *Suite No. I.*
Suite No. 2.
Suite No. 3.
VITTORIA: *Album of representative works.*
WEBER: Pianoforte Concerto No. 2.
Pianoforte Sonata No. 2.
Pianoforte Sonata No. 4.
WELLESZ: *Symphony.*
String Quartet No. 5.

The response was enormous. The record-buying public and connoisseurs alike enjoyed this new game; perhaps they felt voiced and heard, and they became stakeholders, in a way. In a way, for the first time, a project was crowd-sourced conceptually, a beautiful thought experiment!

The results stumped everyone. As reported by *Gramophone*:

> The votes in the Personal Choice showed a greater Catholicism of taste than we had expected. "Examining this list of twenty works without reference to the Personal Choice leads us to believe the public has expensive tastes! Such works as the *Christmas Oratorio*, *Salome*, *Elektra, Fidelio*, the Berlioz operatic excerpts, Dvorak's *Stabat Mater*, Kodaly's *Psalmus Hungaricus*, Beethoven's *Choral Fantasie*, *Boris Godounov*, and the Mahler *8th Symphony*, would each cost several thousand pounds to record. Many of them require huge orchestras, expensive soloists and conductors, and larger choruses.

For the General Choice Competition, there were 750 entries, coming from Great Britain, Northern Ireland, Eire, Australia, Austria, USA, Egypt, Belgium, Sweden, Denmark, Norway, China, Israel, and Switzerland.

The first 20 works, together with the number of votes they obtained, are:

1. Bach. *Christmas Oratorio* 665
2. Beethoven. *Fidelio* 602
3. Schumann. *Complete unrecorded pianoforte works* 576
4. Mozart. *Die Entphrung aus dem Serail* 564
5. Strauss, R. *Salome* 527
6. Handel. An album of arias from the Italian Operas 515
7. Dvorak. *Stabat Mater* 481
8. Berlioz. An album of selected passages from *Les Troyens and La Prise de Troie* 425
9. Tchaikovsky. *Suite No. 3* 410
10. Moussorgsky. *Boris Godounov (Original version)* 322
11. Kodaly. *Psalmus Hungaricus* 304
12. Strauss, R. *Elektra* 298
13. Glinka. An album of representative orchestral works 289
14. Weber. *Pianoforte Concerto No. 2* 269
15. Scriabin. *Preludes for Pianoforte* 267
16. Tchaikovsky. *Suite No. 2* 245
17. Beethoven. *Choral Fantasie* 233
18. Saint Saens. *Variations Op* 231
19. Mahler. *Symphony No. 8* 225
20. Busoni. *Piano Concerto* 219

To understand what may seem like a bizarre act of generosity, some background on the Philharmonic ideals would be necessary. Why should he have cared if the world got to hear music produced and consumed by people—so far removed from his realities? The Philharmonic movement in Western art music stood for an exalted musical sensibility, which while deeply infatuated by the likes of Beethoven, would develop an ear for world music globally. Post World War I, to revive the philharmonic culture, Walter Legge, a classical music record producer for EMI, founded the Philharmonia Society in 1945. Legge, also found the means to re-employ the very best of military musicians who provided music in the battlefield in this new orchestra. The idea was to create a new aesthetic, an alternative society that would produce fare that would elevate the quality of orchestral music. This in the context of London Symphony Orchestra, BBC Symphony Orchestra and the old-vanguard London Philharmonic Orchestra being on the downslide with dwindling monies, audiences, and energy. To fund this ambitious project, he approached JCW who agreed to sponsor the 'Mysore concerts' of the Society. He also thus became the first president of the Philharmonia Concert Society, London, in 1948. The Mysore court and ethos for long had upheld values close to the Philharmonia societies of England. The Maharaja's funding of the Philharmonia Society indicates his deeper intellectual and spiritual commitment to the idea of the 'philharmonia'. The prospect of fostering new music while looking at the world (and not just European music), for musical inspiration, must have resonated with his ever-innovative mind. According to *Gramophone*:

> Many more correspondents have written expressing their admiration for the vision, constructive enterprise and generosity of the young Indian Prince who conceived this plan, and who is making it possible for music lovers throughout the world to learn, enjoy and study works which, but for his knowledge and love of music, would never have been recorded.

In JCW's letter to Sardar Vallabhbhai Patel, we get a sense of how difficult it was to send money overseas; many bureaucratic hurdles had to be jumped before money reached beneficiaries. This was at a time when most other Maharajas in the country were more interested in figuring out financial destinies for their kith and kin, and not sending 10,000 pounds in aid of a remote Western classical producer! The Mysore concerts, as they were publicized, were performed with great grandeur at the Royal Albert Hall, enthralled audiences as they etched sound into history.

PHILHARMONIA CONCERT SOCIETY

President:
H.H. THE MAHARAJA OF MYSORE

MYSORE CONCERTS
1950 - 1951

Monday, February 12th
1951

PROGRAMME
ONE SHILLING

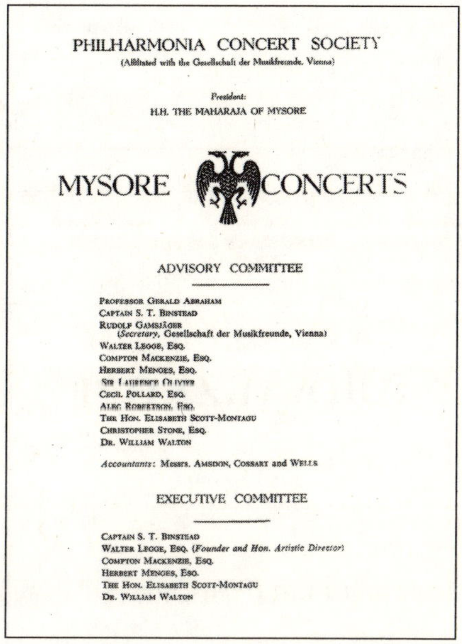

PHILHARMONIA CONCERT SOCIETY
(Affiliated with the Gesellschaft der Musikfreunde, Vienna)

President:
H.H. THE MAHARAJA OF MYSORE

MYSORE CONCERTS

ADVISORY COMMITTEE

Professor Gerald Abraham
Captain S. T. Binstead
Rudolf Gamsjäger
(*Secretary*, Gesellschaft der Musikfreunde, Vienna)
Walter Legge, Esq.
Compton Mackenzie, Esq.
Herbert Menges, Esq.
Sir Laurence Olivier
Cecil Pollard, Esq.
Alec Robertson, Esq.
The Hon. Elisabeth Scott-Montagu
Christopher Stone, Esq.
Dr. William Walton

Accountants: Messrs. Amsdon, Cossart and Wells

EXECUTIVE COMMITTEE

Captain S. T. Binstead
Walter Legge, Esq. (*Founder and Hon. Artistic Director*)
Compton Mackenzie, Esq.
Herbert Menges, Esq.
The Hon. Elisabeth Scott-Montagu
Dr. William Walton

Programme copies and details of the 'Mysore Concerts' organized by the Philharmonia Concert Society and concert announcements at various prestigious venues in London and the rest of the UK between 1950-1952

PHILHARMONIA
CONCERT SOCIETY

President:
H.H. THE MAHARAJA OF MYSORE

MYSORE CONCERTS
1951 - 1952

Wednesday, March 26th
1952

PROGRAMME
ONE SHILLING

DIETRICH
FISCHER-DIESKAU
(Baritone)

GERALD MOORE
Pianoforte

SCHUBERT
"DIE SCHÖNE MÜLLERIN"

THURSDAY, JANUARY 31, 1952
at 7.30 p.m.

KINGSWAY HALL
KINGSWAY, W.C.2

ELISABETH
SCHWARZKOPF

SONG RECITAL

Pianoforte:
GERALD MOORE

STEINWAY PIANOFORTE

MONDAY, FEBRUARY 12, 1951
at 7.30 p.m.

Management: IBBS & TILLETT LTD., 124 WIGMORE STREET, W.1

KINGSWAY HALL
KINGSWAY, W.C.2

IRMGARD
SEEFRIED

WITH

GERALD MOORE
Pianoforte:

WEDNESDAY, MARCH 26th, 1952
at 7.30 p.m.

STEINWAY PIANOFORTE

Management: IBBS & TILLETT LTD., 124 WIGMORE STREET, W.1

Programme copies and details of the 'Mysore Concerts' organized by the Philharmonia Concert Society and concert announcements at various prestigious venues in London and the rest of the UK between 1950-1952

KINGSWAY HALL
Kingsway, W.C.2

PHILHARMONIA CONCERT SOCIETY

President:
H.H. THE MAHARAJA OF MYSORE

Thursday, May 8, at 7.30 p.m.

SCHWARZKOPF
GERALD MOORE

ONLY LONDON LIEDER RECITAL THIS SEASON

Programme includes Songs by
SCHUBERT, BRAHMS, HUGO WOLF, etc.

TICKETS: 7/6, 6/- and 3/-
From Chappell's Box Office, 50 New Bond Street, W.1; usual Ticket Offices, and IBBS & TILLETT LTD., 124 Wigmore Street, W.1 (WELbeck 8418)

ROYAL FESTIVAL HALL
General Manager - T. E. Bean

PHILHARMONIA CONCERT SOCIETY

President:
H.H. THE MAHARAJA OF MYSORE

TWO GREAT FAREWELL CONCERTS
before the EUROPEAN TOUR of the

PHILHARMONIA
ORCHESTRA
Founder and Artistic Director: WALTER LEGGE

and

HERBERT VON
KARAJAN

Tuesday, May 6, at 8 p.m.
MOZART: Divertimento in D major, K.334
STRAUSS: Don Juan
BEETHOVEN: Symphony No. 7

Friday, May 9, at 8 p.m.
HANDEL-HARTY: Water Music
STRAVINSKY: Jeu de cartes
BRAHMS: Symphony No. 1

TICKETS: 12/6, 10/6, 7/6, 6/-, 3/6 and 2/6
From ROYAL FESTIVAL HALL BOX OFFICE (WATerloo 3191); Chappell's Box Office, 50 New Bond Street, W.1; usual Ticket Offices, and
IBBS & TILLETT LTD., 124 Wigmore Street, W.1 (WELbeck 8418)

EUROPEAN TOUR

May 11th - May 31st 1952

PHILHARMONIA
ORCHESTRA
Founder and Artistic Director: WALTER LEGGE

and

HERBERT VON
KARAJAN

May 12	PARIS	Palais de Chaillot
13	PARIS	Palais de Chaillot
14	BERNE	Casino
15	GENEVA	Victoria Hall
16	ZURICH	Tonhalle
17	BASLE	Musiksaal-Casino
18	TURIN	
19	MILAN	La Scala (Opening Concert of the Season)
20	MILAN	La Scala
22	VIENNA	Musikverein (International Music Congress)
23	VIENNA	Musikverein (International Music Congress)
24	LINZ	Turnhalle
26	MUNICH	Deutsches Museum
27	HAMBURG	Musik Halle

ROYAL ALBERT HALL
Manager - C. S. Taylor

PHILHARMONIA CONCERT SOCIETY

President:
H.H. THE MAHARAJA OF MYSORE

Thursday, April 24, at 7.30 p.m.

FURTWÄNGLER
FLAGSTAD

SCHUMANN: Manfred Overture
SCHUMANN: Symphony No. 4
RAVEL: Rhapsodie Espagnol

WAGNER: Five Wesendonck Songs
WAGNER: Closing Scene from Götterdämmerung

Tuesday, June 3, at 7.30 p.m.

KUBELIK
SOLOMON

DVORAK: Scherzo Capriccioso
BRAHMS: Concerto in B flat, No. 2

DVORAK: Symphony No. 5 in E minor — New World

PHILHARMONIA
ORCHESTRA
Founder and Artistic Director: WALTER LEGGE

TICKETS: 12/6, 10/6, 7/6, 6/-, 3/6 and 2/6
From ROYAL ALBERT HALL (KEN. 8212); Chappell's Box Office, 50 New Bond Street, W.1, usual

Programme copies and details of the 'Mysore Concerts' organized by the Philharmonia Concert Society and concert announcements at various prestigious venues in London and the rest of the UK between 1950-1952

The Palace,
Mysore.
15th July 1950

My dear Sardar Patel,

I have received a communication from Sri V.P. Menon of the Ministry of States, New Delhi, intimating that the Ministry of Finance have agreed to release the foreign exchange required for the Philharmonic Concert in London and that orders are being issued to the Reserve Bank accordingly. I am highly grateful to you for having secured for me the required foreign exchange. I am fully conscious of the fact that but for your very strong and valuable recommendation, the Ministry of Finance would not have acceded to my request. By your great gesture, you have placed me and the whole musical world under a deep debt of gratitude.

I always cherish with gratitude your unfailing kindness and courtesy and the gracious consideration

17-7

P.T.O

-2-

you have been pleased to show me in this matter as in all other matters.

With best regards,

Yours sincerely,
Jaya Chamarajendra Wadiyar

Sardar Vallabhbhai Patel,
Hon'ble Deputy Prime Minister of India,
NEW DELHI

Correspondence with Sardar Patel regarding the transfer of funds to support Philharmonia Society and procurement of foreign exchange

13
A FREEMASON OF HIS DESTINY

Brah'mand'a Valaye Maaye
Antarmukha Jyotirmaya Kalyani
Ahinibha Veni Puraani
Antyarahita Kaivalyavihaarini Gati nirjita garini Geervaani

—An ode to the Devi—To whom the universe is a bracelet.

The writings of the Maharaja balance depth and scholarship with a rare awareness commonly missing in writers who write on Indian philosophy. Very few writers have managed to balance depth with clarity, the abstract with the lucid, and keep the focus on the purpose of writing. One striking quality of his writings is that he is quite clear on the what, when and why of content generation. If it is a book like his magnum opus, *Dattatreya*, which is a meta-commentary on the validity of the Advaitha Vedanta approach, then he makes no bones about structuring it as a dense commentary. In contrast, *Religion and Man* is catered to a global audience interested in the Indian experience. In *An Aspect of Indian Aesthetics*, a rather critical analysis about Eastern and Western aesthetics is made, thus clarifying what is unique about both viewpoints. The point of *Gita and Indian Culture* is quite clear from the very first page—he attempts to build bridges of knowledge and chaperone perception of Indian culture in the West. He does this with no overzealous claims of it being the best and no agendas other than to just bring out its intrinsic worth. He offers a beautifully balanced view that neither dismisses all things West nor aggrandizes the East.

This clarity of purpose seems to be the hallmark of his manodharma—be it music, writing or even the idea of designing an opinion poll to really study what kind of classical music is sought by people across the globe for the Philharmonia Society. He elucidates, clarifies, examines, critically evaluates, comments, narrates or unravels a subject, knowing fully well, which 'thought scalpel' he wants to use on what material. A caveat in many commentaries on critically edited Indian shastric texts, or even 'samalochana' vein of interpretive writing on Indian subjects is that complex concepts are described using even higher order jargon or untranslatable text, defeating the very purpose of 'explaining'. Rather amorphous-sounding English words and heavy rhetoric are used to explain densely symbolic imageries in Hindu thought even in writings meant to invite the uninitiated into such experiences.

If one reads the Maharaja's writings, two things are loud and clear. Most of the books, monographs and transcribed lectures were directed towards a passionate mission to 'present' India to the world. His writings pioneer a much-needed body of writings, which open the promise of the Oriental without either the anthropocentric biases of the West or the post-colonial agendas of the East. His psyche embodied such equanimity and he saw many complementarities and inconsistencies on both sides. He is quick to note certain universals to human experience or endeavours, away from and above culture and region. In his book, *An Introduction to Indian Aesthetics*, while surveying the different attitudes to understanding aesthetics, he quotes British philosopher Clive Bell's most eloquent universal truth: 'It is improbable that more nonsense has been written about aesthetics than about anything else!' As he surveys the approaches that Western aesthetics has taken, he remarks, 'There is the Western approach which is chiefly pragmatical, that art concerns itself mainly with the investigation of what is beautiful when we talk or assert ourselves about it.' He makes a compelling argument for how such an approach makes aesthetics merely a branch of critical philosophy. Thus the study of aesthetics is stuck in an observer of experience orientation, rather than as a manual for embodied experience. In the book, he makes the key observation that in India, the core purpose of art is creating religious experience. JCW quotes the *Taittiriya Upanishad's* declaration of this brahman-is-ananda tenet: "*Anando Brahmeti Vyajanat*" (Ananda truly is Brahman, so realize it!) The purpose of all Indian art, thus, he argues, is creating religious experiences, because beauty and the divine are linked. This makes the Indian approach to aesthetics, a science of creating such phenomena. It does this by understanding the intimate relationships between sound and sense in music, form and meaning in visual arts, and vak-artha in literature. He quotes Raghuvamsha to demonstrate the innate link between vak, artha or sound and sense:

Vagarthaviva Sampruktou Vagarthapratipattaye Jagatah pitarou vande Parvati parameshvarou—Raghuvamsha I-1.

He argues that the Indian aesthetic experience is pinned on such sublime truths of the mind, which give access to beauty and finally Ananda.

He is quick to point out that many ancient cultures have resonated with similar approaches, while in India, aesthetics is scientifically understood quite deeply as opposed to many contemporary cultures: 'Therefore all the great nations of the earth approached art as the emphasis of the spirit and the concept of spirituality. Greek art stressed the elements of rhythm, proportion, symmetry and grace; it also emphasised the unity of truth, beauty and goodness, arguing thus for a sane and balanced mind in a healthy and beautiful body.' He contrasts various attitudes world cultures have had in the past: 'In Hebrew art, the emphasis was on the ethical aspect, while the Egyptians delighted in quantity and vastness, and believed in an austere severity of outline as witnessed in some of their monuments like the Pyramids.' He argues that the *Alankara Shastra* is rooted in the Vedanta. As a case-and-point, he describes the concept of Ananda, loosely translated as bliss. The Ananda, either produced through Kavya or Nada, however ephemeral, is seen in Indian thought as a powerful means to passage into higher states of consciousness, and finally the experience of the Brahman.

At a lecture at the Madras Music Academy, while highlighting the importance of Shastras in music, he quips, 'I am sure you will realise the importance of the *"sastra"* side of music, since you are the inheritors of the Indian tradition. You will have a number of problems to face and to solve. For instance, how far is the idea true that a certain time of the day is suited only to a particular Raga, which is after all the product of mere association of sounds?' He is referring to what in cognitive sciences is called the cultural bias, or cultural conditioning. Will the Raaga–Rasa corollary hold true in a cross-cultural paradigm? Will a Norwegian sitting in a smug winterized environment perceive a morning in Raga Bhoopalam? To further illustrate his point, he draws from within the ideologies of the *Alankara Shastra*: 'Again, while it is true that such Raga is the expression of one dominant emotion, can other emotions be introduced within the limits of that Raga, with these emotions being made to act as feeders of the main emotion, very much after the pattern of the judicious admixture of *rasas* in Indian *Kavya*.' His closing statement in the same lecture is most pertinent to the somewhat dogmatic world of South Indian classical music, where a better spirit of inquiry would be welcome. 'You will no doubt approach such problems, in a spirit, in which a reverence for tradition and the critical method for enquiry are harmoniously blended.'

Jivanmukti—the Advaitin Journey

Freedom is a theme often replayed in his inner and outer lives. It is with belief in his free will and faith that he ruled Mysore to its exalted existence. It is his belief in freedom of speech that spurred him to allow free speech in his legislative assembly. It is with this trust in the ability of men to truly act freely and responsibly that he installed democracy in Mysore. It is with this inner freedom that he crusaded through the loss of title, power, money, designations and pain. Jivanmukti was a kind of freedom which he perhaps experienced in his spirit. Noted scholar V. Raghavan observes: 'In and through all this pomp and splendour and frequent travel and activity, his mind was anchored in the poise of the inner spirit.' As he puts it in a nutshell, 'Detachment is liberation in life (*Jivan Mukti*).' The Maharaja's central reverence and devotion to Advaitha Vedanta explains the choice of topics for many philosophical writings: *Atman and Brahman, Religion and Man,* and *Dattatreya: The Way and the Goal.*

Free-will is mired in many confounding connotations in today's world. The idea of freedom, will and free will has had many takers. Baruch Spinoza, hailed as one of the key rationalist thinkers of the 17th century, says, 'He alone is free who lives with free consent under the entire guidance of reason.' Nietzsche said that free will is a theologian's artifice, which makes punishing, condemning and discrimination possible. The general problem with theology being that the existence of free-will must be somewhat explained in the context of divine grace, which is always pushing mortals to act well and right. But in this model, how does one explain poor decisions? How does one explain evil? Many dualist philosophies including the Judeo–Christian philosophies and Dwaitha propound the duality of Jeevatma and Paramatma to explain this black box between intent and action, freedom and determinism. Advaitha Vedanta reconciles this duality in an entirely different way, and interestingly, without the agonizing claims of absolute freedom of choice. As Jean-Paul Sartre (1905–80), quips, 'Condemned to be free!'

Advaitha Vedanta is a positivist philosophy, which asserts that all individuals have equal potential to realize inner freedom. JCW writes in *An Aspect of Indian Aesthetics*: 'The *Samkhya* view is pessimistic, being that nature is not wholly beautiful and pleasant, but is a mixture of *sukha, dukha* and *moha*. Nature does not please all at all times. Therefore for pure bliss, we must look elsewhere than in the real world.' According to Adi Shankara (788 CE–820 CE), the most prominent exponent of Advaitha Vedanta tradition, Advaitha Vedanta asserts that one only needs to look within. It asserts that through vidya, the real self can be accessed and enthroned in the human consciousness. It explains bad decisions, actions and evil as consequences of mada, matsara, kama, moha taking the throne temporarily. JCW notes in his preface to the book, *Dattatreya*: 'The individual can, by austerity and discipline discover the divine in him and establish the superiority of the inner man over environmental conditions. The individual soul may commune with God at any time, at any place and in any historic circumstances.' By enthroning the habit of acting from the true self, there is no difference between Atman and Brahman. Kaivalya (salvation) is realized within and the Jeeva is now free to see clearly, act and will action. This is what the Kaivalya Pada Sutras also speak of: '...Or, to look from another angle, the power of pure consciousness settles in its own pure nature.'—Kaivalya Pada: Sutra 34. Shakta Agamas.

The Advaitha Vedanta–based writings of the Maharaja are significant for another reason. For one, Advaitha Vedanta emphasizes jivanmukti, the powerful idea that freedom and liberation from false consciousness is possible while being alive. This is a stark contrast to other Indian philosophies, which emphasize on videhamukti, or moksha after death. His books are centred on the core concepts of this school: such as Brahman, Brahmavidya, Atman, Maya, Avidya, which are interpreted in a positivist vein. Mysore Hiriyanna (1871–1950), an eminent Indian philosopher, Sanskrit scholar and authority on Indian aesthetics, points to why the Maharaja's books are significant in the realm of Indian philosophy:

> The earliest philosophy of India had a supernatural basis. Asceticism was the natural outcome of it. In course of time, it came to be believed that the highest ideal that man could attain was attainable on this side of death, here and now.

> The full development of this view belongs to the period that followed the composition of the classical Upanishads, but its source can be traced earlier in those passages which refer to *Jivanmukti*. *Jivanmukti* to speak from the purely philosophic standpoint, marks the highest conception of freedom. It is one of the points where Indian philosophy clearly deviates away from Indian religion; for the goal of existence according to this conception is not the attainment of a hypothetical bliss hereafter, but the finding of true freedom on this bank and shoal of time...

The beauty of the Maharaja's life and times was that he was living what he was writing, he was practicing what he thought about. It is as if life constantly tested his reliance on his philosophical ideals on the sands of time. The inspirational message from understanding this relationship between Advaitha Vedanta and his life is that one gets to appreciate the lived-in splendour of a life that lived its axioms. As M. Hiriyanna says, 'The aim of life was no longer conceived as something to be sought for beyond this world, but to be realised here, and if one so willed, now.' An interesting Eastern-take on the 'live free or die' concept!

Many of his writings are somewhat reflecting on his own journey as a sadhaka, seeking to eliminate the binaries of life through a convergent knowledge. In tantric paradigms, the non-dual and pure consciousness of Kaivalya is possible by the union of Shakti the matrix of creation with the male principle of Shiva. Hence transcendence of the binaries of Atman-Brahman, reason-reverence, divine-human remain a dominant theme in his writings. His reliance on the Srividya tantric practice is explained by this inner quest. This also explains why the Devi is the central deity in most of Carnatic compositions, 'The feminine is the will, the knowing and the activity, she is not only the matrix of creation, she is creation.'[1] Only through the *upasana* can this blissful state of Jivanmukti be achieved, the ultimate goal for any tantric *sadhaka*.'[2]

His magnum opus, *Dattatreya: The Way and the Goal,* fits the giant jigsaw puzzle of his life values and penchants. In this book, he takes a fresh look at the concept of Dattatreya from an Advaitha Vedanta perspective. To understand the importance of this effort, one must understand the symbolism of Dattatreya. JCW explains, 'God has three faces—Brahma, Vishnu and Maheswara. The four dogs at His feet are the four Vedas. *Dattatreya* expounds this principle.' Dattatreya is symbolic of a certain unity in Indian theology—a coming together of the disparate and rival philosophies of Brahma, Vishnu and Maheshwara. The unification in spirit of this Trinity represents a point of synthesis and confluence in these micro-theologies in Hinduism. JCW attributes this love and devotion to Dattatreya to his grandmother and mother, who were pious devotees themselves. The book is the first account of the philosophy of Dattatreya in English, with critical study, commentary and analysis. The *Jeevanmukta Gita* and *Avadhuta Gita* are two key texts propagating the supremacy of Vedanta in Indian thought. The Maharaja's book for the first time provides a translation and analysis drawn from various streams of Indian religious thought.

FOREWORD

THIS book is primarily an attempt on the part of the author to rise above ignorance and obtain a glimpse of the truth. The grace of the Lord has been itself the inspiration for this attempt to serve Him. This humble tribute has been written to interest thinking men in this noble subject and induce them to traverse this great road of love and faith. The author is only too conscious of his own limitations; but, as all that there is in him is of Lord Datta, he has ventured on this token of his devotion.

ŚRĪ GURU DATTĀTREYO VIJAYATE

JCW's foreword to his magnum opus, *Dattatreya*, a commentary on the *Avadhuta Gita*

Away from the cluster of writings on Advaita Vedanta–based topics, an eclectic mix of topics feature in his writings, which are best described as ambassadorial. Just like his attitude as a music composer, his writings play 'fill up the blanks', often connecting the dots between two separate subjects, playing commentator, scientist and artist all at once. He often attempts to connect vertical silos of information in Indian knowledge systems with each other or with the world.

The African Affair

Africa held a special place in JCW's heart. He avidly followed African politics, trade and civilizational developments. Two of his publications are about African and Indo-African studies. A mini-research publication is the *African Survey*. Structured like an economics-meets-policy-advocacy paper, the Maharaja makes a case for fostering better cultural, economic and political ties with inter-tropical Africa. He says the publication would have amply served its purpose, if it stimulates a vital discussion on international position in the near East. The study was timely, given the political regeneration of African countries and the emergence of India as an important power in international affairs after Independence. In 1958, a monograph on *Africa and India*, their past, present and future relations was published by him. A paragraph from this book is rather interesting. Throughout the book, he aligns with Pandit Nehru's policy of 'Panchasheel' and that India is looking at Africa as its partner in a post-colonial world. He compares the political strategies of Eisenhower and Nehru. He notes:

> In other words, the United States has lost ground so far, not gained it; among educated Africans, anti-American sentiment is often pronounced. Jawaharlal Nehru is more likely to be the spiritual father of the new Africa than Dwight D. Eisenhower.

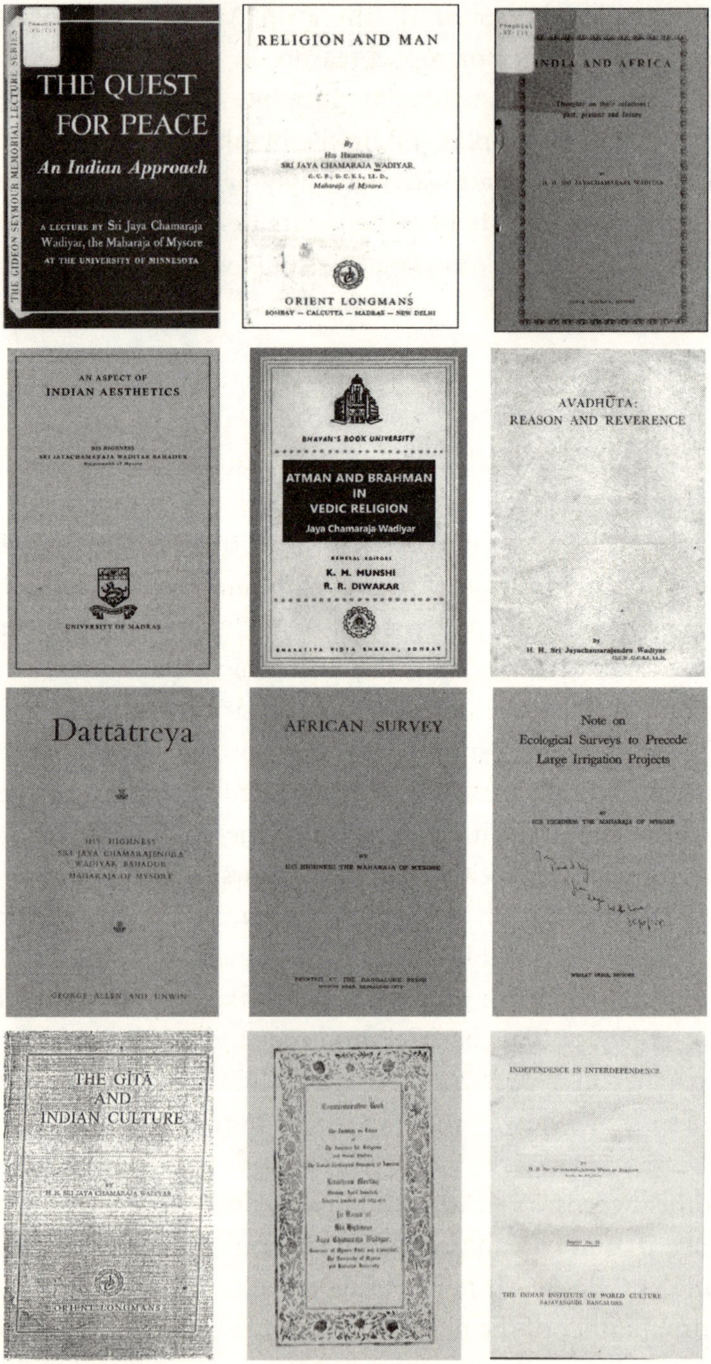

Front covers of JCW's books, publications and writings on philosophy

It is because Nehru has all along unequivocally challenged colonialism and made a plea for African progress.

The role of Indians in Africa today is of even greater significance than yesterday; because India has steadily and unequivocally championed the cause of African Nationalism, in its fight against colonial imperialism. Time and again, the Prime Minister of India has said publicly that there can be no solution to African problems save that which enables the African peoples themselves to decide their future, in consonance with what they consider to be in the best interests of their spiritual well-being. The claims of Africa must first and foremost rest with the Africans.

The democrat in him speaks passionately about the road ahead for Africa and its need to empower voices within. The Maharaja also has supported research that studied the African elephant by several leading conservationalists, which led to a monograph, *The Elephant in East Central Africa*.[3]

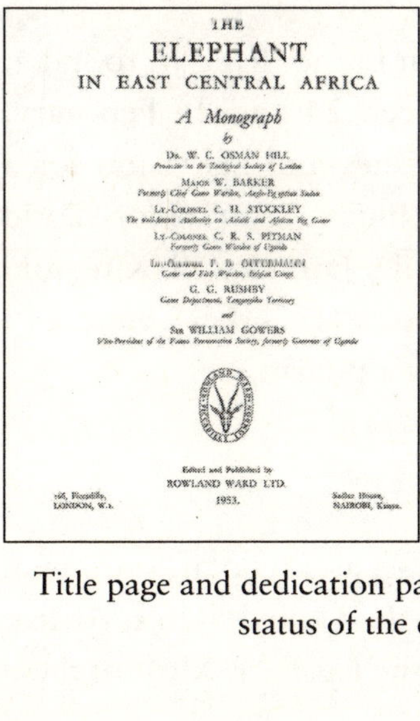

THE

ELEPHANT

IN EAST CENTRAL AFRICA

A Monograph

by

DR. W. C. OSMAN HILL

MAJOR W. BARKER

LT.-COLONEL C. H. STOCKLEY

LT.-COLONEL C. R. S. PITMAN

[illegible]

G. G. RUSHBY

and

SIR WILLIAM GOWERS

Edited and Published by

ROWLAND WARD LTD.

1953.

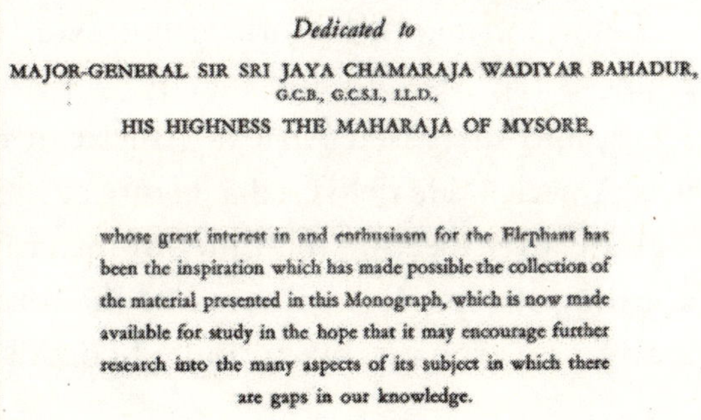

Dedicated to

MAJOR-GENERAL SIR SRI JAYA CHAMARAJA WADIYAR BAHADUR,

G.C.B., G.C.S.I., LL.D.,

HIS HIGHNESS THE MAHARAJA OF MYSORE,

whose great interest in and enthusiasm for the Elephant has been the inspiration which has made possible the collection of the material presented in this Monograph, which is now made available for study in the hope that it may encourage further research into the many aspects of its subject in which there are gaps in our knowledge.

Title page and dedication page of the book commissioned by JCW on the status of the elephant in East Central Africa

He toured the African continent extensively and was a close ally of the Prime Minister of Ghana, Kwame Nkrumah. In a letter to Pandit Nehru, P.C. Alexander, then a bureaucrat in Nehru's secretariat, informs him that a chair for African and Oriental Studies was created at University of Ghana after JCW's suggestion to Nkrumah. He tips off that during JCW's next visit to Ghana, he would be inaugurating this headline-making venture. Later, JCW toured Ghana and delivered the Aggrey–Fraser–Guggisberg Memorial Lecture at the University of Ghana in 1960. The topic of his lecture was 'Traditions, Ideals and Values in the Atomic Age', somewhat reflective of the cultural changes in his world and outside of it.

It was while on one of those lecture tours, that JCW received the dreaded '100 message' on the telegram conveying the sad news of the demise of his mother, Kempu Cheluvaja Ammanni, in Mysore. In the telegram era, code '100' meant death, and would reach the family in a quick instant. Mysore is said to have had telegram services from the time of Nalvadi Krishnaraja Wadiyar, based on Morse Code. The Maharaja aborted the tour plan and returned in great gloom to Mysore—his life would never be the same again, without her trusting net.

Later, during the historic visit of Martin Luther King Jr. to India, King visited Mysore and met JCW between 24 and 26 February, 1959, and discussed African American issues and his vision for a new America. He delivered a lecture at the Indian Institute for World Culture after meeting the Chief Minister B.D. Jatti as well. King told a group of reporters gathered at the airport, 'To other countries I may go as a tourist, but to India I come as a pilgrim.'

The Cultural Ambassador

The Maharaja was in great demand overseas, as a scholar, statesman and thinker. He went on several tours to the United States, Africa, Australia, the Scandinavian countries and the Far East. Most of these were invited lectures, academic tours, coupled with residencies with certain universities. In 1963, he was a special guest of the Australian Federal Government, on a twelve-day visit to various parts of Australia. A newspaper in Canberra described him as 'a Maharaja of many parts who proved to be as dignified and impressive as his title'.

'The Maharajah, who has arrived in Canberra on a goodwill visit, moves with regal dignity and speaks with an academic clarity, which is not surprising.' In a rather short profile, appearing as a strip in the daily, the author covers the juiciest bits of his eclectic personality: 'When free of official duties, the Maharajah is a man with a diversity of interests, classical music and philosophical literature, history, political science, economics, and African affairs attract his attention. He also spends many hours listening to recorded works of Wagner, Mahler, Bach and Beethoven.' The last paragraph lays out a rather interesting perspective on how royals were viewed in that time and age: 'Does he possess the legendary wealth of a Maharaja? He was reported as saying: "We have some amount of wealth, but not as much as people make out. They make it so incredible that I cannot understand it".' The previous year, the Maharaja was invited to deliver several lectures at key American universities. His lecture, 'A Quest for Peace; An Indian Approach,' delivered at the Northrop Memorial Auditorium in 1959, was published by the University of Minneapolis. In the same tour, a whole luncheon was organized in his honour at the Institute of Ethics as part of the Institute for Religious and Social Studies at the Jewish Theological Seminary of America—an honour reserved for few.

If one studies the various subjects of his muse, it is remarkably clear that he kept his intellectual flame burning for all the topics he ever loved. In his *India and Africa* and *African Survey*, one finds he never really let go of his love for political science and international affairs. In his short paper on 'Ecological Surveys to precede large irrigation projects,' his love for wildlife conservation and ecology is clear, consistent with his long-standing activism, leading to him heading the Indian Wildlife Board later in his life. His book, *Atman and Brahman in Vedic Religion,* attempts to provide an Advaitha Vedantic view on the path to salvation, through real knowledge (vidya). *Gita and Indian Culture* attempts to unravel the lucid yet powerful message that the Bhagvad Gita imparts to the world at large. He was indeed a freemason, free within to lay the edifice of his unique legacy of scholarship.

Photographs of JCW's Foreign Travels as a Scholar and Cultural Ambassador

Pictures from JCW's visit to the United States in 1959

Photos from the Maharaja's trip to Australia and the University of Queensland, from where he received his Doctor of Literature degree

Photos from the Maharaja's trip to Australia

Photos from the Maharaja's trip to Australia

The Maharaja registering at The Institute of Ethics luncheon, 20 April 1959, The Jewish Theological Seminary of America, New York City

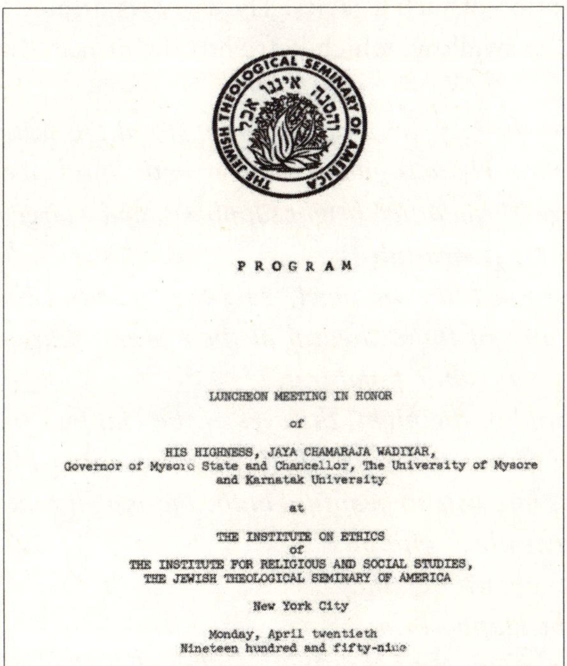

PROGRAM

LUNCHEON MEETING IN HONOR

of

HIS HIGHNESS, JAYA CHAMARAJA WADIYAR,
Governor of Mysore State and Chancellor, The University of Mysore
and Karnatak University

at

THE INSTITUTE ON ETHICS
of
THE INSTITUTE FOR RELIGIOUS AND SOCIAL STUDIES,
THE JEWISH THEOLOGICAL SEMINARY OF AMERICA

New York City

Monday, April twentieth
Nineteen hundred and fifty-nine

Programme of JCW's distinguished lecture and the luncheon given in his honour at the Institute for Ethics

14
THE HAPPY PRINCE

In his short story, 'The Happy Prince', Oscar Wilde in his inimitable style tells the bitter-sweet reality of having a legacy, changing times and the perception of such legacies. The story is narrated through the eyes of a bird, a swallow, which befriends the prince.

> *High above the city, on a tall column, stood the statue of the Happy Prince. He was gilded all over with thin leaves of fine gold, for eyes, he had two bright sapphires, and a large red ruby glowed on his sword-hilt.*
>
> *'He looks just like an angel,' said the Charity Children, as they came out of the cathedral in their bright scarlet cloaks, and their clean, white pinafores.*
>
> *In the cold of the night, the eyes of the Happy Prince were filled with tears, and tears were running down his golden cheeks. His face was so beautiful in the moonlight that the little Swallow was filled with pity.*
>
> *'Who are you?' he said.*
>
> *'I am the Happy Prince.'*
>
> *'Why are you weeping then?' asked the Swallow, 'you have quite drenched me.'*

'When I was alive and had a human heart,' answered the statue, 'I did not know what tears were, for I lived in the Palace of Sans-Souci, where sorrow is not allowed to enter. In the daytime, I played with my companions in the garden, and in the evening, I led the dance in the Great Hall. Round the garden ran a very lofty wall, but I never cared to ask what lay beyond it; everything about me was so beautiful. My courtiers called me the Happy Prince, and happy indeed I was, if pleasure be happiness. So I lived, and so I died. And now that I am dead, they have set me up here so high that I can see all the ugliness and all the misery of my city, and though my heart is made of lead yet I cannot choose but weep.'

JCW's life after 1947 was much like that of this prince. His legacy as a king, a noble one, stood tall, unshakeable; it towered high above. With the transfer of power from that of a sovereign king to a somewhat sartorial Rajapramukh and the job of the Governor of Mysore, his silhouette of power grew thinner. Much like a statue, although identical to the man in form, his administrative powers were now static. Like the statue, he remained magnificent, a heady reminder of a glorious past, standing in majesty even today, and ever so stoic. With his towering presence, he could see, but not move. His life in these new roles were perhaps irksome because unlike a real stone statue, and much like the Happy Prince in Oscar Wilde's story, he got a good glimpse of the pain, hypocrisy and greed that surrounded him.

'Far away,' continued the statue in a low musical voice, 'far away in a little street, there is a poor house. One of the windows is open, and through it I can see a woman seated at a table. Her face is thin and worn, and she has coarse, red hands, all pricked by the needle, for she is a seamstress. She is embroidering passion-flowers on a satin gown for the loveliest

of the Queen's maids-of-honour to wear at the next Court-ball. In a bed in the corner of the room, her little boy is lying ill. He has a fever, and is asking for oranges. His mother has nothing to give him but river water, so he is crying. Swallow, Swallow, little Swallow, will you not bring her the ruby out of my sword-hilt? My feet are fastened to this pedestal and I cannot move.'

He passed over the river, and saw the lanterns hanging to the masts of the ships. He passed over the Ghetto, and saw the old Jews bargaining with each other, and weighing out money in copper scales. At last he came to the poor house and looked in. The boy was tossing feverishly on his bed, and the mother had fallen asleep, she was so tired. In he hopped, and laid the great ruby on the table beside the woman's thimble.

Then the Swallow flew back to the Happy Prince, and told him what he had done. 'It is curious,' he remarked, 'but I feel quite warm now, although it is so cold.'

Nikolai Medtner (5 January 1880–13 November 1951), is still a lesser-known composer in the world of Western classical music. Medtner was a formidable piano virtuoso in his time and was considered a younger Rachimanoff-of-sorts, another Russian piano virtuoso, whom JCW idolized deeply. Medtner was known, like JCW, for his rather keen choices, be it with music or his life with music. He was considered a specialist in Beethoven's music, especially the Fourth Piano Concerto, but seldom played it in concerts. He only played his compositions, and relegated himself to composing in the later part of his life. Born in frigid Moscow, his music sprung melodies that dripped passion. 'Medtner had a natural gift for structure; he was born with the sonata form,' says Paul Stewart, a Canadian pianist who has interpreted his works. 'His compositions are so polyphonic and contrapuntal. It's so dense with melodic material. He has unusual control over melodic material, which develops and fits on top of each other. He composed like a jewellery maker; every single note had a purpose or destiny.' Many hailed Medtner as being born for the sonata form—as an intellectual musician having taken to Beethoven's musical genius in his own way. JCW's idol Rachimanoff himself is said to have dedicated his Fourth Piano Concerto to him, a much younger musician. One can quite understand why JCW was taken in by his music, as there is great resonance in approach to composition and beauty. Medtner was a stickler for the sonata form, and JCW, for the Carnatic kriti. For both, melody and structure are central to their style of composition. Perhaps the most interesting observation is that both seem to compose with a keen eye for sound, beyond musical vocabulary and syntax. Medtner's music is full of melodic soundscapes; JCW's full of sonic imageries using word and melody.

If anything was wrong with Medtner's music, it was the time and place of his birth. First the Russian Revolution broke out in October 1917, drowning his tunes initially, and later World War I played havoc with his ability to record, perform or move out of his country. Post moving to London, Medtner almost never performed, only taught, played and composed privately. Towards the end of his career, World War II made it difficult for him to have his music recorded or performed, because of crumbling orchestra companies and a war-economy. He did not have the faintest clue that a tornado of hope and benefaction from Mysore would ensure that most of his compositions were recorded for posterity. Out of the blue, his trade commissioner in London received a letter from JCW:

> The Palace, Mysore.
> 19th October, 1946.
> Dear Captain Binstead,
>
> This letter is to inform you that His Highness is specially interested in the music of Nicolas Medtner, a great modern composer and pianist, and wishes to form a 'Nicolas Medtner Society', through which it may be possible to make live in the history of music the compositions of a great composer as interpreted by himself. [...]

> How best can the music of a great master of the piano be perpetuated in a fitting manner?
>
> It may be possible to have it done as was done before (viz., the Delius, English Music, and the Beethoven Piano Sonata Societies) through publishing a series of albums of 8 or 10 records each, covering completely the whole range of Medtner's compositions. His Highness would be willing to come forward at once with a donation of £2,000 (later £5,000) towards getting such a Society started. Perhaps HMV, who have already given an album of delightful Medtner pieces, or Columbia, may take up the work of recording Medtner's compositions.
>
> His Highness suggests the three Piano Concertos, all his piano music, the songs (a goodly selection) the Violin and Piano Sonatas, Sonata-Vocalise, Improvisations, etc. [...]
>
> His Highness is uncertain how far such an enterprise would be successful, but would like to have your reactions, after consulting numerous musical friends. [...]
>
> May I suggest that direct contact with the composer himself would be desirable, as he may be happy and eager to help in the formation of the Society with the generous help and patronage of His Highness?

Soon an advisory committee was cooked up by Binstead, with the music-literati including Compton Mackenzie and his brother-in-law Christopher Stone (joint editors of the *Gramophone*) and recording producer Walter Legge, who went on to seek JCW's help for his Philharmonic Orchestra. Upon hearing of this strange and kind benefactor, Medtner's reaction was thus: 'He moved towards his pianoforte, which stood just by the window of the drawing room. The spring sunshine caught his countenance as he played for us a Fairy Tale—and how appropriate—for it must have seemed to Medtner like a fairytale!' His wife Anna noted that in the autumn of his life, the project gave him new life and energy. It is not clear if they ever met, but Medtner dedicated his third concerto to JCW. The

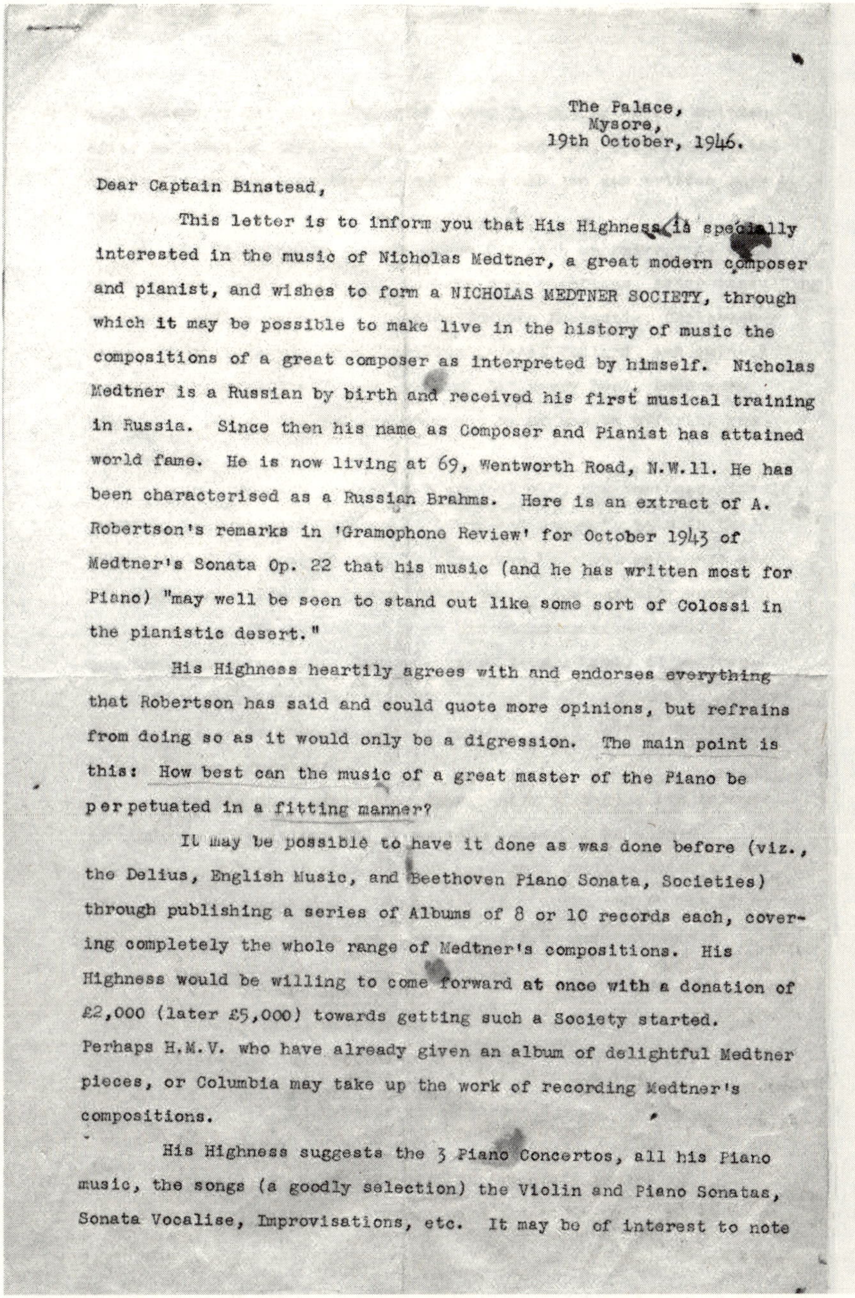

The Palace,
Mysore,
19th October, 1946.

Dear Captain Binstead,

This letter is to inform you that His Highness is specially interested in the music of Nicholas Medtner, a great modern composer and pianist, and wishes to form a NICHOLAS MEDTNER SOCIETY, through which it may be possible to make live in the history of music the compositions of a great composer as interpreted by himself. Nicholas Medtner is a Russian by birth and received his first musical training in Russia. Since then his name as Composer and Pianist has attained world fame. He is now living at 69, Wentworth Road, N.W.11. He has been characterised as a Russian Brahms. Here is an extract of A. Robertson's remarks in 'Gramophone Review' for October 1943 of Medtner's Sonata Op. 22 that his music (and he has written most for Piano) "may well be seen to stand out like some sort of Colossi in the pianistic desert."

His Highness heartily agrees with and endorses everything that Robertson has said and could quote more opinions, but refrains from doing so as it would only be a digression. The main point is this: How best can the music of a great master of the Piano be perpetuated in a fitting manner?

It may be possible to have it done as was done before (viz., the Delius, English Music, and Beethoven Piano Sonata, Societies) through publishing a series of Albums of 8 or 10 records each, covering completely the whole range of Medtner's compositions. His Highness would be willing to come forward at once with a donation of £2,000 (later £5,000) towards getting such a Society started. Perhaps H.M.V. who have already given an album of delightful Medtner pieces, or Columbia may take up the work of recording Medtner's compositions.

His Highness suggests the 3 Piano Concertos, all his Piano music, the songs (a goodly selection) the Violin and Piano Sonatas, Sonata Vocalise, Improvisations, etc. It may be of interest to note

Correspondence between JCW and Medtner from 1946 till the time of Medtner's demise in 1951

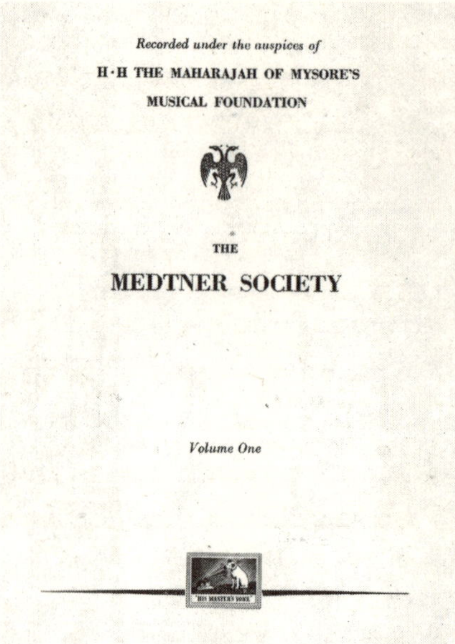

Recorded under the auspices of

H·H THE MAHARAJAH OF MYSORE'S

MUSICAL FOUNDATION

THE

MEDTNER SOCIETY

Volume One

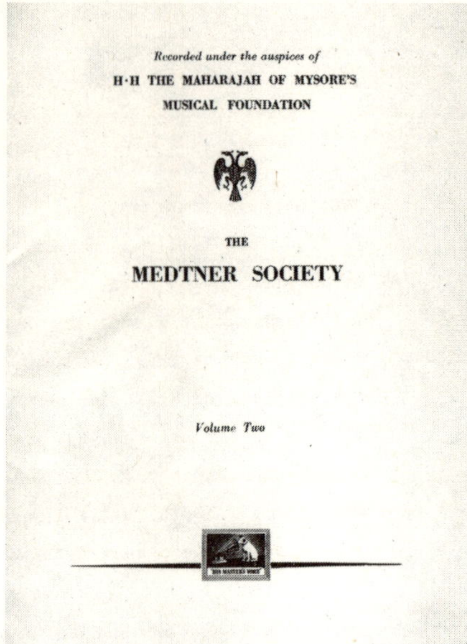

Recorded under the auspices of

H·H THE MAHARAJAH OF MYSORE'S

MUSICAL FOUNDATION

THE

MEDTNER SOCIETY

Volume Two

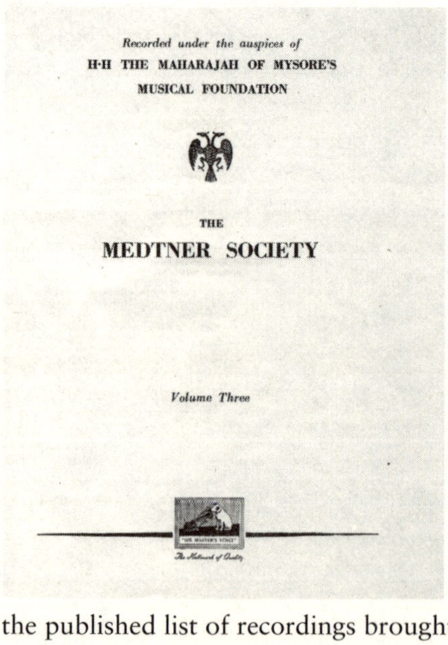

Recorded under the auspices of

H·H THE MAHARAJAH OF MYSORE'S

MUSICAL FOUNDATION

THE

MEDTNER SOCIETY

Volume Three

Front pages of the published list of recordings brought out by JCW's Musical Foundation through the Medtner Society. Over sixty of Medtner's works were recorded and made available through this initiative

Nikolai Medtner

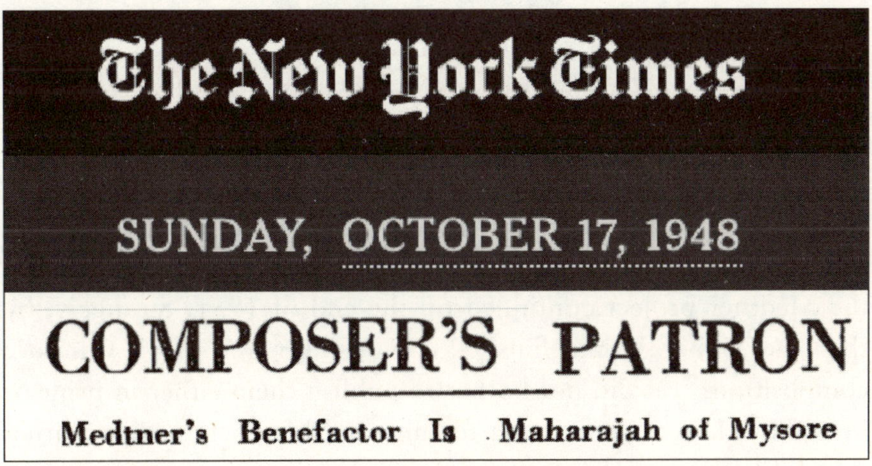

The New York Times

SUNDAY, OCTOBER 17, 1948

COMPOSER'S PATRON

Medtner's Benefactor Is Maharajah of Mysore

Headline of an article carried in the *New York Times*, 17 October 1948, about JCW's support to document the creative genius of Medtner in gramophone records

first recordings made under the auspices of the Medtner Society—the Canzona matinata and Sonata tragica, on 19 March 1947—initiated a series of historic and standalone recordings available of the master. Medtner recorded his three piano concertos, as well as his sonatas, chamber music, numerous songs and shorter works. He must have passed away in great peace, as he saw most of his compositions come to life between 1948 and 1949.The Medtner Society founded in 1948, lives on even today, championing the cause of this very original voice in Western classical music.

Gramophone disc inner sticker labels of Medtner's third concerto dedicated to JCW

In another universe in Mysore, the music grew terse in JCW's own life. Despite growing financial woes and tussles with the government of Mysore, and later the government of Karnataka, his funding to the Medtner project continued till the end of 1951. Strangely, by then the Maharaja had finished composing many of his Carnatic compositions, yet did not bother to publish them either in print or in audio. He was spending a fortune and life energies in curating musical legacies of others instead. There is no surviving recording of him playing the piano either, except for memories of his family members who speak of his affair with the keys.

Most clearly, unlike the other princes of the time, such acts of benevolence came at a time when most of his peers were busy consolidating their own legacies and funds. Fully aware of the song-and-dance sequences that were being played out in other princely kingdoms in garnering money, JCW quips in a letter to his chief minister K.C. Reddy:

> You might have perhaps read in the newspapers that the Nizam of Hyderabad has created with the assent of the Government of India, a trust of 16 crores of rupees in favour of his sons. It is reported that this trust is in addition to other trusts amounting to some crores that have been created by him. When compared to this and to the private properties owned and possessed by other rulers, the so-called private property of Mysore palace pales into insignificance. It is not known why a decision on this question is pending so long.

> *'Swallow, Swallow, little Swallow,' said the Prince, 'far away across the city, I see a young man in a garret. He is leaning over a desk covered with papers, and in a tumbler by his side there is a bunch of withered violets. His hair is brown and crisp, and his lips are red as a pomegranate, and he has large and dreamy eyes. He is trying to finish a play for the Director of the Theatre, but he is too cold to write any more. There is no fire in the grate, and hunger has made him faint.*
>
> *'Alas! I have no ruby now,' said the Prince; 'my eyes are all that I have left. They are made of rare sapphires, which were brought out of India a thousand years ago. Pluck out one of them and take it to him. He will sell it to the jeweller, and buy food and firewood, and finish his play.'*

Richard Strauss was no Medtner. When he passed away, he left behind a massive amount of composed work, in literally every major genre at that time: tone poems, lieders, orchestral works, keyboard and chamber works, solo instruments with orchestras, vocal and choral works. Strauss was also on the cover of *TIME* magazine in 1927, denoting his national and international fame while alive.

Criticized for his political diplomacy in not being anti-Nazi party, he held many powerful positions in Nazi Germany including the head of the Reichsmusikkammer, which was criticized for propagating 'good German music' as opposed to Jewish composers, atonal music and jazz. Towards the end of his life, he was embittered by the developments in post-war Germany, where his wealth was seized and he was forced to live a meagre existence. He wrote the *Four Last Songs*, on the subject of dying in 1948: 'Frühling', 'September', 'Beim Schlafengehen', and the haunting 'Im Abendrot' (At Sunset). The last one, 'Im Abendrot' (At Sunset), ends with the line 'Is this perhaps death?' Writing to the most celebrated Wagnerian Soprano Kirsten Flagstad in 1949, he noted: '...I have the pleasure to provide to you my *Four Last Songs* with orchestra, which are currently in print in London; to give their premier performance in an orchestral concert with a first class conductor and orchestra...' In a most stark answer to his last song, it was death for him after this. Strauss passed away without hearing his very last songs performed. JCW decided to sponsor its premiere and live recording at Royal Albert Hall with Wilhelm Furtwängler conducting the Philharmonia Orchestra, with Flagstad as the soprano, just as Strauss has wished! This patronage came at a huge cost of some $5000, monumental and massive at that time. This historic recording is still hailed as 'one of the greatest romances in the history of the gramophone'.

At home in Mysore, matters were very much like how they had been for Richard Strauss in post-war Germany. Impoverished by war, and battling newfound-'bureau-crazy', which was chipping away at his spirit, his desk penned many songs of protest. In the letter dated 31 January 1949, to the Chief Secretary, it is stated that:

> ...the buildings belonging to the Palace and occupied by the military units will have to be acquired by the government and the value thereof has to be paid by the government to Palace funds, including the value for the lands on which these buildings have been constructed. Acquisition of buildings necessarily implies payment of compensation at the rates

prevailing at the time of acquisition and not at the time of original construction. The compensation now claimed is well below the market rates. Hence I shall be glad if you could kindly have this question settled immediately.

As clearly written in his letter to Sri K.C. Reddy, Chief Minister to the government of Mysore, Bengaluru, dated 20 December 1950, the irritations with a new financial reality had begun:

After the reduction of the Civil List from 42 lakhs to 26 lakhs, we are finding it extremely difficult to balance the palace budget. A sum of 26 lakhs would have been adequate in normal times before the war, but in these abnormal days, when the prices of almost all commodities are soaring up every day, the sum would be rather inadequate to meet even normal expenditure. We are paying a sum of 6.5 lakhs of rupees towards the pay of the Palace employees and a sum of 3.5 to 4 lakhs of rupees towards the dearness allowance alone. It is learnt that the private properties of the other rulers in India have been finalised and settled, and that it is only in Mysore that this question remains unsettled still. Your not having settled these questions for a long time puts me into a very embarrassing position. As I am most anxious that these questions should not be kept pending any longer. I shall be very pleased if you could kindly settle them very quickly.

'Dear little Swallow,' said the Prince, 'you tell me of marvellous things, but more marvellous than anything is the suffering of men and of women. There is no Mystery so great as Misery. Fly over my city, little Swallow, and tell me what you see there.'

The swallow flew over the great city, and saw the rich making merry in their beautiful houses, while the beggars were sitting at the gates. He flew into dark lanes, and saw the white faces of starving children looking out listlessly at the black streets. Under the archway of a bridge two little boys were lying in one another's arms to try and keep themselves warm. 'How hungry we are!' they said. 'You must not lie here,' shouted the Watchman, and they wandered out into the rain.

Then he flew back and told the Prince what he had seen.

'I am covered with fine gold,' said the Prince, 'you must take it off, leaf by leaf, and give it to my poor; the living always think that gold can make them happy.'

Leaf after leaf of the fine gold the Swallow picked off, till the Happy Prince looked quite dull and grey. Leaf after leaf of the fine gold he brought to the poor, and the children's faces grew rosier, and they laughed and played games in the street. 'We have bread now!' they cried.

The sudden demise of my father and uncle had struck a severe blow on my mind. My mind leaned more and more towards Adhyatma. I was face to face before the cycle of birth and death. I had to resolve the tangle.

At that critical moment came succour—Isavasya Upanishad. I studied it with the help of its translation. My mind was steadied. I wanted to read the Vedas and the Upanishads in their original Sanskrit language. I earnestly pursued the learning of Sanskrit.

Then another thought crossed my mind. I had the good fortune of having the needed facility to learn Sanskrit. How many people have that privilege? Our people must be enabled to have access to this great heritage through their own language.

This noble intent initiated another mammoth service to the preservation of Indian knowledge systems. The *Sri Jayachamarajendra Granthamala* was started—with the goal of translating the greatest of Sanskrit works to Kannada. It was a gigantic undertaking, to recruit and manage an army of Sanskrit and Kannada scholars and editors. The entire *Rig Veda* was translated to Kannada in thirty-five large volumes, the first volume appearing in 1948 and the last released in 1965! Despite his descent from the throne and through challenging times, he kept his commitment to the project, liquidating quite many private properties to fund this gift to Kannadigas and Indians to come. Late H. Gangadhara Shastry, court astrologer and Dharmadhikari of Mysore Palace, who himself has contributed substantially to the above works, has stated that the Maharaja used to study each and every one of these works and discuss them with the authors. It seems on a festival night on Shivaratri, he was summoned in the middle of the night and advised to simplify the use of some difficult Kannada words in one of the books. (See Appendix—for a list of books published under this series.)

It is in testing times that the man shows remarkable character and grace. One must be the king of one's inner kingdom to maintain this poise, when everything you know as your identity is soon to be stripped. It takes an emperor of heart to respond to such situational adversity with the inner poise of an Avadhuta—it is as if he channelled all this chaos to fuel his creative and benefactorial pursuits. To do this when one is a king is one thing, but to do it while one's own ancestral legacy is being methodically disbanded calls for a strength of purpose beyond duty. It is as if JCW continued to perform his Rajadharma, fully oblivious to political times and changes. Such acts of fortitude are only possible by a maverick, and a powerful one at that.

Pages from the *Jayachamarajendra Granthamala series*

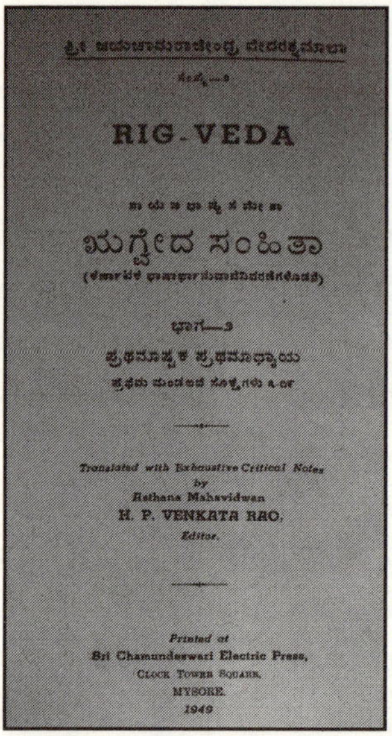

RIG-VEDA

ಋಗ್ವೇದ ಸಂಹಿತಾ

Translated with Exhaustive Critical Notes
by
Asthana Mahavidwan
H. P. VENKATA RAO,
Editor.

Printed at
Sri Chamundeswari Electric Press,
Clock Tower Square,
MYSORE.
1949

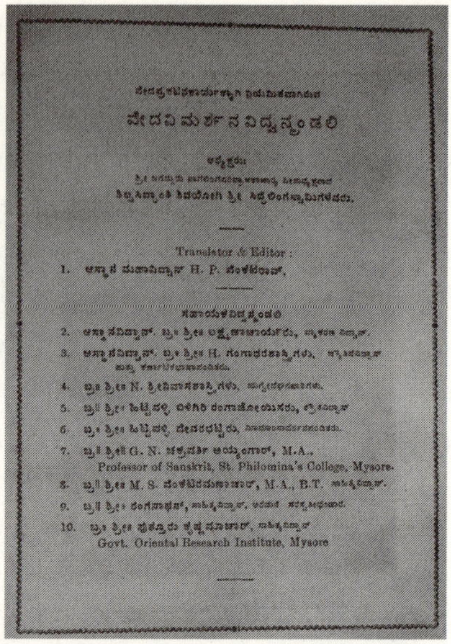

ವೇದವಿಮರ್ಶನವಿದ್ವನ್ಮಂಡಲಿ

Translator & Editor :

1. H. P.
4. N.
7. G. N. M.A.,
Professor of Sanskrit, St. Philomina's College, Mysore.
8. M. S. M.A., B.T.
10. Govt. Oriental Research Institute, Mysore

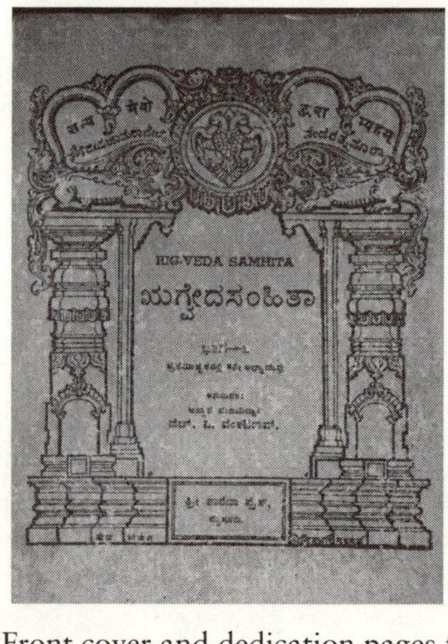

Front cover and dedication pages from the *Jayachamarajendra Granthamala* series. The Maharaja funded the translation of *Rigveda Samhita* in Kannada, the only available translation of this Rigvedic treasure; a gift for Kannadigas and Indic scholars

At that moment a curious crack sounded inside the statue, as if something had broken. The fact is that the leaden heart had snapped right in two. It certainly was a dreadfully hard frost. Early the next morning the Mayor was walking in the square below in company with the Town Councillors. As they passed the column, he looked up at the statue: 'Dear me! How shabby the Happy Prince looks!' he said.

'How shabby indeed!' cried the Town Councillors, who always agreed with the Mayor; and they went up to look at it.

So they pulled down the statue of the Happy Prince. 'As he is no longer beautiful, he is no longer useful,' said the Art Professor at the University.

It is common knowledge that the Mysore rulers were having a civil list of their own for the past many decades, when such a thing as a civil list was unknown in any other state in India. The entire state income formed more or less the Ruler's Civil List, and they were not utilising any portion of the state revenue beyond their civil list for their personal expenditure. Besides, the distinction between the private properties belonging to the palace and the state properties has been maintained in the Mysore state right from the beginning.

All of the information that is available in the palace office regarding palace private properties has been furnished to government without any reservation. If inspite of it, the government feels any doubt or suspicion in the matter, I have already told you that I have absolutely no objection to your deputing an officer of the status of a Deputy Commissioner specifically for this purpose for a month or two, so that he could go round, make enquiries, examine the available records and satisfy himself about the correctness of the information furnished. I am most anxious that you should see to it that the settlement is expedited, since this question is pending for a long time.[1]

The deep embitterment had begun, within and around him. The only solace was his 'chitprabhananda'—the bliss that emanated from within. That inner bliss continued to touch the lives of others through acts of benevolence remembered even today. In 1954, Ramanathan Krishnan, a 17-year-old became the first Asian player to win the boys' singles title at Wimbledon. Ramanathan Krishnan's inclusion and first trip to Wimbledon was funded by JCW. E.A.S. Prasanna, famous cricketer/off-spin bowler, fondly remembers how the Maharaja took the trouble to personally convince his father to let him travel to the West Indies as part of the Indian cricket team.

During this time, his investment in faith and Rajadharma remained undeterred. He built three temples in Mysore city. The most famous Bhuvaneshwari Temple located inside the Mysore Palace lies on the northern side of the Palace Fort with Varahaswamy temple to its south. It was constructed by JCW in the year 1951, along with the installation of a copper Surya Mandala, a family heirloom inside the temple. A special pooja is offered every Rathasapthami day to this mandala. The main idol of Bhuvaneshwari was carved by the famous sculptor of Mysore, Shilpa Siddhanti Siddalingaswamy, who also initiated the Maharaja into the secrets of Srividya Upasana. In 1953, a unique Gayathri temple came into being in the temple premises—located in the south-east corner of the fort in a direction opposite to the ancient Trinayaneshara swamy temple. Gayathri Devi is depicted with five faces (Panchamukhi) representing the Pancha pranas—Prana, Apana, Vyana, Udana and Samana, and the three forms of Gayathri Devi—Savithri, Gayathri and Saraswathi—documenting the iconographical and mythological knowledge associated with the Gayathri concept.

Far away from the hustle bustle of Mysore palace, a quaint temple constructed by him weaves a story of him seeking an heir for Mysore. While visiting the Kamakameshwari Temple behind Pasupatinath Temple in Nepal, the Maharaja made a vow that if blessed with a male progeny, he would construct a temple for the unique iconography of Kama Kameshwari. Lord Shiva here is depicted in human form with Kameshwari, the one who drives and fulfils the desires of her devotees. The iconography of Kama Kameshwari is very rare, as compared to the temples devoted to the various avatars of Shiva, such as Bhairava, Sadashiva, Dakshinamurthy, etc. Built in a fascinating medley of the Dravidian and Mysore sculptural styles, the main idol symbolises the coming together of the desired and the desirer. Indeed the Maharaja's desire for a son came true on 20 February 1953, with the birth of Srikantadatta Narasimharaja Wadiyar, after which the temple was consecrated in 1954. All three Temples were sculpted by the Maharaja's Guru and famous sculptor, Shilpi Siddalingaswamy.

Then they melted the statue in a furnace, and the Mayor held a meeting of the Corporation to decide what was to be done with the metal. 'We must have another statue, of course,' he said, 'and it shall be a statue of myself.' 'Of myself,' said each of the Town Councillors, and they quarrelled. When I last heard of them they were quarrelling still.

'What a strange thing!' said the overseer of the workmen at the foundry. 'This broken lead heart will not melt in the furnace. We must throw it away.' So they threw it on a dust-heap where the dead Swallow was also lying.

'Bring me the two most precious things in the city,' said God to one of His Angels; and the Angel brought Him the leaden heart and the dead bird.

'You have rightly chosen,' said God, 'for in my garden of Paradise this little bird shall sing for evermore, and in my city of gold the Happy Prince shall praise me.'

The temples built by JCW in the Mysore
Palace temple premises

The temples built by JCW in the Mysore Palace temple premises

In an interview to Bernard Weinraub of the *New York Times* in 1973, after the stripping of privy purses to all Indian Royalty, JCW waxes in a melancholy vein: 'Sometimes one thinks of the past. One thinks of the entertaining, of playing a role. It was quite pleasant, of course, but there's no sense lingering on the past, is there? You have to make the best of what's available now.' Weinraub describes the Maharaja's new durbar as 'the ailing Maharaja of Mysore in a dimly lit room piled high with books, magazines and phonograph records.' His real companions, his music, his books and his knowledge vestitures had not deserted him. At the prospect of turning over the Mysore palace to the government, he said, 'It is being done with great regret, but what can one do? I'll just occupy a couple of rooms, I'm not quite sure. I'll do some travelling, perhaps some lecturing, things like that.'

'I have no real bitterness,' he added. 'I think of my mother and father. How they entertained! It was so long ago, but I do think of it. One likes to recall it like a dream, a nice dream.' With the Dussehra festival abandoned, the throne a grim reminder of lost power, the privy purse abolished, and the financial vice gripping at his spirit, his health suffered. In his last few years, the Maharaja is said to have been quite reclusive. According to family accounts, the passing away of his first child, Smt. Gayatri Devi, in 1974, due to cancer wounded him deeply and he never really emotionally recovered from it till his end.

Just before he passed away on 23 September 1974, the Maharaja travelled to Shringeri, the abode of Sharade, the Goddess of knowledge—his last pilgrimage. His Carnatic kriti, 'Vandeham Sada Sharadaam' must have been on his lips as it is today on the lips of devotees who hear this kriti during the several utsavas at Shringeri. As he sought the darshan of the Jagadguru, whom he revered deeply, he is said to have told the Jagadguru that this would be his last trip to Shringeri. As he passed onto the lap of the Mother Goddess, the world mourned a scholar, a benefactor, a king, a figure whose destinies were entwined with Mysore's in more ways than one. Mysore had lost its last Maharaja.

15
THE MAVERICK MANODHARMA

Talking Cantonese while you think in Sanskrit? Thinking about Carnatic swaras in cycle of fifths? Jazz be-bop scats in Carnatic sollukattu? A Spinoz-ian take on Advaitha Vedanta? Maverick geniuses work this way. Life's mystical energies speak through them to produce work that remains unboxed, fresh, standalone, and untarnished. Even the timeline of when and how his many passions held centrestage in JCW's life is a case in point. It is well-documented in writings about JCW that he dreamt of a life as a concert pianist, wanted to study with the famous pianist Rachimanoff and was even accepted as his student. The marvellous Mysore throne usurped those dreams as a whole kingdom came his way. Strangely, there is no documented evidence of his piano performances except an anecdotal recollection by some at Bangalore's Gayana Samaja. This could be because like horse riding, hunting, ritual worship and other pursuits, playing music was a private affair for the royals. There are no available concert announcement records of his piano recitals either as a soloist or with his musically gifted sister, Rani Vijaya Devi. After his coronation, he found a new passion for Carnatic music; he devoured Carnatic music theory and composition in a few years. His musical enterprise was captured in 97-odd Carnatic compositions, not a piano concerto, or a symphony. He never really returned to Carnatic composition in the 1950s as per available records and was consumed by living out his dreams in Western Classical music by reviving the Philharmonic Orchestra and starting the Medtner Society between 1947 and 1951. Somewhat simultaneously, his most ambitious service to Kannada literature in the form of the Jayachamaraja Granthamala and Vedrathnamala had started, which went on till 1965. All of this went on, amidst great political din surrounding him while being Governor of Mysore and Madras. He found redemption in research and writing, and behold, his magnum opus, *Dattatreya: The Way and the Goal,* was published in 1957. Post his exit as Governor of Madras, he donned a new role, as an ambassador of Indian culture and lectured abroad at many prestigious universities in the United States, Australia and Africa. A spate of illnesses had started to slow his endeavours down by the late 1960s and a couple of years before his death, he is reported to have turned inward, studying philosophy and adhyatmic literature. His life was like a river, sometimes in great spate, sometimes in tranquil flow, sometimes subterranean, and sometimes in a river-fall.

Manodharma could be understood as the sense, sensibilities and sensorialities which govern a person's position on life's dilemmas, uncertainties and predicaments. Neuropsychologically, every person, as a product of his genes, context, education and life experiences, brings a certain 'operating system' that governs his actions, reactions, decisions, and creative exposition. A person's manodharma is at the core of his self-expression. In Carnatic music, musical improvisation is called manodharma, as it is this 'sense' of the mind, which powers one's musical attitudes to curating beautiful experiences through sound. It is an unconscious determinant, something that the person himself may not be perhaps aware of—a certain framework of values, memory and method. In a way, it's the 'man' at the steering wheel of an individual's mind.

A Manodharma of Synthesis and Confluence

A maverick's manodharma is the only constant between seemingly disconnected behaviour and attitudes in the outer sphere. It explains the motivations behind actions that are undertaken in the most unpredictable of places, almost irreverent to strife and in the most testing of times. The Maharaja's stories of benefaction point to this. His efforts to give new life to the Philharmonia Orchestra in London were done while the most excruciatingly painful transitions of power were happening in his life. Yet, it was done, and in great style. Much like his description of the sea (one of the tutors of the Avadhuta in Hindu literature). In his lecture on 'Reason and Reverence', he describes: 'The sea is calm and sublime, unfathomable and extensive. When huge floods swell it, it does not overflow its boundary or wane in the dry season, affluence does not intoxicate him nor does provocation depress him. He is neither elated by the one nor depressed by the other, very much like the ocean.' In another interesting quote from the same lecture, he advocates how a yogi must sport his atman: 'So must the Yogi or *Avadhuta* sport his own *Atman,* carefree, unconcerned and immersed only in bliss.'

In his many divergent mediums of expression: music, poetry, philosophical commentary, and curative writing, there are some beautiful convergences. His manodharma is one that finds beauty in synthesis. Melding old with the new; new harmonic vocabularies in an older form of Carnatic kriti. A new perspective on an ancient *Avadhuta Gita*. Synthesizing knowledge on wildlife conservation and ecology into administrative schemes. His manodharma strove to make journeys; the unbounded journey from the form to the formless, from darkness to light, from death to immortality—as the very first shloka of the *Avadhuta Gita* prays for:

asato ma sadgamaya
tamaso ma jyotirgamaya
mrtyorma amrtam gamaya
om shanti shanti shanti

Lead me from the untruth to the truth
Lead me from darkness to light
Lead me from death to immortality
Om Peace Peace Peace

Another unshakeable aspect of his manodharma lurks behind all the machinations of poetry, prosody and prose: a firm awareness of the nature of truth, in the contemporaneity of truth. His realized perception within that true knowledge is affirmed in the current. It is as if he knew that the pursuit of knowledge is moving forward—not about putting your back to the past but backing the present into the future. His numerous study tours, on the study of African civilization, the Scandinavian countries and Australia, were from the manodharma of a seeker of truth—a student of knowledge, seeking to construct knowledge based on his experience. Not a mere consumer of knowledge of what is read, memorized and uttered. Even though he was a voracious reader and a bibliophile beyond cure, his pursuit of truth was firmly engaged in the many 'thought pots' he cooked himself. Much like the Kannada adage, *'Pratyaksha kandaru, pramanisi nodu'* (Even if you witness a truth unravel, examine it). His manodharma was one of great equanimity. Many scholars fall into the trap of intellectual activism—trying to resurrect older knowledge, hypotheses or dogmas. Many in the spirit of post-modernist scientific jingoism shun all older knowledge, trying to make fire all over again!

The Maharaja was a Freemason. His inner quest for freedom is a dominant theme in his poetry as well. Such imageries are strewn all over his Carnatic kritis and his writings. He describes the Devi as the 'Antarmukha Jyotirmaya Kalyani'—the auspicious one, who reigns as the inner light, and the one who gives 'Antyarahita kaivalya'—the eternal kaivalya or jeevanmukti. In a lecture as part of the Freemason Society, a society of men who believed in being architects of self, communities and realities, he succinctly describes his greatest motivations. One can also say that it is this spirit to illuminate and be illuminated that informs many of his adhyatmic writings:

> Light—Light—and more Light is what all of us need in abundant measure. Most of us would remember the story of that Greek Philosopher Diogenes, who used to walk about the streets of Athens with a lighted lantern in his hand even during the day time. Children used to follow him about and make fun of him for doing that. But when intelligent and grown up folk asked him why he carried a lighted lantern, Diogenes used to say, 'What we need in the world is intellectual illumination'.

In the life of the Maharaja, one finds beautiful life attitudes, orientations to the 'problem' of should East meet the West? Can one adore the classical yet subscribe to the idea of changing classicism? Can one seek the vintage and viable at the same time? Can one use intercultural engagements to enhance one's identity in one's tradition? His life leaves us with such sublime questions—his manodharma leading the way, pointing to the unseen. It is his manodharma that generations to come should remember and emulate.

A King-Sized Life

Everything about the Maharaja was in addition to regal, king-size. King-size in the real metaphorical sense of the word too. In Dr S. Krishnamurthy's book, *Sangeetha Samaya,* he recounts how when the Maharaja went hunting, he only shot elephants and tigers. Secondly, he had a preference for solo elephants with a tusk-size of four–five feet, which in today's world would be considered a mammoth! This mammoth-size fancy is expressed in many other choices of his life. If he were to wield the pen, it would be to comment on the mammoth texts of Vedantic absolutism—the Avadhuta Gita and the Jeevanmukta Gita. If he composed, each piece was to be a formidable 'game'. It was to be in heavy prosodical Sanskrit, with the most difficult metres and taalas and rare Ragas. There was a decisive expression of his persona in every aspect he touched. If he thought of administrative modules, they were ambitious multi-pronged five-year plans—a five-year plan for developing Mysore's irrigational resources at two crores in 1946! The genius of that idea was to change the attitude of administration from a manage-troubleshoot mode to a proactive envision-incentivize-grow mode. Interestingly, all of the changes and losses in his life were king-size too. To relinquish the power over Mysore was a gigantic change, so was dealing with the abolition of the Rajapramukh title, and later the privy purse.

Many princely states contributed towards India's battle against the Axis. It was with this king-size vision and administrative foresight that JCW thought of an indigenous aircraft hub, not just for Mysore, but also for the country at large. His generosity was also king-size and king-like. Whether it was funding Ramanathan Krishnan's efforts in tennis or funding E.A.S. Prasanna's sojourn to the West Indies, his actions were always large-hearted. It was not sufficient to help fund the recording of Nikolai Medtner's music, he went all out and created a Medtner Society, which remains active even today. His activism for the ancient and Indian knowledge systems were of mammoth proportions. His translation project of the Rig Veda is perhaps the biggest undertaking in India's recent history, running into two decades of research, translation and publication-related activities. He was not satisfied with merely organizing a seminar or two on this topic. As he mentions in the first chapter of *Dattatreya*, that Ishvaranugraha was so strong in his inner world that the divine force operated through him as a river in rise. He felt very strongly for the Hindu crusade in a world of religious evangelism and prejudice. Thus was co-founded the Vishwa Hindu Parishad (VHP) on 29 August 1964, a global consortium to further the sustenance of Sanatana Dharma. VHP has continued its activism and service for the cause of Hinduism in a world of great anthropocentric bias and Western-dominated Indology. At the second meeting in New Delhi on 24 November 1964, it was announced that 'a great fillip to the activities of the Parishad was provided by HH the Maharaja of Mysore, Shri. Jaya Chamaraja Wadiyar by accepting to be the President of the Parishad and Sir C.P. Ramaswamy Aiyar as Vice-President'.

'Diligent practice of religion and morality,' according to him, 'could solve the problems of Hindu society as of other societies of the world'. He stressed the cultivation of spirituality and non-violence in everyday life:

> There are many social and religious problems in Hindu society to be solved without delay. And this can be done only by the cultivation of ethical and spiritual qualities. To the Hindu belonging to any sect or creed, the spiritual values of truth (*satya*) and non-violence (*ahimsa*) come first, and the biological values like strength and vitality and material values, like wealth and pleasure, occupy only a subordinate place.

What makes such a life 'maverickian' is not the large breadth of its engagements. His deep patriotism for Hindu culture did not prevent him from perceiving great value in the music of a Medtner, whose religion was perhaps only music. His adroit command over adhyatma did not trap him in the guiles of a critic or a pondering philosopher, but allowed him to be one who jumped into the arena, to make music, to write, to think, to feel, be judged and criticized. His acute sense of classicism in Carnatic music did not blind him to the beauties of European music. Even in such aesthetically disconnected musical traditions, he perceived a certain unity. A quote from his book *Dattatreya* sums it succinctly: 'Knowledge of undifferentiated purity springs in the inspired men, only by the grace of God and saves them from great peril.'

When enumerated as a mere list of achievements of the Maharaja, one may simply dismiss them as duties of an able lord, leader or scholar, but it is only upon closer inspection that one can find the workings of a genius—a mind that is firmly crowned in divine grace, drenched by a creative shakti. A colossus of arts, and a life of titanic significance. His Majesty indeed!

NOTES AND REFERENCES

2: The Philosopher on the Throne

1. The Divine Right of Kings was a doctrine used by monarchies in Europe and Britain to legitimize perpetuation of the idea of dynasty and keeping the mantle in hereditary succession.
2. Absolute monarchy is a concept of transfer of leadership rights based on lineage. French philosopher and leader of the enlightenment Voltaire opposed this idea and delineated the qualities of monarch away from mere pedigree.
3. *Katha Upanishad*, Adhyaya I, valli 2-9.
4. Read more about his contributions to India's role in World War II and to national building in chapters 'Administrative Marvels' and 'Sovereign Souvenirs'.

3: The Wadiyar Legacy

1. Barbara Ramusack, *The Indian Princes and their States* (Cambridge: Cambridge University Press), 2003
2. Mohammad Iqbal Chawla, *Wavell and the Dying Days of the Raj: Britain's Penultimate Viceroy in India* (Karachi: Oxford University Press), 2011
3. Residency Records of Mysore/ IO: RR/2 (37/354): Resident of Mysore to the Government of India, 23 December 1920.

4. Tony McClenaghan, *Indian Princely Medals*, (Lancer Publishers), 1996.
5. Makara, the mascot of the Hoysala empire, an anthropomorphic entity with the mouth of a crocodile, ears of a cow, eyes of a monkey, body of a pig, feet of a lion and tail of a peacock.
6. Sharabha, was a mythical eight-legged fusion of man, eagle and lion, an anthropomorphic entity, enshrined in many temples of the Chola period such as the Kampaheshwarar Temple, near Thanjavur. The iconography of the Sharabha is diverse and has changed over many centuries.
7. John Marshall, *Taxila: An Illustrated Account of Archaeological Excavations* (revised edition), (Cambridge: Cambridge University Press), 2013.
8. Alan Dundes (ed.), *Sacred Narrative Readings in the Theory of Myth* (Berkeley: University of California Press), 1984.
9. *Critical Edition of Mahabharata* by Vedavyasa, edited by the likes of V. S. Sukhtankar, S. K. Belvalkar, S. K. De, Prof. Dr. R. N. Dandekar. The Critical Edition enjoys the status of being one of the most prestigious and appreciated editorial works of the world. This edition was prepared with painstaking effort by scholars over a period of about five decades, after consulting 1,259 manuscripts.
10. P.V. Nanjaraje Urs, *Mysooru–Noorinnooru Varshagala Hinde*, (Abhiruchi Prakashana), 2011.
11. D.S. Achuta Rao (au.) and S. Settar (ed.), *Administrative and Social History of Mysore Under The Wodeyars (1600-1800 CE)*, (Manipal University Press), 2017.
12. Shama Rao, *Modern Mysore*, (Chennai: Higginbothams), 1936.
13. Irfan Habib, *Confronting Colonialism Resistance and Modernization Under Haidar Ali and Tipu Sultan* (Delhi: Tulika Books), 1999.
14. Vikram Sampath, *Splendours of Royal Mysore: The Untold Story of the Wodeyars*, (New Delhi: Rupa Publications), 2008
15. Responding to Mahatma Gandhi's Quit India Movement, a tiny village of patriots in Issur, Shikaripur Taluk of Shimoga (Shivamogga) declared themselves free from colonial rule and established a small self-governing apparatus. Enraged, the British army was sent in to annex the village. Upon hearing the news of Issuru's rebellion, JCW launched into talks with the British administration and coined the

immortal phrase, "*Esuru kottaru Issuru kodevu*" (We'll give you many villages but not Issuru). He convinced the Governor General to condone the death sentences of the freedom fighters, and refused to allow direct presence of the British in Issur either.

5: Brandishing a Mysore Brand

1. Margaret H. Cousins and James H. Cousins, *We Two Together*, (Madras: Ganesh and Co.), 1950.
2. Aya Ikagame, *Royalty in Colonial and Post-Colonial India: A Historical Anthropology of Mysore from 1799 to the Present*, (University of Edinburgh: Ph.D Dissertation) 2007.
3. Walter Legge, *Words and Music*, (Gerald Duckworth & Co Ltd), 1998.
4. Read more about Mysore Concerts in Royal Albert Hall in Chapter 'A Mysorean Philharmonia in London'.

6: Chitprabhananda—on the Throne of Melody

1. Palace communications, Karnataka State Archives.
2. Maharaja wrote two books on Africa: *African Survey* and *India and Africa* and also funded an in-depth research and publication of a monograph on East Central African Elephant by W.C. Osman Hill, Professor of Zoological Society, London.

7: Administrative Marvels

1. Personal correspondence, Todhunter to Ismail, 27 March 1941
2. Speech on the occasion of the opening of the All-India Bangalore War Services Exhibition on 10 June 1943.
3. Speech on the occasion of the opening of the All-India Bangalore War Services Exhibition, 10 June 1943.
4. Bjorn Hettne, *The Political Economy of Indirect Rule. Mysore 1881–1971* (London and Malmo: Curzon Press), 1978. p. 402.
5. P. T. George, 'Land System and Laws in Mysore State', *Artha Vijñana : Journal of the Gokhale Institute of Politics and Economics, 1970.*

6. Ibid., p. 123.
7. F. Buchanan, *A Journey From Madras Through the Countries of Mysore, Canara and Malabar*. 2nd Edition (London: East Indian Company), 1807.

8: An Instrument of Freedom

1. John Wood, Penderel Moon, David M. Blake, Stephen R. Ashton, 'Dividing the Jewel: Mountbatten and the Transfer of Power to India and Pakistan', *Pacific Affairs*, Universityof British Columbia, 1985.
2. V.P. Menon, *Integration of the Indian States* (Sangam Books Ltd), 1956.
3. John McLeod, *Sovereignty, Power, Control: Politics in the State of Western India, 1916–1947*, Leiden: Brill, 1999.
4. R. P. Bhargava, *The Chamber of Princes* (Northern Book Centre), 1991.
5. Winston Churchill, Speech, Constitutional Club, March 1931.
6. Arthur Berriedale Keith, *A Constitutional History of India, 1600–1935*, (London: London Press), 1969.
7. Ian Copland, 'Congress Paternalism: The "High Command" and the Struggle for Freedom in Princely India', in Jim Masselos, *Struggling and Ruling: The Indian National Congress 1885–1985* (New Delhi: Sterling Publishers), 1987, pp. 121–140.
8. Rosita Forbes, *India of the Princes*, (London: Right Book Club), 1939.

9: The Saga of the Sceptre

1. K. Chengalaraya Reddy, *Progress of Education in Mysore State, 1916-1922*, Bangalore, 1922, pp. 69-70.
2. Doreswamy, H. S., *Horatada Ditta Hejjegalu*, Bangalore, 1972, pp. 26-30; *Report on the Administration of Mysore*,1938, (Bengaluru: Karnataka State Archives), 1938, pp. 6-7.
3. On 25 April 1938, a group of villagers organized a Satyagraha, seeking freedom from British rule. Due to escalations and mounting pressure, indiscriminate firing from police resulted in the death of thirty-five people.

4. V. P. Menon, *Integration of the Indian States*, (New Delhi: Sangam Books Ltd), 1956.
5. Proceedings of the 6th Session of the Mysore Congress, Bangalore 1946, pp. 20-24; Confidential Files, No. 40 of 1942-43, Daily Abstract of Information on Civil Disobedience Movement, Karnataka. State Archives, Bangalore; 91 Secret Files, S.B. 188/42-43/October 2, 1942, 34 of 1942-1943, Karnataka State Archives, Bangalore.

10: The Democrat in the Durbar

1. All letter correspondences from S. Gopal, *Selected Works of Jawaharlal Nehru (1 November–December 31, 1958) - Vol. 45*: Second series, Vol. 45, Jawaharlal Nehru Memorial Fund, 2012.

11: Sovereign Souvenirs

1. Dr Shanti Swarup Bhatnagar played a significant role in the vision and building of a network of scientific institutions, policies and operation vision for India's Science and Technology endeavours. He was the Founder Director of Council of Scientific & Industrial Research (CSIR) and is credited with having been instrumental in establishing 12 national laboratories. The CSIR-CFTRI has been a national laboratory since its inception.
2. Ramachandra Guha and Madhav Gadgil, *This Fissured Land: An Ecological History of India* (New Delhi: Oxford India Perennials Series), 2012.
3. Speech on the occasion of the laying of the foundation stone of Sri Jayachamarajendra Institute of Indian Medicine in Bangalore, 11 December 1943.

12: A Mysorean Philharmonia in London

1. Basil Deane, *Gramophone* magazine, December 1950, p. 141.
2. Maharaja of Mysore's letter to Walter Legge, 30 December 1950.
3. *Gramophone*, April 1950, pp. 197–98

13: A Freemason of His Destiny

1. Rita Sherma (au.), Alf Hiltebeitel and Kathleen M. Erndl (eds), *Is the Goddess a Feminist?: The Politics of South Asian Goddesses*, (New York: New York University Press), 2000.
2. Teun Goudriaan, *Hindu Tantric and Śākta Literature*, (Otto Harrassowitz Verlag), 1981, pp. 39–40.
3. Osman Hill et al., *The Elephant in East Central Africa*, (London: Rowland Ward Limited), 1953.

14: The Happy Prince

1. Letter addressed to Sri. KC Reddy, Chief Minister, Government of Mysore, Bengaluru, 2 November 1950.

APPENDICES

Appendix 1: List of Wadiyar Rulers of Mysore

Adi Yaduraya (1399–1423)

Hiriya Bettada Chamaraja Wadiyar I (1423–1459)

Thimma Raja Wadiyar I (1459–1478)

Hiriya Chamarajarasa Wadiyar II (1478–1513)

Hiriya Bettada Chamaraja Wadiyar III (1513–1553)

Thimma Raja Wadiyar II (1553–1572)

Boala Chamaraja Wadiyar IV (1572–1576)

Bettada Chamaraja Wadiyar V (1576–1578)

Raja Wadiyar I (1578–1617)

Chamarajarasa Wadiyar VI (1617–1637)

Raja Wadiyar II (1637–1638)

Ranadheera Kanteerava Narasaraja Wadiyar I (1638–1659)

Dodda Devaraja Wadiyar (1659–1673)

Chikka Devaraja Wadiyar (1613–1704)

Kanteerava Maharaja Wadiyar (1704–1714)

Dodda Krishnaraja Wadiyar I (1714–1732)

Chamaraja Wadiyar VII (1732–1734)

(Immadi) Krishnaraja Wadiyar II (1734–1766)

Nanaja Raja Wadiyar (1766–1770)

Bettada Chamaraja Wadiyar VIII (1770–1776)

Khasa Chamaraja Wadiyar IX (1766–1796)

(Mummadi) Krishnaraja Wadiyar III (1799–1868)

Chamaraja Wadiyar X (1868–1894)

Vani Vilas Sannidhana, queen of Chamaraja Wadiyar X, was Regent from 1894–1902.

(Nalvadi) Krishnaraja Wadiyar IV (1902–1940)

Sri Jaya Chamaraja Wadiyar XI (1940–1947)

Appendix 2: JCW'S Family Members

Sisters:

- Princess Vijaya Lakshmi Ammanni, later Rani Vijaya Devi of Kotda Sangani.
- Princess Sujaya Kantha Ammanni, later Thakurani Sahiba of Sanand.
- Princess Jaya Chamunda Ammanni Avaru, later Maharani Sri Jaya Chamunda Ammanni Sahiba, Maharani of Bharatpur.

Wives:

- Maharani Satya Prema Kumari of Jigni.
- Maharani Tripura Sundari Ammanni Avaru

Children:

- Princess Gayatri Devi Avaru (1946–1974)
- Princess Meenakshi Devi Avaru (1951–2015)
- Maharaja Sri Srikantadatta Narasimharaja Wadiyar (1953–2013).
- Princess Kamakshi Devi Avaru, born 1954

- Princess Indrakshi Devi Avaru, born 1956
- Princess Vishalakshi Devi Avaru, (1962–2018)

Appendix 3: Imperial Honours Bestowed Upon JCW

- Knight Grand Cross of the Most Honourable Order of the Bath (GCB) in 1946.
- Knight Grand Commander of the Most Exalted Order of the Star of India (GCSI), 1945.

Appendix 4: List of Books and Essays by JCW

- *The Quest for Peace: An Indian Approach* (Minneapolis: University of Minnesota), 1959.
- *Dattatreya: The Way and the Goal* (London: Allen & Unwin), 1957.
- *The Gita and Indian Culture* (Bombay: Orient Longman) 1963.
- Religion And Man (Bombay: Orient Longman), 1965. Based on Prof. Ranade Series Lectures instituted at Karnataka University in 1961.
- *Avadhuta: Reason & Reverence* (Bangalore: Indian Institute of World Culture), 1958.
- *An Aspect of Indian Aesthetics*, University of Madras, 1956.
- 'Puranas as the Vehicles of India's Philosophy of History', *Journal Purana*, Issue #5, 1963.
- 'Advaita Philosophy', *Sringeri Souvenir Volume*, 1965, pp. 62–64.
- 'Sri Suresvaracharya', *Sringeri Souvenir Volume*, 1970, pp. 1–8.
- M.P. Pandit, *Kundalini Yoga: A Brief Study of Sir John Woodroffe's 'Serpent Power'* (New Age Books), 2004.
- 'The Virtuous Way of Life', *Mountain Path*, July 1964.

- Note on Ecological Surveys to Precede Large Irrigation Projects, Wesley Press, Mysore; 1955.
- African Survey, Bangalore Press, 1955.

Appendix 5: List of Books Published Under the *Sri Jayachamarajendra Granthamala* Series

- *Rigveda* – in 35 parts
- *Shankaracharya's Stotras* – in 2 parts
- *Mukapamcashati*
- *Kamakalpa Tarustava*
- *TripurasundarI Manasika Puja*
- *Gurugita*
- *Shivagita*
- *Mahamasta Purashcarana Vidhih*
- *Shodashi Puja Kalpa*
- *Bhuvaneshvari Puja Kalpa*
- *Rudra Mahanyasa Prayoga*
- *Suktagalu*

Puranagalu:

- *Devi Bhagavata* in 5 parts; translated by Edatore Chandrashekarashastri (year 1942–43)
- *Shiva Purana*
- *Shiva Rahasya*
- *Skanda Mahapurana*
- *Kalika Purana* in 2 parts by Hasanada Pandit Venkatarav (28 May 1944)
- *Varaha Purana*
- *Bhavishya Purana*

- *Ganesha Purana*
- *Vamana Purana*
- *Kanci Mahatmye*
- *Vishnu Dharmottara Purana Brahmanda Purana*
- *Naradiya Purana*
- *Rama Mantra Mahime (Agastya Samhite)*
- *Narasimha Purana*
- *Samba Purana*
- *Saura Purana*
- *Adi Purana*
- *Kalki Purana*
- *Matsya Purana*
- *Kurma Purana*
- *Shiva Tatva Sudhanidhih* - By ve.brall es. Sitaramashastri (24 August 1949)
- *Halasya Mahatmye*
- *Gargya Samhita*
- *Brahma Vyevarta Purana*
- *Brahma Purana*
- *Shamkara Samhite*
- *Padmapurana*
- *Vishnu Purana* in three parts: Translated by Pandita Ganjam
- *Timannayya,* 1948

Mantrashastra - Sahasranama - Upanishat:

- *Parivasya Rahasya*
- *Tripuratapinyupanishat*
- *Lalitatrishati Bhashya*
- *Tripura Rahasya*

- *Shrikamda Sarartha Bhodhini*
- *Suta Samhite*
- *Vanadurgopanishat*
- *Sharada Sahasranama*
- *Ganesha Sahasranama*
- *Dakshinamurti Sahasranama*
- *Shiva Puja Paddhati*

Appendix 6: List of Irrigational Projects Completed During the Reign of JCW

Anjanapura Reservoir

Bheemanahalli Reservoir

Markaronahalli Reservoir

Nellikere Reservoir

Gopalapura Reservoir

Lakkavalli-Bhadra Reservoir

Nugu Reservoir

Bhairamangala Reservoir

Kanva Dam and Reservoir

Hirebhaskara Dam and Kargal Dam Reservoirs

Honnamachanahalli Lake

Markandeya Lake

Parashuramapura Lake

Molkalmooru Lake

Shimsha Yedadande Canal

Mundakere Yedadande Canal

Soolekere Reservoir and Canals

Allapura Bridge and Canal

Bhadra Yedadande Canal

Vedavathi Dam and Canals

Ramadevaru Dam and North Canal

Sakkrebayalu Dam

Thirthahalli Tunga Bridge

Kanakanahalli Arkavathi Bridge

Holenarasipuradalli Hemavathi Bridge

INDEX

Note: page locators/page numbers in *italics* denote images, maps, box items

ABOUT THE AUTHOR

DR DEEPTI NAVARATNA is a musician-neuroscientist whose interests span the arts, science and history. She is a Chevening Clore Fellow (2021–22) and is recognized as one of the most dynamic cultural leaders across the globe. She is the first Indian woman to have performed at the Parliament of World Religions in 2021. She is currently the T.V. Raman Pai Chair Professor of Excellence at the National Institute for Advanced Studies, Bangalore.

Read more about the author at: www.deeptinavaratna.net

JCW (second from left) with Chou En Lai (centre), the first Premier of the People's Republic of China, and the Chinese delegation

With Ho Chi Minh, Prime Minister of the Democratic Republic of Vietnam

With the First Secretary of the Communist Party of the Soviet Union, Nikita Khrushchev, noted artist Svetoslav Roerich and Chief Minister Kadidal Manjappa, among others

With Pope Paul VI, Head of the Catholic Church and sovereign of the Vatican City State

With Indonesian President Suharto and wife Tiyan Suharto, and Karnataka Chief Minister S. Nijalingappa

With the King of Saudi Arabia, his delegation and Chief Minister of Karnataka, Kengal Hanumanthaiah

With Mirza Ismail, Dewan of Mysore from 1926-1941

With Jnanpith Award winner and noted Kannada poet, Kuvempu

(Left) At a reception for an international delegate at the Governor's residence

With Veerendra Heggade at the Dussera celebrations in Mysore

With his spiritual mentor Sringeri Jagadguru

With Pandit Jawaharlal Nehru, Chief Minister B.D. Jatti and members of his cabinet

(Seated, centre) With international delegates who travelled to the Scout Jamboree and President Dr Sarvepalli Radhakrishnan

With Pandit Nehru at a United Nations meeting

With Dr Radhakrishnan and Chief Minister Kengal Hanumanthaiah, and other political leaders

With Zakir Husain, Indian economist and the third President of India

With Governor General of India C. Rajagopalachari

With Queen Elizabeth II, Queen Empress of the United Kingdom and Commonwealth Realms

(Fourth from left) With several national leaders, including Smt. Sarojini Naidu, Dr Zakir Husain, Dr Radhakrishnan, Lal Bahadur Shastri, Dr Karan Singh and Sardar Vallabhbhai Patel